ED SCHOOL FOLLIES

ED SCHOOL FOLLIES

The Miseducation of America's Teachers

Rita Kramer

THE FREE PRESS
A Division of Macmillan, Inc.
NEW YORK

Maxwell Macmillan Canada
TORONTO

The Free Press
A Division of Macmillan, Inc.
866 Third Avenue, New York, N.Y. 10022

Maxwell Macmillan Canada, Inc.
1200 Eglinton Avenue East
Suite 200
Don Mills, Ontario M3C 3N1

Macmillan, Inc. is part of the Maxwell Communication
Group of Companies.

Printed in the United States of America

printing number
2 3 4 5 6 7 8 9 10

Library of Congress Cataloging-in-Publication Data

Kramer, Rita.
   Ed school follies : the miseducation of America's teachers / Rita
Kramer.
     p. cm.
  Includes index.
  ISBN 0–02–917642–5
  1. Teachers—Training of—United States. I. Title. II. Title:
Miseducation of America's teachers.
LB1715.K64 1991
370'.71'0973—dc20
                                        91–9774
                                         CIP

Contents

Acknowledgments

I would like to thank the faculty, administration, and students of the schools which welcomed me and hope they will not be too dismayed by some of my observations. In the long run, I hope they will find I have been helpful to them and will not regret their hospitality. I also want to thank my husband, Yale Kramer, for patient debriefing after my many trips and for his helpful suggestions along the way. I am deeply grateful to the Committee for the Free World, whose support made the research possible, and most of all to Midge Decter, who planted the idea, watered it, and watched it grow, and then did the necessary job of weeding. Her unfailing interest and good-humored encouragement kept me going to ed schools even when I felt like dropping out.

New York
January 1991

Introduction

Learning to Teach

What is the trouble with America's schools? This is a question that has been at the forefront of the national consciousness for decades, at least since the Soviets launched Sputnik in the 1950s and we were told that Johnny couldn't read. Since then, the crisis of American education has been proclaimed and described again and again, inspiring a miscellany of panaceas promising reform, only to be followed by new revelations of pedagogical pathology, new diagnoses, new prescriptions, new therapy. The patient, despite all these efforts, does not seem to be improving.

We have seen the new math come and go, along with the open classroom, and neither changes in the curriculum nor changes in the way it is taught seem to have made enough of a difference. Too many Johnnies still can't read, or write, or add, subtract, or multiply. Too many of our elementary pupils are unprepared for high school, and too many of our high schools' graduates are ignorant of the most basic facts about their country's institutions and its past, unacquainted with the literature and art that are the heritage of civilization, unable to make sense of science or technology.

Why?

There are many ways to answer the question. The schools are responsive to conditions in society and to its values. They have to

1

deal with the children who come through their doors, and with the effects on them of the breakdown of the family, the general permissiveness and loss of respect for authority, the drug epidemic, the effects of television—its form as well as its content—all of which influence young minds. But none of these factors strikes at the heart of the matter, none explains why our schools teach so little to so many children. It is not a matter of money, buildings, materials. The essential ingredients in the learning process are the pupil and the teacher. When we talk about education, we are talking about teaching—who does it and how well—and about what is being taught.

Wanting to know who our teachers are—where they are coming from; how they are being prepared for their critical work with the young and by whom and in what way; what they seem to be making of their training; what their expectations are for their future—in the fall of 1988 I set out on a voyage of which this book is the log.

I spent a year visiting schools, colleges, and departments of education in various parts of the country, sitting in on classes in large public and private universities, smaller private colleges, and the quondam normal schools that are now part of state systems. Wanting to get as representative a sample as possible of the schools, colleges, and departments of education that make up the "ed school" world, I visited institutions in the Northeast as well as the Northwest, on the West Coast as well as in the Southeast, the Midwest, the Southwest. I did not cover all parts of the country, and I visited only a small fraction of the close to 1,300 existing teacher-training institutions, but they were far enough apart and varied enough in character to provide a general picture of their world today and what goes on in it.

Everywhere I went, I talked with faculty, students, and administrators of teacher-preparation programs, and I visited elementary and high schools where education students did practice teaching. I asked many of the student teachers I met, as well as their teachers: Why did you go into teaching? What do you think schools are for? What is the teacher's job? And I asked the student teachers, What do you see yourself doing as a teacher? Next year? In ten years?

What I saw and heard in "ed school" was a revelation.

When I began this project, it was without an agenda. I set out to see what was out there in the world of ed schools, with only one question already clearly formulated. It had to do with the pool of prospective teachers. I was curious about the effects of the two great social upheavals of our time on the teaching profession, traditionally populated by women and minorities, which used to mean not only blacks but second-generation Americans, the children of immigrants on the way up the social ladder or the upwardly mobile children of workers who were the first generation of their families to go beyond high school. Both women and blacks had many other options now. How many of them, I wondered, were going into teaching? What I found was that there were more women and fewer blacks than I expected.

While young women no longer automatically go into teaching until they find husbands or, failing to marry, remain as the ubiquitous "spinster" teachers of my childhood, today large numbers of older women with children, whether married or single parents, are reentering the labor force by choosing to become teachers. Why there are relatively few blacks preparing for a career in teaching despite the many kinds of affirmative action programs designed to encourage them to do so would not become as quickly obvious as why so many women are still doing so.

Who are the nation's teachers? According to figures made available at the end of 1986, 70 percent of the country's two-and-a-half million public school teachers are women—76 percent at the elementary and 51 percent at the secondary level—and 9 percent of the current teaching force is classified as "minority," of which 6 percent are black. Another fact about the teaching force is that it is currently the most unionized occupation in the country, with 80 percent of public school teachers belonging to a union, as contrasted with only 12 percent of college graduates employed full time year-round.*

In the late 1980s, enrollment in undergraduate teacher-education programs had been steadily increasing in response to the job market; there were more positions available and they were paying more. (Data compiled by the American Federation of Teachers in 1985 showed that every state in the nation raised its average salary for teachers at rates higher than inflation and higher than those of other government employees; the average salary for teachers was over $25,000 a year, higher than annual earnings of workers in the private sector in every state in 1986.) Who are these prospective teachers?

According to a survey by the American Association of Colleges for Teacher Education in 1989, teaching as a career does not seem to be attracting increasing numbers of blacks and other minorities, who continue to constitute only about 5 percent of the enrollment,

* The figures are from C. Emily Feistritzer, "Teacher Crisis: Myth or Reality?" (Washington, D.C.: National Center for Education Information, 1986).

which remains primarily white and female. The median age of the students enrolled in undergraduate teaching programs is 24. A quarter of them are married, many have children at home and many work part-time. The survey also found that more than three-quarters of the graduates of colleges of education preparing to teach in elementary school had no academic major other than education. Almost as many had no academic minor.

The requirements for admission to the more than twelve hundred various kinds of institutions that prepare teachers for state certification vary wildly. The large public universities responsible for producing more than half of the nation's teachers are more selective than small private institutions, which usually enroll education students earlier in their careers—before they can be said to have had a general academic education—and which rarely reject an education applicant. Also varying from state to state are the requirements for certification that determine what will be required in order to graduate from a teacher-preparation program.

Some states with large numbers of inner-city problem schools are issuing emergency credentials to fill their teaching needs. Noncredentialed teachers are paid on a per diem basis, although they may be employed on a regular schedule, a makeshift if not hypocritical solution. Some of these people may be better qualified academically and better teachers than those whose credentials depend merely on having accumulated the prescribed number of education course credits in college.

In other states, notably New Jersey, alternative routes are openly designed to circumvent traditional teacher education programs altogether, issuing a provisional certificate that lets a qualified college graduate teach while fulfilling the pedagogical requirements for certification. Alternative certification programs are intended to serve a diverse population including blacks and members of other minority groups and older people—former teachers returning to the field, and midcareer changers and retirees who would like to teach.

The assumption is that these people already have an adequate general education and can be taught what they need to know about the theory and activity of teaching while they are doing it. This may be truer of the older applicants than of the recent college graduates, who, while they may have the advantage of not being overburdened with knowledge of pedagogy, may not be overburdened with general knowledge either. That, of course, depends on the standards of the colleges and universities from which they have graduated.

Schools of education as such are only about 150 years old. In 1839 Horace Mann established the first of the state institutions to train teachers for the nation's common schools by acquainting them with the principles or "norms" of classroom instruction. These single-purpose institutions devoted to vocational practice, which came to be known as "normal" schools, were largely staffed by faculty with teaching experience but no academic credentials. Those they enrolled, the majority of them women, were taking what amounted to a step upward on the socioeconomic ladder.

In the early years of this century, the normal schools began to evolve into four-year teachers' colleges, which could grant degrees enabling their graduates to teach not just in the elementary grades but in the increasingly important high schools. Eventually they became general purpose state colleges and universities, part of the expanding system of public institutions of higher education that gained momentum in the years following World War II, when the federal government and state legislatures appropriated unprecedented sums for the education of returning veterans. As a result, an apprenticeship model was replaced by that of professional training and scholarship, and to the preparation of classroom practitioners was added that of educational bureaucrats.

The quest for academic status and acceptance as an equal of the other professional faculties such as law and medicine led to the abandonment on many college and university campuses of the connection with the lowly women who taught children in elementary classrooms.* Those who are trained in the vocations of law and medicine profess to know more than their clients about their fields and their clients' needs; they work independently and not under bureaucratic control; and they possess a fixed body of specific knowledge. In contrast, teachers are directed in their daily work by political bodies outside of their field, and their training institutions have no agreed-on disciplinary content. This may help to explain why, as Glazer puts it, "They never seem to be long secure in their adoption of any curriculum and mode of training, and they undertake 'radical revolutions' every decade or so." Professors were too busy inventing a discipline of education to concern themselves with the present realities of the public schools. That was left to the less elite—and less selective—institutions. And even at those, more and more courses in theory began to supplement practice teaching under the influence

---

* An interesting discussion of the characteristics of the various professions and their respective training institutions is Nathan Glazer's "The Schools of the Minor Professions," in *Minerva*, Vol. XII, No. 3, July 1974 (London).

of the graduate school culture, with its emphasis on the scientific study of education rather than on the practical training of teachers.

Today graduate schools and departments of education exist alongside the other professional faculties like law and medicine, business, and engineering in the large prestigious research-oriented universities, both private and public, from which their influence emanates. Harvard's and Berkeley's schools of education are not in the business of training classroom teachers. More devoted to research, grantsmanship, publication, and the other trappings of scholarship that define academic pursuit than to teacher training, they produce a leadership cadre for the educational establishment: professors and deans of other education faculties, high-level administrators, superintendents, principals—all those whose careers in education lie outside the classroom. Their eye is on policy and theory, not practice, but the theories they generate—their interpretations of their findings on how children learn and how teachers should teach—influence what is taught in teacher-training programs and thus eventually in the nation's classrooms.

There are some 150 graduate schools of education in the United States today, comprising less than 10 percent of the thirteen hundred institutions—from small private colleges with religious affiliations to major state campuses—that prepare teachers. The influence of the most prestigious dozen or so of the graduate schools is enormous. Their deans and their alumni elsewhere in the education establishment sit on—and often chair—the boards and commissions empaneled by government and foundations to pronounce on matters affecting the schools. Those pronouncements then define the direction of policy in the years until another blue-ribbon panel issues another report explaining why matters haven't improved much since the last one.

As normal schools evolved into state teachers colleges and eventually became absorbed into university graduate schools of education, there remained a number of colleges of education, both on private campuses and publicly supported ones, that provided teacher-training programs for undergraduates. Notoriously nonselective, they offered three or four years of concentration on pedagogy to students barely out of high school, whose general education was slighted while they prepared to devote themselves to the education of others. On the one hand, graduate schools were producing specialists in such matters as the psychology and philosophy of education while, on the other, undergraduate programs were turning out classroom teachers with minimal background in the subjects they were destined to teach. All of them knew more about how to teach than what to teach.*

By the close of the 1970s, most of the country's teachers were coming not from the education schools and departments of liberal arts colleges and elite universities but from the upgraded state teachers' colleges, less well known, less selective, and less demanding. They had already come under attack in numerous works two of whose titles told the story: *Educational Wastelands* and *The Miseducation of American Teachers*. Gradually, the idea began to take hold among critics that undergraduate teacher education should be abolished altogether and replaced with a liberal arts education followed by a fifth year of education courses and practice teaching leading to a master's degree in teaching. A year of internship in the schools would precede taking on full classroom responsibility. This was the recommendation of both of the much-publicized reports issued in 1988, that of the Holmes Group of deans of leading graduate schools of education in research universities and that of the Carnegie Corporation's Task Force on Teaching as a Profession, a group of business leaders and government, union, and school officials.†

Both groups saw the move to place all teacher education at the graduate level as a step toward improving the quality of teaching. Teachers would be professionals if they were certified only after graduate professional study. Professional education would replace vocational training and people who knew something they had studied as undergraduates would turn to the matter of how to teach it in graduate school.

Would this bring better people into the classroom? There were those, like Peabody College's Dean Willis D. Hawley, who disagreed with the Holmes and Carnegie reports' recommendations and maintained that a solid liberal arts background could be integrated with course work on learning theory and teaching methods while at the same time getting future teachers into the classroom much earlier in their careers. And there were still others who sought to circumvent the existing systems of teacher training altogether—both graduate and undergraduate—for alternative routes.

* For a general overview of this topic, see Geraldine Joncich Clifford and James W. Guthrie, *Ed School: A Brief for Professional Education* (Chicago: University of Chicago Press, 1988). See also Harry Judge, *American Graduate Schools of Education: A View from Abroad* (New York: Ford Foundation: 1982).

† Holmes Group, *Tomorrow's Teachers: A Report of the Holmes Group* (East Lansing, Mich.: Holmes Group, 1986); Carnegie Task Force on Teaching as a Profession, *A Nation Prepared: Teachers for the 21st Century* (New York: Carnegie Forum on Education and the Economy, 1986).

Since the federal government's move into the education scene in the late 1950s and subsequent legislation, a vast education industry has proliferated in response to the availability of funds for mandated programs addressed to problems of racial integration, the disadvantaged, education of the handicapped and of the non-English speaking, and so on. Government-funded research projects are ubiquitous on campuses and in consulting firms all over the country. Publications abound, with reports and surveys filling data banks and spilling over library shelves.

As federal money was becoming available to those in the education field, another change was being put into place. The "new left" social scientists who came on the scene in the late 1960s began to reinterpret American history and sociology from a preponderantly Marxist point of view, and nowhere were the revisionists more radical than in the field of schooling. The books by Kozol, Goodman, Illich, and others became best sellers and their ideas about the relationship between school and society, teacher and pupil, permeated the ed school world, both in terms of what was taught and how research was designed, carried out, and interpreted.

With a few exceptions, such as Teachers College of Columbia University and the College of Education at Michigan State University, the leading institutions in the field of education largely shy away from identification with the preparation of the elementary school teaching force. They are more intent on proving that education is an academic discipline with its own subject matter worthy of a place alongside the other university schools and departments. To that end they emphasize graduate education, research, and publication. The training of primary school teachers thus devolves upon the second-tier institutions, from small private colleges to large state universities, less selective in admissions and less demanding of those they admit.

In the year I spent observing these programs, I saw examples of both systems and came to think that such structural changes neither address the real problem nor provide a real solution. To show why, I propose to take my readers back to the beginning as I retrace my steps through the ed school world. They may not share all my feelings and judgments about everything I have seen, but I invite them to look at it with me, to join me in the classrooms and corridors and off-campus haunts I visited during a year-long odyssey among some of the schools and departments of colleges and universities that prepare teachers to instruct schoolchildren in America today.

PART ONE

The Northeast

1

❧ —— ❧

Teachers College

From Progressive Education to Peace Education

The journey began on the way up the steps leading to the entrance to Teachers College, the graduate school of education at the uptown edge of Columbia University in New York City. Arguably the country's most venerable teacher-training institution, TC is the fount of progressive education and the source of innumerable trend-setting projects and influential publications in the field. There facing me on the massive wooden door of the red brick building was a sign pointing the way to "Conflict Management Training for Educators." Conflict Management? Then it occurred to me that perhaps what was meant by conflict management was discipline.

I found my way to a large lecture hall, took a seat, and looked around me. I was immediately cheered by what I saw and surprised by my own thought: How nice that all these lively, attractive young people want to be teachers! A tall, blond young woman in tight jeans and boots was talking to a young man in a ski sweater and a black woman in a pin-striped suit. I judged there were over a hundred students filing in or already seated. My impression was that there were more whites than blacks, more women than men, but it was a close call.

I turned to a young woman in the row behind me to ask if I could see the assignment sheet and book list I'd heard her discussing with the person next to her. She was wearing orange high-top sneakers, and above an oversize drab sweater, her hair shot out in all directions with that wild, unkempt look it takes a certain degree of artfulness to achieve. I asked if she was a classroom teacher. No, she told me, she was preservice. She'd taken a liberal arts degree and was here to get her education credits. She told me she'd majored in science. It seemed like a good idea to know something substantive first and then worry about how to teach it. Others in the room, the in-service teachers already in the classroom, had taken undergraduate degrees in education and were student teaching while getting their master's degrees.

I asked where she'd gone to college and was mildly surprised when she answered Harvard. How come, I asked, she'd decided to come here to Columbia rather than going on to Harvard's prestigious Graduate School of Education. She had wanted to come here, she told me, because of the Peace Ed program. She wanted to teach peace to kids. It was the most important thing in the world right now, teaching children how to think about nuclear war, arms control, interpersonal negotiation. You had "to like work it into all subjects, not just science." It was an issue relevant to everything, to high school English and junior high social studies just as much as elementary school biology.

By now the professor, a dark-haired woman in a bright red dress, had taken her place at the lectern at the front of the room and was enthusiastically explaining that TC not only aimed at preparing its students to teach but also to assume leadership roles in the teaching profession. Today's session of Problems of Curriculums and Teaching would deal with teacher research, which she explained was research undertaken by teachers in their classrooms in order to improve their classroom practice. It had gotten under way here at TC in the 1940s when the faculty began to question "traditional linear research" undertaken by university professors within the parameters of such methods as statistical analysis of experimental and control groups and designed to be published in professional journals. Teacher research was, by contrast—and here she pronounced each word slowly, pausing after each word so note-takers could get it all down—"a teacher . . . action . . . oriented . . . mode of developing staff development strategy."

Next to me, a young man chewed soundlessly as the crumbs from a large muffin wafted down on his notebook. As an example of such research she described a project dealing with teacher satisfaction in the New York City schools, which had demonstrated that effective teaching was accomplished by teachers who felt committed, engaged, and who *loved* teaching because they enjoyed what she would call the three Rs—respect, recognition, and reinforcement from their peers, administrators, parents, and students.

Such research, the professor pointed out, was based on teachers' reports of their own observations in the classroom. The problem under study exists in the here and now, as distinct from the static world of scholarship in which, because of the time lag involved in publication, conditions may have changed and the problem may very well no longer even exist in the way it was studied. The language of the research is also direct, "teacher-like," rather than abstract, boring—some groans and laughter from the listeners here—and pedagogical. For teachers, she went on, it was a matter of professionalism, of taking charge of their own continued learning, not just for purposes of fulfilling the requirements of college courses or accreditation, but for the purpose of setting their own goals. She would now introduce, by way of illustration, three teachers who had been studying their own practice in the public schools of Scarsdale, a wealthy community in New York's Westchester County that has long enjoyed a reputation as one of the best school systems in the country.

Taking her place at the lectern was a short, feisty-looking middle-aged woman with a stylish hairdo, wearing a well-tailored suit, who taught writing to fifth-graders. She told the class that observing and reflecting on what went on in one's classroom and changing strategies that didn't work meant "taking charge, developing ourselves as teachers, being responsible for our own growth." She had recorded her classroom experience in a log that was projected on the screen in front of us ("I observed and listened to Amy reading . . ."). Concentrating on the progress of Amy, a child who had had trouble learning to write and been identified as "learning disabled," this teacher had kept notes, watched for signs of improvement and recorded them, and in the end had succeeded. Taken out of the isolated one-on-one situation with a special education teacher and made part of the classroom community, Amy had moved beyond the primitive stilted efforts at writing we saw projected on the screen to legible, more articulate, even playful prose.

Focusing on one child, the teacher felt, had taught her something she could apply to the others; "How she learned became part of *my* learning, affected the way I would deal with them all. Reflecting on my own teaching strategies led to changes in my teaching and in myself."

I would have sent a child of mine to her classroom, to any school that employed teachers like her, like a shot.

The colleague who followed her was a crowd pleaser, a man in his sixties who appeared in shirtsleeves, tieless, rumpled, slightly stooped, self-deprecating. If his predecessor had seemed the personification of the self-possessed, well-spoken, well-groomed urban Jewish woman most often found teaching gifted children in the better Eastern suburban schools, he might have been sent by central casting to play the Mister Chips of 1960s America: a man now ready to bow out to the applause of young students grateful to have been more amused and appreciated than prodded and challenged. (The young in this room did indeed applaud him when he finished amusing them.)

His research consisted of querying his students, at the beginning and again at the end of their high-school math course, on their thoughts about the use of the electronic calculators he had introduced to them. He showed us what percentage of his students had "a favorable response" to the use of calculators at the end of the course compared to the percentage at the outset. He made gentle fun of parents who worried that their kids couldn't do arithmetic "the old way" (laughter) and who didn't appreciate the importance of concepts over computation. How many times, he asked with a rhetorical twinkle, do you have to add a column of twelve figures in real life?

The young black woman in the pin-striped suit wanted to know how the girls in his class felt about using the computer. What about "the myth that boys do better than girls in math?" After a *pro forma* protestation of his nonsexism and a somewhat apologetic acknowledgement that things were changing, he told her that for the most part, and with exceptions of course, boys did.

My first-grade teacher followed him to the podium. I knew it wasn't really Miss Callahan, who would have been well into her second century by now, but it did occur to me that there was a quality that many teachers of the very young seemed to have—an innocence akin to that of their charges, or perhaps just a lack of the cynicism so ubiquitous in our time. Wherever they may come from they suggest the Midwest, and soap, and gingerbread and hymnals. There must be something constantly renewing about attendance at the miraculous unfolding of the ability to recognize letters and then words and to connect them with each other to tell a story. Which, indeed, was what she was talking about. She had tossed out her basal readers and workbooks ("nobody in the class seemed to miss them") and substituted "real books" from the school library. As her pupils thrived, she reported on her progress to her "support group" of fellow teachers, gaining confidence from them, she implied, as she imparted it to the children. Most of what she reported seemed a matter of documenting things like the importance of selecting and arranging the books in such a way as to make them attractive; the fact that children don't always understand what they've read and don't always say so, making it important to talk about the reading afterward; and that the children love to imitate grown-ups, sitting in the teacher's chair to read aloud. She told of the children, asked to bring in their favorite books from home, carrying in full shopping bags and sounding like salesmen as they told each other, "You'd love this one."

The muffin-eater sitting next to me wanted to know, "How much extra work was this for you?" She smiled at him—beamed, actually. "When you love what you're doing," she told him, "it's not extra work. I was so involved, so interested, I'd be writing up my notes at lunchtime." What we were talking about here, I thought, was not methodology but character. Only one of them can be taught.

Another question from pin-stripe, who began her remarks with, "Last year I had some children who could read really nice." At this stage of the game, no one corrected her.

The student teachers seemed to appreciate the fact that what they had just been listening to could really be of help to them in the classroom. Hands shot up all over the room to ask questions like, Where do you get the books? How do you handle competition between the kids? What do you do when parents complain that their kids aren't learning phonics?" Her answer to that one brought down the house. "Don't *tell* them you don't teach phonics," she said. Then added, "You do." They all smiled and nodded, as though they understood quite well what she meant.

The first thing I heard when I entered the room where the seminar on Education for Peace, Disarmament and the Control of Nuclear Weapons was meeting was a young woman's voice saying, "I can't stand it. I just can't stand reading about it. I skip past the bloody parts." Another young woman responded, "I know what you mean. I can't watch those things either. I turn away. Or I turn it off."

There were fourteen in the room, three faculty members, seven young women and two young men students, and two visitors, a young man from the Sudan and myself. Things got underway with "a few general announcements." One of the instructors—everyone was on a first-name basis and I'll call her Marian—recommended that everyone get a copy of the study guide and reader produced to accompany Channel 13's program entitled "The Nuclear Age." Then one of the students, a young woman in a voluminous sweater and pants, wearing a large red button that read "Another Woman Against Bush" (this was late in October of 1988), reminded all present that on that evening the same local educational TV channel would be repeating *Rosie the Riveter*, a film that she said showed "how women were encouraged to enter the"—and here she made little quotation marks with her fingers in the air and looked significantly around the room—"war effort"—pause for ironic effect—"and what happened to them afterward." Marian then announced that there would be no class the following Tuesday evening so that everyone could vote. "For peace," added one of the students. "That's the purpose of our vote," Marian agreed. "To vote for peace."

The class had already met several times before. Everyone had been given a reading list of books dealing with the Vietnam War, and this evening some of the students would report on what they'd read, after which there would be discussion of how these works could be used "to teach peace." Asked what they'd read, various students mentioned the novels *Going After Cacciato*, *Running Dog*, *Fields of Fire*, and *A Rumor of War*, and the nonfiction titles *Dispatches*, *To Heal a Nation*, and *The Face of Battle*. The Woman Against Bush— I'll call her Gloria—said she had read a book called *Women in Revolution*, "to get the perspective of women in the Vietnam War."

The student who reported on *Going After Cacciato* said the theme of the book was how to escape from war, and proceeded to give what sounded like an intelligent and fairly sophisticated account of the book's structure as it intertwined narrative sections of fantasy and reality. She quoted a passage: "War kills and maims, rips up the land, makes orphans and widows . . ." and another line: "It's the same in Nam or Okinawa." She didn't say what was the same. I assumed what was meant was the subjective experience of the soldier in the field, not necessarily the reason for his presence there. I remembered what had brought about the presence of American soldiers on Okinawa, and their presence there seemed a less debatable issue than the presence of American soldiers in Vietnam.

Another student mentioned the film *Hearts and Minds* and said what she had learned from the novels and memoirs by Americans about their experiences in Vietnam was that they felt shame at what they were doing, seeing it from the Vietnamese point of view. One author had written about finding on a dead young Vietcong soldier a photograph of him looking proud in his uniform. Marian said it reminded her of a faded and torn photograph her grandfather had given her that showed her own father grinning in his World War I uniform. "He was only seventeen," she said, "and he had no idea then what was in store for him."

True enough, I thought. War is dreadful, and the suffering and the cutting short of young lives is tragic, but it's not that simple. The assumption being made here was that if you identified with the individuals on the other side, you wouldn't fight them. But— no one was asking this—what if they didn't identify with you? What would happen to you then? The Vietnam War seemed an easier subject for the kind of thinking that was going on here than certain other wars I could think of, past and present. What about wars of religious fanaticism? What about wars of racial genocide? What about the Nazis? Should we have remained "at peace" until we were annihilated, up the chimney with our racial impurities? What about self-defense? Should we have remained "at peace" when our navy was attacked at Pearl Harbor? If anybody was thinking of distinguishing between wars and wars along any of these lines, no one was saying so.

One of the book reports was given by a young Chinese student, a graceful, slender girl with delicate features. She was quoting from Chinese books in library bindings, and she introduced her presentation by saying, "Americans were against the Vietnam War because it caused dissension, and because they lost. But war is wrong because it brings suffering to both sides." Then she read figures telling how many had died, how many were injured, how many missing on both sides. The figures were from an article in a magazine which she held up to show the pictures of destruction and death and maiming caused by U.S. bombs and chemical weapons. There was an intake of breath around the room, and sounds of disgust. Then, in somewhat halting English, she translated from the books in front of her. She described them as volumes of letters which had been written by Vietnamese eyewitnesses to friends and relatives. From across the room the small volumes looked like bound pamphlets. In a soft and lilting voice she translated the text which told how American soldiers had routinely killed Vietnamese women in a ritual they called Holy Mother Mary Suffering, nailing them to crosses, then raping, and finally eviscerating them. She went on in this vein quoting from one book after another. There was no comment, no question from anyone in the room.

When we broke for coffee, I took advantage of the moment, with everyone milling around and talking, to approach her and ask if I might see the magazines and books she had been reading from. She was very gracious about showing them to me and, when I asked, translated for me the place and year of publication. It was North Vietnam. The books had been published in 1964, the magazine in 1968.

The class now broke up into small groups, to discuss "how violence affects both its victims and perpetrators" and "whether we can teach about war and consider alternatives to war without these accounts, which are so painful." In my group were Gloria, the feminist; a history professor who was one of the course instructors; a student from India; and Ellen, a pale young woman with nervous hands who kept pulling a ring on and off a finger when she was not gesturing in talk. Gloria wanted to make the point that war grew out of the cultural emphasis on winning as purpose, and that it was connected with sexual violence. She told us she had learned that from reading Susan Brownmiller, a name she pronounced with the slight pause of respect that might precede the name of a great philosopher or religious leader. War involved the desecration of the female. War was about domination. In war you destroy the enemy's possessions, one of which is the female. "I think it has a lot to do with something I'm very concerned about in this country right now, which is what's going on in colleges everywhere. Date rape and gang rape. It's the cult of masculinity in fraternities, the same as war."

Ellen spread her hands out in a gesture of pleading. "War is never a way of solving things," she pronounced. Ignoring the non sequitur, the group agreed that masculinity was equated with violence. At this point, the history professor let us in on something. With an engaging grin (meant to disarm?) he declared himself to be a Civil War buff. He loved reading about battles. He asked us to consider Sherman's March. A perfect example of what war did to men. Before long what starts as an orderly march inevitably becomes a swathe of indiscriminate destruction—burning, looting, raping, robbing. He asked us to consider which was worse—the Ghurkas in the Falklands trained to crawl into bunkers and slit the throats of their enemies or the person who lobs a shell into them from fifteen miles away. Wasn't the Ghurka way "more honest," involving more human contact? As the others nodded in agreement he added, "Sticking a bayonet in someone's throat is less numbing than sitting here in Columbia at a computer and simulating the destruction of hundreds of thousands of people." Less numbing. I would have to think about that.

Then he added a paradoxical thought. What, he asked, about some of the other qualities that appear in men at war, qualities other than cruelty. What about loyalty to friends, the case in which a man risks his life in a cause he knows to be hopeless just in order to save someone else? Silence. Gloria frowned, Ellen twisted her ring. After a moment in which the professor seemed stranded alone on his paradox, Gloria suggested we consider, as the evening's agenda had asked the groups to do, the question of how to introduce peace education into the elementary school curriculum.

Gloria provided the first strategy. Role playing. Providing scenarios the children could relate to, like games in which someone is forced to lose. "Then ask them how did it feel to be the loser, to be humiliated? That way you get rid of competition. You introduce cooperative play instead of competitive games." Appreciative nods from the group. Gloria turns to Bob, who has come in late and joined our group.

"More social studies," Bob says emphatically. "Get them to look at different cultures, to respect the culture of those we fought with, so they understand them as people. We're all people," he announces. "Oh, yes," Ellen says, "that's so important, and it's so lacking in our culture!" "We only learn about victory," Bob goes on, "not about what was done to achieve it. We glorify war. We have to demystify it. That should be part of the curriculum from first, second, third grade on. It's a lot easier the younger they are."

How do you introduce the subject, the history professor asks, looking around the group. Gloria doesn't think you should try to do it through reading books about war and violence—the group agrees that's not developmentally appropriate for the early grades— "so you have to get at it in other ways. Like taking them to the UN. It's so moving. You get a sense of peace making."

At this point the groups come together for "some sharing." Chairs are moved around and everyone goes back to the large U-shaped table in the center of the room. Marian begins, "We have to have children really understand what war is all about." Gloria is ready for this. "War has to do with the male sex role. The cult of masculinity." From the other side of the table a young woman adds, "That's where the nonfemale image of God comes into play." Ellen agrees. "If they had feminine figures of God would they treat women that way, like rape them and everything?"

The rhetorical question hangs in the air as Marian continues, "We have to educate this country for peace through cooperative learning. We have to start really young, even before school. Now that most mothers are working, the kids go off at two or three."

But, she emphasizes, it has to be done right. One of the students asks what she means. "Can you give an example of bad peace education?" She can. "The early stage of nuclear education, in which we gave information to students about the technology and the effects with no prior assessment of their emotional receptivity. We frightened them. To frighten is a bad approach. There was a lot of criticism. And we ought to address the politics of it, the values. Like sex education," she adds, "it works best where the community is involved." She adds that three of the city's school districts now include in their curricula a program developed by Educators for Social Responsibility.

On the way out I find myself walking down the hall with Gloria, who tells me, in answer to my question, that she teaches at a small college where she is the head of the Department of Gender Studies. "Women's studies and peace education are connected," she says, as though afraid I may have missed the point.

In the weeks that followed, I saw different kinds of classes on different levels at Teachers College, dealing with different aspects of schooling and taught by professors and instructors with different styles to different kinds of students. I began to see that at the end I would have to ask myself what it was that made them in some way seem so much the same.

There was the course in Curriculum Design. Before the class, I talked with the instructor, a man who had been a professor for thirty years, a teacher for a while before that. I asked what he thought about the influential Holmes Report, which had recommended that future teachers all take a liberal arts degree in some subject such as English or science and then take a graduate degree in education, thus replicating the professionalism of medicine and law.

He wasn't sure that was such a good idea. "We've been trying to get teachers into the classroom with kids earlier," he said. "If you don't have any contact with kids through four years of college, how do you know you want to teach?" He also disagreed with the thinking of then-Secretary of Education William Bennett and the influential Department of Education report *A Nation at Risk*.

"They complain that only the least competent go into teaching, those with the lowest SAT scores. But I'm not sure high SAT scores are the best indicator of what makes a good teacher. Other factors may be important. We know that effective teachers of gifted children aren't necessarily geniuses, and how much science do you need to know to be a good elementary school science teacher? Not as much as a physicist, surely, but just how much?"

It has become a commonplace to say that first-class minds are not to be found in schools of education. This is a question I would be considering many times in the months ahead. Are first-class minds what we need in the nation's classrooms, and if so, at what levels? Or is it something else we need, and if so, what?

"But the real problem in the schools," the professor went on, shifting, if not changing, the subject, "is the disadvantaged. And there to really make a difference you have to change society. Meanwhile, we get a new batch each year. . . . But we are teaching better. The latest National Assessment shows kids in compensatory educational programs doing better. It shows that our urban schools are not quite the cesspools they were.

"The question is, who decides to become a teacher? The Carnegie Report shows it's not just money, but the environment for success that matters. The women's movement has made a great difference in the pool of applicants. Women have more options than they used to, not just teaching and nursing, and so do members of minority groups. As a matter of fact, right here many minority scholarships go begging, ironically enough, while some deserving whites don't get help."

The class in curriculum design was the closest to the intellectual level of a graduate course in the liberal arts or law of any that I saw. It was also deadly dull. The professor, whether from pedagogical principle or existential fatigue, lectured in a practiced tone from a text which seemed to have long ago ceased to excite him, although it stimulated a fury of note taking on the part of his students.

The authors of current programs to reform the schools—Boyer, Adler, Goodlad, and others—were compared, and changing philosophies of recent decades were described in a movement from an emphasis on alternatives and options to more rigorous standards and core studies. Behind the questions of what we should teach and how we should teach it were philosophical assumptions about the child and society. The students would have to demonstrate a familiarity with all this in order to earn the degree that would open the doors to administrative positions and higher institutions of learning. And if they thought about these distinctions and analyzed the assumptions behind them it might even make them better at deciding what should go on in their classrooms or the classrooms of those they would be supervising.

Certainly such matters are outside and above the concerns of most teachers, but these people are being trained as the leaders of their field and it is they who will deal with the questions of what to teach and how to organize it. They pay a lot for this training—the tuition at City College is one-fourth of that at Teachers College. It will enable them to become the elite of the education world, and their seriousness is made evident in the quiet that pervades the room except for the droning voice of the lecturer and the scratch of pens on paper.

The deadly boredom of listening to a lecture being read (maybe this is one of the things they are learning about teaching) makes them grateful for a little professorial joke, however weak, to offset the slow creep of time, prevent the wandering mind. Are any of them standing back from the lecture as I am trying to do, analyzing the analyzer as he distinguishes, illustrates, emphasizes? Do they feel as I do, somewhere behind the apparent objectivity, a subtle bias in favor of those philosophers of education who feel its purpose to be less the preservation of the traditions of the past than a contribution to social change in the future? After all, this is Teachers College, where tradition is the tradition of progressive education, of John Dewey and William Heard Kilpatrick.

A reference to Whitehead prompts the first raised hand: "Who?" The student is irritated; she doesn't know what to write down. "Alfred North Whitehead," the professor repeats slowly, and quotes a passage from *The Aims of Education* about "the fatal disconnection of subjects" in the modern curriculum. "The best that can be said of it is, that it is a rapid table of contents which a deity might run over in his mind while he was thinking of creating a world, and had not yet determined how to put it together."

On another plane entirely from the consideration of how philosophies of education would influence the teacher and the taught is the preservice course intended to prepare elementary school teachers for the classroom.

This course was taught, whether intentionally or not, in imitation, or what often seemed like a parody, of a grade-school class. Seated around separate tables in groups of six or eight, the class divided into teams of two to consider an exercise in the practical arts. They were to suggest creative ways in which to make use of such materials as wallpaper sample books, bottle caps, egg cartons, and toothpicks in the absence of other supplies for teaching some subject on a grade level from kindergarten to sixth.

The group at my table included a woman in her late thirties whose own child had just entered school and who was student teaching and working for her degree, and two young women who were teaching at two of the city's most prestigious private girls' schools.

Another was student teaching in a New Jersey middle school, and two were teaching in nursery schools. Two professors and a couple of assistants roamed the room, looked over shoulders, praised the creative suggestions that were being put forward for using paper plates to illustrate fractions and old newspapers to suggest social science projects. Suddenly, one of the assistants stood up, clapped her hands and began to sing, "If you're happy and you know it, clap your hands . . ." At all the tables, her pupils joined in, through all the choruses: "If you're happy and you know it, stamp your feet . . . say hurrah . . . do all three." An object lesson, it was explained, on how to help children make the transition from one activity to the next.

A poem by Walter de la Mare was read out loud, slowly and with emphatic expression. We were invited to be children repeating the refrain of "someone" with the instructor. This was an illustration of what is referred to as classroom "community acts" meant to take the place of "too much paper and pencil." In another exercise designed to convey the perspective of a young child, everyone was asked to get down on the floor and look up at one of the professors standing on her desk. There was general agreement that the teacher looked pretty big from down there.

When the class returned and regrouped, it was as though everyone had grown up during the break. The clapping and singing, the reciting and sitting on the floor had evidently been purposeful pedagogic strategies. Now we were grown-ups again, learning about children, not acting like them. A recapitulation of what they had covered in the last class reminded them that educational theorists such as Plato had concerned themselves with what people ought to be, defining the ideally educated person, whereas psychological learning theories started from a definition of what people are actually like, specifically how they grow and develop. From there the instructor moved inevitably to the theories of Erikson, Bruner, Piaget— and Kohlberg, the moralist of the 1960s who preached the "higher idealism" of the period's adolescents and thus entered the pantheon of developmental psychologists.

These young teachers are, then, being encouraged to study child development, and to make their own learning a continuing process. Meanwhile, *their* teacher is illustrating what she tells *them* to do— not expect too much of children: deal with the concrete rather than the abstract; make sure students can understand a task before expecting them to perform it. She tells them to study one child in their class, to try to remember themselves at that age.

When the class ends there is a sense of finality, as though the curtain were ringing down at the end of a play. It has been an orchestrated event, and an effective one. An illustration, in sum, of a well-planned lesson.

For anyone needing to be reminded, a tour of classrooms in action provides a vivid reminder of how much the teacher influences the taught. I attend another course for student teachers, most of them older, more practiced. Some, like a young woman who taught for three years in Florida, have come to study here as full-time doctoral students. Others include an elementary school principal and a supervisor of teachers in New Jersey who stay at their jobs while working course by course toward their doctorates and a move up the professional ladder.

When they break into small groups of three and four for discussion, I join two men and a woman who prove to be bright, articulate, and in one case witty, and a fourth, a young man in a military camouflage suit who seems to be out of his depth. Each group has read the autobiography of a teacher. The subject here is Herbert Kohl. They talk about his teaching strategies, his view of what children are like. Each group will present its report to the whole class two weeks from now.

"Let's come together as a group now" is the signal; clustered chairs are moved back into rows. The professor wants to know whether they think suggested reforms in student teaching reflect the concerns of the student teachers here. The discussion that follows releases a downpour of the jargon bequeathed by the human potential movement to the corporate and academic worlds. "Role playing, getting involved, task-oriented, priority goals, peer interaction, feedback, role models, support groups . . ." Finally the light of real experience breaks through.

"Student teaching is boot camp." "It should be more like an internship." "Less paper work, busy work. More responsibility." "The cooperating teacher shouldn't be your adversary. Shouldn't feel you're a threat. Should trust you." "You do all the marking, she gives the grades at the end without doing any of the correcting." "Three hundred hours just isn't enough. You need an entire year." "More preparation time." "More opportunity to observe experienced teachers in action, see how they do it." Others wished "I had been computer literate," "I had more feedback—any feedback—from cooperating teachers," "Had more contact with other student teachers experiencing similar situations," "Had somebody to teach me that the job was limitless and no matter how much I did, there was always more to do—somebody to teach me to relax, say no, take time for me."

Woven through complaints of not enough time and not enough money ("If we were paid more we could stay at it longer, learn more before we get out there on our own") was a steady refrain of caring, sharing, "compassion." Many if not most of these teachers talk about things like feeling, warmth, empathy more than they do about skills, training, discipline. They long for "a humane, progressive education instead of what's out there. The emphasis on a controlled classroom scares me."

Not all of them see it that way, though. A teacher with four years' experience in the public schools speaks up. "All the talk about being reflective, being creative—it has nothing to do with the reality of what teaching is all about. What you need to learn is how to plan bus routes, how to put together a cafeteria schedule, how to move a class from one room to another, how to line kids up in the playground."

It seems fitting that so much of the process of educating teachers in this democratic society takes place in groups, stressing the sense of community rather than the individual. Returning to their small groups to discuss the papers they've read on teaching methods, another exercise gets under way in forging a consensus to report to the larger group. Not everyone will have to read everything that's assigned; some of it will be summarized by members of the other groups.

My group has hit a snag. The young man in the camouflage suit is not following the argument, wants to talk about himself ("I says to my supervisor"). Everyone listens respectfully to his complaint that the author of the paper on teaching methods they're discussing says bad things about inner-city schools, that he talks about the debris outside, the grating on the windows. A moment's pause, then a young woman in the group says that the author's point is that despite these disadvantages, it's what goes on *inside* —in the classroom—that counts. "Oh, yeah," says the young man. He smiles and shrugs. "I get mixed up reading so many books at once."

By the time the class ends the professor has elicited a summary of their assigned paper from each group and listed salient points from each on the board under various headings. On the resulting chart she points out to them how underlying values influence ultimate goals and determine one's idea of what good teaching is. How they will want to teach will depend on how they define the aim of education—for instance, a mature adaptation to life's problems versus raising achievement test scores.

It is not explicitly said. It does not need to be. It is there in the tone, the expression. The job of the teacher, the function of the school, is not to impart knowledge, at least not knowledge of the testable kind. It is not primarily a matter of the skills which are attained through the mastery of language, symbol, and abstract thought. It is to foster life adjustment—to "treat," as it were, the whole child. Here at Teachers College teaching is thought of as one of the helping professions, akin to social work—a kind of social therapy.

In one class the unspoken was made explicit, and here—and only here—it met with some argument. The course was entitled School Improvement, and the argument, surprisingly enough to me at that point, came not from the students but from the professor.

The discussion began with the catchword of the previous decade, "teacher burnout." There was a familiar recitation of its causes: the pressures brought about by the number of decisions a teacher has to make in a given hour; the pressures imposed by the need to maintain control in the urban classroom; the pressures caused by the teachers' sense of not being in charge of their own professional lives. They felt unfulfilled.

Walking around in front of the room and gesturing as he describes the fulfilled teacher, this professor gives the feeling of exemplifying what he is describing. "Everything they do matters. They tell their kids, 'If you don't read *To Kill a Mockingbird*, your lives won't be what they could be.' They have a reverence, a passion for their subject, whether it's 'The Idylls of the King,' Thomas Jefferson, a Mozart divertimento, or reading *Phèdre* in French 5." This is the first time I have heard mention of such things here at TC.

He talks about mastering teaching strategies and the importance of consistency. If a paper is assigned for Thursday and it isn't turned in on Thursday, in his view a grade should be deducted. Just as there are learning styles, there are also teaching styles, and what one's students learn is the test of them.

This is the signal for disagreement. "We have to get away from the emphasis on tests," a slight young woman with long hair says plaintively. Outcomes, excellence, accountability, achievement scores are identified in succession by members of the class as the shibboleths of the 1980s. Instead, these educators think (feel?), teachers should be "caring," should "feel good about themselves" and help their pupils feel good about *themselves*. A member of the class says heatedly, "The idea that if kids don't achieve you're not a good teacher is absurd!"

This graduate-level class is made up of present and future school administrators.

Election Day had come and gone when I returned to Teachers College. Everywhere—in the hallways, the cafeteria, the classrooms, the restrooms—the event was referred to in the shorthand way in which people who know they agree with each other signal that agreement. Sentences did not need finishing, shrugs and shakes of the head were enough. Reactions ranged from disbelief to indignation: clearly, educators had their work cut out for them. And nowhere would they be found readier to undertake the challenge presented by the American public's blunders than here in one of the country's premier teacher-training institutions.

SCENE FROM A CLASSROOM

The place: A large lecture hall in Teachers College.

The time: A winter afternoon in the education course careers of about a hundred and fifty graduate students, shortly after the inauguration of George Bush.

The cast: The students and an elderly professor who is reputed to be the most popular member of the faculty here. I have come to her course on Social Philosophy and Education to see why.

The professor enters from the left, takes her place at the lectern facing the students seated in the rows rising to the back of the auditorium, and passes to those in the front row several stacks of papers. These are the Marx-Engels reprints, she tells them, and those who wish to can pay her three dollars each next time. "It's voluntary and philanthropic," she says.

She begins with some introductory comments on the Frankfurt School and Walter Benjamin, who "looked at what coerces consciousness—bureaucracy, the media, the anonymous forces of an administered society." She takes out of her bulging briefcase the first of a number of clippings, books, papers, magazines she will read from or refer to during the class.

THE PROFESSOR: It's important to keep in mind in a course like this the voiceless, the powerless—women, the lamed, the destitute, the disenfranchised, the slave—those whom Dostoevsky called "trodden, offended." We are not hearing from the scarred, the homeless, those the community has abandoned. We have to ask what individualism means to the dislocated. The world is being torn apart. Just read *Time* today. AIDS . . . privatism . . . that terrible election campaign just over (sounds of agreement, indignation, from the class) with its peculiar emphasis on competence, without a heart, its despicable mean-spiritedness and racism.

This is a society with norms of success, effectiveness, efficiency, based on exploitation, imperialism, slavery, on British education with its proper canonical curriculum. The American idea of freedom is freedom from being interfered with, freedom *from*, rather than freedom *for*. But you *achieve* freedom by resisting something. When I was a young wife and mother, I was stifled. I couldn't get out of the playground. My God, there were so many things I wanted to do! But I was married to a doctor, locked in to a bourgeois routine of baked potatoes and naps that was a barrier to my own fulfillment. I needed a door to some space. I got a neighbor to care for my child and I went back to school.

The students are by now rapt.

THE PROFESSOR (continues): Teaching is work in community relations. You have to beware of the dangers of imposing the views of the haves on people less fortunate. This society pushes possessions. We must emancipate ourselves from these pressures, not be guilty of "cultural invasion." We have to do something about our preoccupation with rewards and competition in this country, with material accumulations. Is that what education ought to be? It serves the values of those in power. It has never fundamentally altered the economic structure. What if we could make a difference in human structures? There is a moral lack of care in this society.

A STUDENT: I sort of think we've got to make ourselves happy first.

ANOTHER STUDENT: Most business people have no real commitment.

ANOTHER STUDENT: We are a society notoriously bad about funding poverty programs because we link them with work.

THE PROFESSOR: I am disgusted by the reliance on philanthropy instead of federal and state government responsibility.

STUDENT: An artist should be *paid* for doing what he likes, even if it's sitting on the porch and playing the guitar.

ANOTHER STUDENT: Malevolent market forces . . . (The phrase hangs there, not even a sentence.)

THE PROFESSOR: That's true. (She says this after almost every comment.)

STUDENT: What scares me in the U.S. today is commitment to others is being squashed. People are like losing it.

The professor tells them she's planning to march in Washington for abortion rights that spring. "Let's make a big noise," she says.

At this point a student asks a question appropriate to the title of the course.

STUDENT: "What do we mean by social science?"

THE PROFESSOR: Social science is a normative concept, not just descriptive. It's about creating a more rational and sane society. Books like *Cultural Literacy* and *The Closing of the American Mind*, these attacks on "relativism"—they are *afraid* of multiplicity, uncertainty. Relativism is a *good* thing. Our aim should be to involve as many people with their multiple voices as possible. Let everyone be heard from. There are no "objective standards," there is no such thing as "objective norms."

The Professor refers to Hannah Arendt's *Eichmann in Jerusalem*. The students don't know who Eichmann was; she has to explain. She says, regarding Arendt's position on an objective moral law, "She disapproves, *ex post facto*. There is no such law. Nobody voted on, nobody passed that law." This last elicits laughter.

A black student says, "Here in America we have a Charles Murray who makes our Holocaust seem rational." She says that Charles Murray argues that black babies should not be born, that he is advocating genocide. No one questions, no one disagrees.

THE PROFESSOR (continuing): "Inalienable rights"—what does that mean? What objective thing is there? It was invented to do away with the divine right of kings. We act as if there were such a thing.

These student teachers are being encouraged to "transform" a world they know almost nothing about, either in the complexity of its present arrangements or the various routes by which it became the way it is. They know next to nothing of past disasters or triumphs, successes and mistakes. And nothing of the relentless way in which human nature reasserts itself in age after age, inconveniently limiting the possibilities for the most ambitious social plans. Sure of themselves as only those ignorant of history can be, they feel no need for tolerance of their own imperfect but relatively free society. All they know is that it isn't everything they think it should be. To them, that seems enough evidence for an indictment.

2

⚜ ——— ⚜

The State University of New York

Playing at Pedagogy

The State University of New York is the nation's largest university system, with about 390,000 students on over sixty-four campuses. The SUNY campus at Plattsburgh is in what people who live there call the North Country, almost at the Canadian border. It is an economically depressed area of the state, with no industry, little manufacturing, and only two main customers for services—the university itself and the nearby air force base. I have been told that the area is beautiful from spring into fall, but on this morning of a cold grey early December day the campus has a bleak look. The buildings are boxes of the anonymous institutional style that could be anywhere in the world. The residence hall where I have spent the night could be a budget ski lodge here in the Adirondacks except for the hand-lettered and Xeroxed signs around the elevator and the front door urging votes for various candidates running for the student assembly.

In the dining hall a string of Christmas lights flashes alternate little pulses of red, green, blue, orange, a disembodied plastic Santa's cheeks puff out with rosy jollity over a tinsel beard, a string of letters spells out the season's greetings, and youngsters move around to the ubiquitous unheard murmuring beats of an invisible radio or television set. Just as the buildings here in no way resemble the spires and towers of the Ivy League's attempts to take on the Old World's history and traditions, these young people, despite the universal uniform of studenthood, seem different from their cosmopolitan counterparts. In their jeans and camouflage suits, their leather and down jackets buttoned up against the cold, they move about among tables laden with Sugar Crisps, granola, griddle cakes, Danish pastries, help themselves to two, three glasses of orange juice, tropical fruit punch, chocolate milk and sit down in pairs, threes, foursomes.

They are as rosy-cheeked as Santa, wild-haired, always smiling, and, like the campus around them, plain, modern, functional, and a-historical. Not university students so much as American kids. Talking to them, one finds them, like their campus, without a sense of the past and not yet old enough to have acquired their own patina. Cheerful, helpful, artless, guileless American kids. Here at this breakfast table it dawns on me that I have left the coastal culture and the international perspective behind with Teachers College and New York City. Here in the North Country we are in what is usually referred to as middle America.

Sitting at the conference table in his modern managerial-style office, the boyish-looking president of the university has made me welcome and told me a little about the Center for Teacher Education. A 2.5 grade average—the equivalent of a $B-$ or $C+$—is the only entrance requirement for its undergraduate program. About one-third of the students come from the Long Island towns and other suburbs of New York City; about one-third from other parts of the state, mostly from the district around Albany, the state capital; the remaining third grew up around here in the north. Only 4 percent belong to that vast student population still euphemistically referred to as "minority," meaning all groups classified other than white. There is, however, the president tells me, much "multicultural" representation in the area. He explains that "around here, 'multicultural' means rural." The public schools to which student teachers will be assigned for two eight-week periods have their share of poor, disadvantaged children from single-parent families who live in "the projects." Only, unlike those in the inner cities, these are white.

As for some of the problems characteristic of this kind of student body, the president thinks the students need "a warm, caring, supportive environment, role models and mentors." If students drink and take drugs, he says, it is because "they have low self-esteem and don't know who they are." As for their academic shortcomings, if the faculty complains that they can't read or write, "Whose fault is that? *Their* teachers were trained by the same teachers who are complaining about them now."

The program here is well thought out and looks good on paper. It also sounds good as explained to me by the pleasant young assistant professor who will be teaching the section I'm about to visit. The program is divided into "blocks," the first of which—foundations—encompasses child development, child psychology, the history and philosophy of education, special education and teaching the gifted. These are supplemented with courses in language arts and writing on educational issues. The second-year block deals with curriculum and instruction, both elementary and secondary, includes courses on the teaching of mathematics and science, and is followed by an entire semester of student teaching.

The iconography of ed schools changes subtly from institution to institution. The earnest social exhortations of signs and posters in the hallways and classrooms of Teachers College have given way here to something lighter. A bumper sticker over the instructor's desk says "If you can read this, thank a teacher." And as I take a seat in a classroom (originally part of a defunct demonstration elementary school that now houses the Center for Teacher Education and Educational Services) I see over the blackboard at the front of the room, in large clear script, the legend: "We Choose to Feel Special and Worthwhile No Matter What."

The hour begins with the usual shuffling of papers to be returned, announcements about the upcoming final exam, and summary of the preceding class. They had been talking about classroom management, about the physical setup of the classroom and "how it impacts on the teaching—learning situation." Now they are moving to the question of assessment, from "issues of planning and implementing instruction" to "evaluating" it. In short, tests.

Appropriately enough, they are to begin with a short quiz. As I watch the young professor move from table to table handing out copies of the purple-lettered worksheet, smiling, calling the students—mostly young women—by name as he answers their questions, it strikes me that in his neat suit and tie, mustache and glasses, and pleasant manner, he could be a middle-management corporate executive anywhere in America. And he would not only be making a considerably higher salary, he would not be expected to spend his evenings making up worksheets and grading examination papers. What makes him—or others—choose teaching as a profession?

At the moment, surrounded as I am by students, I can only put this question to young women. Amy says, "I love little kids. I grew up with five older brothers and sisters and my mom always had foster kids and baby sat." Lucy has a four-year-old son. "When he gets to school I'll have the same working hours he does." Laurie too "loves kids." She actually beams when she says the words, as though they are completely new.

"Loving kids" as the motive for choosing a teaching career, the idea that at every level school should provide "a warm, caring environment," are axioms that go unquestioned, as the reactions to the questionnaire on grading and testing make clear. Some of the questions on the worksheet are: Do you think a student's IQ should be taken into consideration in his or her grade? Should effort play a part in a student's grade? Where do you stand on at least one large test for each marking period? Is the student's social class a factor? Where do you stand on the idea of a grading curve—an equal number of people receiving low grades and high grades?

Tabulation of the answers reveals that the main concern of these future teachers is not inspiring good students but protecting the average and the poor ones. "You should look at the effort, the amount of participation, not the intelligence level." Not surprisingly, they think of themselves as "average," of their own IQs as "normal," and that "achievement has nothing to do with IQ." They want everyone to end up with a passing grade—in school, in society, in life.

To that end in the discussion that follows they suggest various Byzantine ways of begging the question of standards. "What about the third-grader who tries," one of them asks, "but just can't learn to read?" "Mark him for effort." "Don't use grades to discourage him." "Use grades as positive reinforcement." "There are some who strive but it's tough for them. So the struggle should count." "Why not separate things—give him a *D* for achievement and an *A* for effort." The last solution elicits laughter from everyone—a manifestation of the good-natured attitude that seems to characterize their personalities as well as their positions.

The only question raised to challenge these views is, "What if you pass a poor student on to a situation where he can't survive?" The focus is still not on any objective goal but on the well-being of the individual student. But now the instructor steps in and asks the class, "What *are* grades for? Why do we give grades?" "They make us." (Laughter) "To get feedback about achievement." "To keep track of overall improvement. Moving from an *F* to a *C* means more than getting *A* all the time." "To have something to tell the parents." "For the teacher's benefit—to see how effective you are."

The responses give the instructor an opening to remind them of some of the reading they've been assigned in their textbook this semester. "Bloom's taxonomy . . . judgment based on criteria . . ." Blank faces. They looked alive when giving their opinions, recounting their experiences. Faced with an abstract argument, they seem to go dead. He perseveres nevertheless, reminding them of the agenda: planning, which involves setting goals; implementing; evaluating, which involves having some objective criteria. They're not disrespect-ful, they don't argue, but one can see they're not buying it. They don't like the idea of objective criteria for grading. They want to make allowances for poor performance and, if possible, rule out failure altogether. In the end he finds a common area of agreement between himself, a teacher of teachers, and his pupils who will fan out to the public schools to teach children, including three of his own: "A lot of the learning that goes on in a classroom is not based on performance objectives."

Between classes, in the hallway where a knot of students stands around the coffee cart, some of them tell me why they want to be teachers. One young man says a lot of his friends are teachers. Another says he wants to be a role model for boys. "There are too many single-parent families today, boys growing up with only their mothers at home. Somebody has to teach them values and character." Two women in their thirties agree that "it's the best profession if you want to raise a family." One of them has stayed home taking care of her three children, and now that the youngest has started school she's decided to become a teacher rather than pursue her original career as a dietician, so that she'll have the same schedule as her children. A younger woman says simply, "I've always wanted to be a teacher. When I was a kid I always played school." Over and over again I found women's expressed reasons for going into teaching to be personal and practical; where idealism entered the picture was with the young men.

Perhaps it was a coincidence, but one of the liveliest and most interest-ing classes I visited was also the one with the largest number of young men—seven out of twenty-six. It was also the one in which I was most aware of the craft with which the instructor—I'll call him Professor Harrison—choreographed the classroom event. He had a clear agenda in mind and knew his students well enough to be able to play their positions off against each other as he kept the discussion moving toward the point he wanted to reach. Like the earlier class, this one—Elementary Curriculum and Instruction—was in Block II. Here too the atmosphere was good-humored and the laughter frequent. But the discussion was less weighted with unexamined statements of preference and more clearly tied to the ideas of various writers on pedagogical issues. The students had read the texts, gone out to teach in the schools, then returned to write statements based on their experiences. Today was for tying it all together. The subject under review as I took my seat was classroom management.

"You need to know what you're doing and why," Professor Harrison was telling the class. A compact grey-haired man with a trim beard and confident bearing, he perched on a table at the front of the class with his arms folded; his eyes moved from one student's face to another's as he engaged them in dialogue. There were no merely rhetorical questions, no merely pat answers. No doubt about it, something was going on in this room. If nothing else, a demonstration of effective classroom management.

"What about the kid who doesn't pay attention but knows the answers?" asks a young man. "It must be Aaron again," says one of his tablemates, and there is general laughter. (They not only know each other, they know each other's pupils.) This leads Harrison to comment on "the teaching act as a control mechanism" and "playing 'Gotcha,' where you think you'll turn the child around by humiliating him." A student remembers being made to write "I will behave" one hundred times and how he used carbon paper to get the job done. Harrison is sarcastic about the use of learning as punishment and tells an engrossing story about his own daughter, whom he calls "Polly Perfect" (evidently one of a familiar cast of characters here) to illustrate his point. He mentions body language and asks for their own memories of their school days. Someone remembers a teacher who spent the entire term looking out the window at the flagpole instead of at the students while she lectured. Harrison comments, "That could only happen in high school. In elementary school the teacher's eyes seemed to bore through your skull and bare all the secrets of your soul." He suggests they examine their facial expressions in a mirror. "Do you know how wimpy your stern look looks?" Someone gives an example of a valuable tool for classroom management—Valium.

The jokes aren't stoppers. They're all used by Harrison to make a point, to serve as an example of something that was said by one of the authors they have read or illustrated by a classroom experience one of them has reported. Some of these young women have children in school and their comments are full of references to the classroom experiences their own children are having. One of them objects vehemently to giving out external rewards like red and gold star stickers. Harrison does not minimize her concern. This, he says, is the trouble with American society—"the generic idea of the value of competition, that there must be winners and losers." This vision of inevitable inequality is "not humanistic."

He ends the morning by reading to the class from a paper one of them has written. It is clear that he regards it as an ideal, not just because it is well written but because he approves of its position. A good teacher, the student writes, "will create an environment conducive to learning . . . in which rules are not arbitrary, and are not enforced for the purpose of controlling students. Rules and their enforcement must be consistent and based on individual rights so the students will respect them; they must be fair, taking into account the individual backgrounds and abilities of students."

It has been a long morning, and not once have I heard any mention of content in the curriculum. Instead, they are talking about "building self-esteem through assertive role playing in peer situations."

At lunch with some members of the faculty, we talk about the National Teachers Examination. Everyone agrees that it is a scandal. There is some disagreement, however, about the nature of the scandal. A young man I have not met before thinks the fact that a third of the teachers in Texas could not pass the examination means that it discriminates against minorities. A woman who is herself from the South disagrees indignantly. It was so simple a test of basics that no one unable to pass it should be certified to teach. "I wouldn't want *my* children taught by anyone without basic language, in some dialect. Speech is the key to mainstream culture. Speech and writing." Again, the fairness doctrine has run up against the issue of standards. And Professor Harrison tells me that half of his students didn't know at the beginning of the term what "ism" added to a word meant. "We can't presume our students know anything," he says. "They've never even learned the states and their capitals."

I didn't know it, but I was about to witness a demonstration of Harrison's point. The class in Exploring Education Issues through

Writing was led by the woman who at lunch had upheld the idea of standards for elementary school teachers. The students were all women, of varying ages but mostly young, with impassive expressions and an inability to utter more than ten words without the insertion of "like."

Professor Cleary began by saying we would be "workshopping on transactional communication situations." The first situation was "bypassing." We would be "barnstorming on bypassing." Bypassing, I discovered, looking at the paper in front of the young woman next to me, occurs when communicators miss each other with their meanings. The text for this lesson seemed to consist of simpleminded thoughts expressed in jargon.

One of the young women responds to a request for a classroom example: "If the child is having a lot of problems you'll try to find like what interests this particular child." Cleary agrees that there is no one general way to teach a subject; the approach must be adjusted to each child's individual learning style. The assumption here is that once that style is found, everyone will succeed, in contrast to the expectation in other, less egalitarian societies, that inevitably some won't make it.

"I was wrong to say something they didn't understand," says a student teacher. She had asked the class to "give me the characteristics of a square." She confesses, "I went too fast for them."

Before the class ends I have heard one of the student teachers say, "I'm done talking," and the professor say, "When I was your all's age . . ." It seemed that the best one could hope for is that young teachers like these might prove adequate for the care—if hardly the instruction—of the very young.

It was impossible not to admire the three supervising teachers from the local schools I talked with, together with some of their student teachers from this program. The supervisors had all been teaching for a number of years—the oldest, although she hardly looked it, for seventeen—and they talked earnestly and sympathetically about the problems in the district schools: the children from the air force base whose fathers were often away for long periods of time; the working mothers who were not there when their children came home from school; the parents in the housing projects who were unable to help their children with homework because they themselves functioned at a low level of literacy and had no computation skills; the single teenage mothers who, like their black counterparts in the inner city slums, lacked the resources to be nurturing, being hardly more than children themselves. Some of their pupils came to school without having had breakfast; others had parents who never listened to them.

The only appropriate word for these teachers' attitude toward their job and their charges is "dedicated." Asked how they felt about having to fill so many roles in addition to giving instruction—being social workers, therapists, surrogate parents, and in other ways expected to make up for some of their pupils' deficits—they responded not with a complaint about their tasks but with a judgment about the best way to go about fulfilling them. They simply took it for granted that they would try to do whatever was asked of them. "It's our job. If we don't do it," said one, "who will?"

They talked about the group of student teachers who had organized an after-school program, about the teacher who had taken a child home for a visit when she found he had never seen a dishwasher, the time a parents' meeting had been called to discuss the introduction of a sex-education program for kindergarten through twelfth grade and only two parents showed up, and the number of schools with no parent–teacher organization at all. One of them said, "When they leave my room I want to be able to feel I've helped them cope with what they'll have to deal with—and that they'll be excited to come back on Monday morning."

Other teachers said, "The caring part of it, reaching out and helping kids and making a difference—that's all part of the job. It *has* to be," and "If you open your eyes and see there are problems at home, you can't just do nothing. A child can't learn in school if there are problems at home, so you have to get to the bottom of their problems if you're going to teach them." They all agreed that administrative duties often got in the way of being "instructional leaders."

But the improvised coffee hour at dusk in a children's schoolroom left me with even more questions than I had come with. Was this a self-selected group of the very best who were meeting with me on their own time after school hours? Would the less thoughtful, less articulate young women I had observed preparing to be teachers here grow into equally responsible and inspiring adults? Or were there forces of social change at work—for instance, the greater number of career options opened up for women in recent years—drawing off the best and the brightest into other fields?

I brought these questions with me to the classrooms I visited later. In one, dealing with the secondary level, students had read an article about an innovative school in West Germany. Their comments ranged from "I liked it" through "It was very interesting" to "I liked it a lot." One student found it "too praisable," by which he was revealed to have meant "too uncritical." Discussion consisted at first of repeating and summarizing the contents of the article. Pressed for comment, they came up with "I'm just like, you know, it wouldn't work here." "I don't think it would work that good." "I think . . . I think . . . I think . . ."

A class in Elementary Foundations of Education proved elementary indeed. A room full of girls, all of whom seemed to have spent more time thinking about the arrangement of their hair that morning than about the theories of child development, educational psychology, and the history and philosophy of education which they were presumably here to discuss. Peggy, Sharon, Lynne, and Mary Beth, like members of the other groups of four or five, had prepared descriptions of a philosophy of education for their classmates. These were shallow summaries in a paragraph or two of complex ideas that most members of the class would be spared having to read in their original forms, purple printed pages decorated with little drawings evidently meant to supplement the meager text. The definition of "perennialism," the subject of this morning's first presentation, was given in the form of a flower whose petals were labeled "truth," "beauty," and "goodness," the leaves "classical" and "realism," and the stem "Great Books." Mortimer Adler was identified as the leading proponent of this school of thought and the phrase "liberal education" was mentioned. The group carrying out this assignment had gone to the library and taken out some of the great books, which they had brought to class and arranged on a table. Displayed were worn library copies of Aeschylus, Dante, Machiavelli, Plato, Aristotle, Homer. Some of the girls walked to the table and looked at the books, but did not bother opening any of them.

One member of the class, when called on for discussion, volunteered, "Liberal arts is not what we're interested in. Here you want to start learning about your life." She went on, "We've been doing liberal arts all our lives in school. Now I want to learn about teaching little children." During the break I asked her what liberal arts she had studied. She told me she'd taken courses in psychology, economics, and sociology. She was nineteen, and what she knew about the liberal arts was that she wasn't interested in them.

Most of her classmates agreed. "I like school and stuff, but . . ." trailed off into a shrug. "The teachers here," said another, "they're so knowledgeable of their courses." Another said, "You get burned out in college." "We could argue till we're blue in the face, we all have different opinions, so why argue? We want to get out of school, get out there and teach." They took a vote, and only one out of the twenty-four voted for a system that would require four years of liberal arts prior to teacher training courses. "Why waste four years on this liberal arts stuff after nineteen years of straight education?" was the way Michele put it.

The "existentialists" fared somewhat better than the "perennialists" in the morning's demonstrations. The printed description was simple but clear, and verbal rather than visual. ("The individuals make responsible choices freely . . . allow students to freely select topics for study . . . make the school fit the child instead of making the child fit the school.")

Asked by the instructor how they wanted to present their topic, the young ladies representing existentialism said they would act out a classroom situation illustrating it. While four of them sat on the floor pretending to do different things, the fifth, playing teacher, asked how they wanted to spend the next hour. Two voted for a science project, one voted with her feet, saying she would go out in the playground and pretended to open a door and leave the imaginary classroom, and the fourth had no opinion. The science project was to consist of making an Albert Einstein puppet. "How do you feel about that?" the pretend teacher asked the fourth pupil, in an unconscious parody of the Summerhill kind of school one assumes they had in mind. A little more pretending to be children, a lot of giggling, and the real professor sits by, smiling as she watches. The pretend teacher looks at her pupils' imaginary handiwork and says, "That was a really nice group activity."

The hour is drawing to a close, and from her seat at the side of the room the earnest and attractive young professor tries to stimulate questions from the group. A few of the students make statements about whether they liked or did not like the kind of school depicted and whether they thought it would or would not "work." Most sentences are finished with something like "da*da* da*da*," as in, "If the teacher just says, 'Do this,' da*da* da*da* . . ." Or, "The teacher's gonna be like, well . . ."

Summing up, the professor asks the class, "Do you think an existential education person would be a conformist or a nonconformist?" Several students call out, "*non*conformist." "Good," she says, smiling.

Later that day I had a chance to see the same course—Elementary Foundations of Education—taught very differently. Professor West, as I'll call him, was a middle-aged man who could have been the father of his young associate who had taught the earlier section. And in the context of this institution he might be said to be so, having been, as I later learned, one of the original designers of the program.

His students had been asked to do a fair amount of reading from the works of Dewey, Piaget, Adler, and other major educational theorists and to add to their written summaries of these authors' positions relevant notes on their own practice teaching experiences. They were then to organize these examples under various headings in a notebook to which they would be able to refer and to which they were urged to add new thoughts and new illustrations in the years to come. While most of the questions these students were asking seemed to be about putting the thinker in question into the right section of their notebooks, the questions about classification necessarily required some understanding of the ideas involved.

It strikes me that not only is Dr. West older and more experienced than the professor in the earlier section of the course, his students, too, both women and a few men, seem a few years older and, it must be said, more intelligent—whether this was intentional on the part of the administration or for some other reason. These students were preparing to defend the positions represented by the choices they had made in organizing their notebooks with a degree of concern that indicated a respect for the task itself and for the teacher who had set it for them.

When I talked later with Dr. West about the discrepancy between this class and the earlier one, he tactfully declined to discuss his colleagues but said, "The teaching profession doesn't have any consistent validated rationale for what they do, so there's no consistency between schools—at another SUNY campus nearby, things are totally different from what we do here—or even between the way Block I and Block II are taught here in the same institution by different teachers." He hoped that putting together a handbook of concepts and sources for future use would provide these students with "a basic reference framework, the ability to defend their positions on change or validate their concepts with administration, parents, and fellow teachers." It was the most ambitious, yet also the most practical and least pretentious, goal I had so far observed anyone having set for himself and his students. It was hard work for them to meet his standards, hard work for him to keep at them, showing how. In the process, he was teaching them more about how to teach effectively than anyone I'd yet observed. I wasn't going to be able to use that old chestnut, ". . . and those who can't teach, teach teachers" anymore. Not for a while, anyway.

PART TWO

The Southeast

3

Austin Peay State University

Standards and Starfish

Clarksville, Tennessee, where Austin Peay State University—named for a former governor—is located, is a town of approximately 6,500. The largest employer is Fort Campbell, a military base just over the border in Kentucky with around 30,000 Mobile Brigade personnel and dependents. The next largest employer is the county school system. In recent years the Clarksville Coca-Cola bottling plant has been automated ("The only jobs they have for college boys now is moving trucks of cases around," says a local resident). Japanese automobile and auto parts manufacturers have set up plants in the area; they hire locally and send their recruits to Japan for training. Goods and services are provided by retailers and wholesalers in a newly developed regional shopping center. ("It's killed downtown Clarksville" is the local's comment.) The Clarksville newspaper, the daily *Leaf-Chronicle*, circulation 19,000, gained a moment of notoriety when a syndicated *Chicago Tribune* columnist revealed that it had refused to print and then stopped buying his column because he was "bashing" then-candidates Bush and Quayle.

Austin Peay evolved from a rural academy in the early years of the nineteenth century and a Protestant church-affiliated college at the turn of the twentieth; it became a normal school for the training of teachers in the late 1920s. As such, it offered a two-year program intended to prepare teachers for the poor rural district schools. Part of the Tennessee state system for roughly the past quarter century, along with its education courses it has for about ten years also offered bachelor's and master's degrees in arts and sciences. Its history and its present-day character are fairly typical, in both its strengths and weaknesses, of the quondam normal schools in less urbanized areas of the country.

The chairman of the education department has been at Austin Peay for twenty years, long enough to give him a perspective on the current wave of school reform. "The reform movement has affected the public perception of and thus the demands on teachers," he says, "so reform in the children's classroom is accompanied by reform in the teacher-education classroom. Standards have been raised by means of competency tests and grade requirements. That's all to the good; it makes the job better. But if there's a teacher shortage we'll have to lower standards again.

"We expect too much of teachers today," he adds. "The pool isn't worse, the expectations are higher."

At a school like Austin Peay, the tradition is very much a practical one and the emphasis is on classroom teaching methods as distinct from the issues of theory and policy that pervade the education schools and departments of the large research-oriented multipurpose universities. Most of the students grew up in the area and many are already raising their own families there. They are intimately aware of the needs of the community and the problems of the local schools, and they are here to qualify for a job and learn how to do that job effectively within the framework of the State Board of Education rules and regulations. In required courses like Foundations of Education, they will be exposed to such topics as historical influences and trends in American education, curriculum in a multicultural society, philosophical ideas in education, and the influence of socio-cultural forces on learning, as well as such issues as teacher supply and demand, organizations and politics, Constitutional rights of teachers and students and legal aspects of discipline policies, teacher dismissals, grievance procedures, and collective bargaining. But the heart of the matter for them is in such courses as Instructional Strategies. They want to know how to manage kids, and how to get the material across—how, as one of them put it, to survive in the classroom.

The instructional strategy being explained to the class on the day of my visit is questioning. You cannot get much more practical than this—a course that explains and demonstrates such specifics of classroom management and instructional technique as how to ask questions. The professor is a tall, rangy, bespectacled man of middle years in shirtsleeves, easygoing and thoroughly confident. He shows a short film in which teacher models demonstrate the skills he has in mind. It's a "minicourse" made by a film company and published by a large textbook house from material developed by a research firm. A lot of hands have gone into producing this demonstration of how to question students, breaking the subject down into how to make use of pausing, how to handle incorrect responses, and how to call on nonvolunteers. This approach is called microteaching. The students fill out lesson forms and checklists to establish their understanding of what is being taught. They are given a format to follow and will be videotaped practicing what they have seen demonstrated and heard discussed, after which they'll see themselves on the VCR and "critique" their own and each other's teaching. Everything is clearly spelled out for them; they only have to follow the examples.

The method should be foolproof. At the very least, it should provide a certain confidence as well as a basic repertoire of approaches for the novice teacher. This is a significant advantage when so many complain of feeling thrown to the wolves, overwhelmed, at a loss when they first begin practice teaching or take over their first class. At worst, of course, it could produce a certain mechanical tendency in the teacher.

Can one be taught to respond to others? Dr. Banner, as I'll call him, shows the students how to redirect questions in order to avoid being the central presence in the classroom. "The bottom line," he tells them, "is to decrease teacher talk and increase student talk." Nobody questions this goal. Yet he himself lectures uninterruptedly, holding both the floor and their attention. And there's no question that they're getting more out of his talk than they would out of each other's. On the other hand, perhaps the teacher *should* in many if not all cases be the dominant member of the class. Banner disarmingly confesses to being less than a perfect teacher himself, one for whom enlightenment came too late in his professional life to change his ways.

Among the students I find myself talking with at the break is a burly bearded man in his late forties who tells me he's retired from the military, has trained as an X-ray technician, but has decided to switch into teaching. He's seen his own kids respond to good teachers and bad ones and thinks that despite the lack of money in teaching, it's what he'd like to do. "I guess you could say I'm altruistic." Still, it bothers him that teachers are being asked to do so many—and perhaps incompatible—things. "Too much is being put on them— to be babysitters, figure out bus schedules and run the cafeteria, recognize learning disorders and deal with them . . ." The list goes on.

After the break, Dr. Banner offers more examples of ways teach- ers can move a discussion along "without making the teacher more important than the student." Like so much of what one hears in the world of professional educators, this is intended to be democratic and to discourage elitism. Yet his own teaching, as we have already seen, differs from the advice he gives his students, knowing as he does more than they do and being good at presenting what he knows.

He is also fond of the clinical model and tells the class about supervising a student teacher who felt demoralized because a student in his high school class always fell asleep. "You try what you can," he told him, "but maybe the kid is working at a filling station all night, just waiting to drop out of school. You can't be successful every time with every student. It's like being a doctor or a lawyer— you can't expect to win every time."

He seems conscious, too, of owing his students a return on their investment: not only the tuition they pay but the fact that some of them got up at five in the morning and drove from a nearby town, "another world," to be here at seven for the earliest class. He tells them, "Get your kids thinking in the right direction in the first few minutes. If you spend that time taking roll and all the other housekeeping malarkey we have to go through before getting on to more important things, it'll be like what we used to say on the farm when we didn't put the hay up right—it'll be a snowball come winter."

The unspoken assumption of what he tells them is that the teach- er's job is to interest the student, not, as in the traditional European model that predated the child study movement, progressive educa- tion, and the democratization of schooling, that it is the student's responsibility to learn, however the material is presented. Neither the authority of the teacher nor that of the text dominates the Ameri- can classroom, where the purpose of learning, and the test by which it is judged, is ultilitarian.

"Use 'why' words," Banner tells his students, offering them tips on how to phrase their teaching so as to "relate previously acquired information to new information in order to develop new concepts. Ask them to justify, explain, relate. Ask them if they can find a parallel."

The purpose of learning, he tells them, is "to be able to use it, to apply it to new situations."

In the faculty staff room, a time to unwind over a cup of coffee. "This is where we bitch about these things," says one of the professors, pointing to a cartoon on the wall that lists "working conditions: lousy pay, overcrowded classrooms, nitpicking bureaucrats, ding-dong school boards, disrespectful kids, indifferent parents."

I have just heard him telling a class of young men and women about to start the first field experience of their teaching careers, "You must be honest and above reproach in all things. You are an educator—one who leads." The discussion centered around "how cultural forces influence school and learning." He told them, "We have to think about the social implications of what we teach" and mentioned recent court cases involving such issues as godless human-ism in the curriculum and whether a student had a right to wear a hat in class. They would have to become versed in the law pertaining to grievance procedures and student rights. He reminded them that state law required the preparation of an individualized educational program for every child and that "counseling is part of what we have to do." They would have to know each child's background, "the conditions under which children survive, what they bring to school."

He told them about his wife, a ninth-grade English teacher ex-pecting to teach *Julius Caesar* and finding herself faced with a roomful of students who could not write a simple declarative sentence, unac-quainted with the five basic parts of speech, unable to spell or to read a simple magazine article. He advised those who expected to teach in the rural county schools to "get a wide distribution of courses in addition to your specialty. You may have to be a part-time speech teacher or coach the cheerleading team. And don't keep a messy room. It will get you in trouble with the janitor—and he has status.

"When the public sees us delivering on student achievement, when SAT scores increase—that's what will make us professionals. That's more significant than salaries."

Here, as in most states today, a course in special education is required for teacher certification. Special education is a term that no longer seems quite fitting, since the intention of Public Law 94–142—perhaps the most influential piece of federal legislation affecting the schools since the early days of desegregation following the Brown decision—is to bring all kinds of handicapped children out of special situations and into the regular classroom. It mandates, for a wide spectrum of "exceptional" children—which includes such disparate categories as the mentally retarded, blind, deaf, orthopedically handicapped, health impaired, learning disabled, behavior disordered, emotionally disturbed, and gifted and talented—a free and appropriate education in the least restrictive setting. That setting is the regular public school classroom, and the practice of enrolling all of the above kinds of children there is known as mainstreaming. Today, every public school teacher can expect, and must be trained, to deal with all such children to some extent.

The class on special education training was meeting for the first time on the day that I attended, and by the time it ended I felt touched by the almost evangelical fervor in the young woman who taught it. Here is where in our day those dedicated to a life of service go. Many would-be teachers enter the field out of the same impulses that might once have led them into nursing or a religious order. They yearn to do good.

It is impossible not to admire and respect the ideals expressed by this fresh-faced young woman who bends over the lectern to exhort her students to "make an opportunity for all the children in America," to think of themselves not just as teachers but as "social engineers—put *that* on your credit card application"—who "hold tomorrow in the palm of your hand. Just think," she says, "all our future scientists, governors, artists, are now in preschool. You have a chance to shape their intelligence, teach them how to think. Small obstacles like blindness shouldn't be allowed to stand in the way.

"There is no average," she tells them. "Everyone is unique, different, special, and we are all learners on a journey together. What's important is the trip. Think of this course as an introduction to teaching and learning. Despite their disabilities and defects, these children are more like us than different, and teaching them you will find out a lot about how *you* learn, pick up special tricks that will make you a good communicator."

When she tells them about the self-confidence gained by a young retarded woman she taught how to swim at a summer camp, she makes it seem unimportant that she says, "Between this young woman and I . . ." She tells them they'll be visiting a school for children with multiple devastating handicaps where they'll see things that will be hard for them to face, but where they'll also see blind children pushing the wheelchairs of children who can't walk. And she tells them that the answer to the question, "Who is acceptable?" is "Everyone."

Many longtime teachers are less than enthusiastic about what they see as attempts like these to reform society through the schools, not necessarily because they disagree with the intended reforms but because they feel the effort can't be undertaken without slighting other things the schools—and only the schools—can and should do.

Typical of such critics, a teacher for ten years before becoming a teacher of teachers for the last ten and whose subject is English literature (now referred to in the professional jargon as language arts), is the woman who feels that "as we're extending the base, those at the top are being slighted." It bothers her that many prospective teachers are not much more proficient in grammar, punctuation, and pronunciation than those they would teach. "In these rural areas the southern dialect is a problem," she says. "There are ingrained colloquial speech patterns like 'I seen you,' 'I come by yesterday,' or 'Where did I put my book at?' and they don't get corrected by reading as they once might have. They don't read."

This teacher is among those who applaud recent enactment of competency requirements like the Pre-Professional Skills Test, a basic achievement test that weeds out the most unqualified. But she agrees with the department chairman that such requirements are at the mercy of the marketplace. Standards are lowered whenever the pool of teacher applicants shrinks. (This is one of the arguments for alternative routes to teacher certification drawing on the population of the well-educated and talented who may not have had traditional education courses; but in any case that argument is not a consideration in this part of the country, away from urban centers and the large universities where such ideas tend to originate.)

"What we're seeing here in the rural picture," she tells me over styrofoam cups of coffee in her small, pleasant book-lined office, "is more nontraditional families. That means not only more poor single mothers with kids entering the public schools. It means a lot of women going back to work who have one or two kids. They're deciding to become teachers because they know they can handle kids. They've managed households and taught Bible classes or worked in day care and they know they can manage a classroom in places like Big Rock and Palmira and Bumpus Mills. They're the best students we have."

Some of those students are in the Children's Literature class I visited. When asked for titles of favorite books read in childhood and still remembered, they mention the books they had recently read to their own children: the *Little House* books of Laura Ingalls Wilder, Beverly Cleary's books, *Charlotte's Web, Curious George,* and Dr. Seuss all kept company with Nancy Drew and the Happy Hollisters. Offsetting the sense of continuity inspired by these familiar titles and authors, however, were comments like one from a student who said, "I remember this book, my momma read it to me? I can't think of the name. It was about this girl and she had long golden hair." At this point several voices call out, "Rapunzel!" and the speaker sinks back in her chair, looking exhausted from the effort to remember what turns out on further questioning to have been the Disney version of some fairy tales. The professor improbably suggests that they familiarize themselves with the titles and authors on a list of winners of the prestigious Newbery Medal awarded each year for a distinguished children's book "so you'll know about them and even if you haven't read them you'll be able to talk about them."

The subject of reading is, like so many parts of the curriculum, a controversial one—not only what should be read but how the basic skill of reading should be taught. Research is cited and experts quoted as the argument goes on between the proponents of a traditional phonics approach, learning to sound out the letters that make up words, and what in its present incarnation is called the "whole language" approach, learning to recognize words in context. In a graduate school of education at a large research-oriented university one is likely to hear discussion of the research and the opinions of experts. Here at a teacher training institution, whether it's called a school, a college, or a university, one gets a more down-to-earth direct response to the question, What do you think of the whole-language approach to reading?

"A disaster," is the verdict. An experienced classroom teacher whose earliest first-graders now have children in school themselves says, "It probably *is* how children learn if they learn from the crib, if they absorb books on their mother's lap from babyhood, if they grow up surrounded by words, signs, labels, but you can't start that way at age five when there's been no previous exposure." Another reminder that the diversity of our society imposes different kinds of tasks on the teachers of different kinds of children with different needs.

How family, social class, and economic status influence the goals and practices of the classroom teacher was the subject of a graduate seminar called Social-Cultural Foundations of Education. Some of the students in the course are teaching early grades of children from the lower-end housing projects in the region and they talk about the low self-esteem of these children and the high frequency of dropouts as they get older. The professor, whom I'll call Dr. Boone, tells the others, "You will not escape the opportunity, the obligation, of working with these kids."

Looking over the textbook for the course, the sixth edition of a standard work entitled *Society and Education*, I realize how powerful the publishers of textbooks really are. Here are statements about class and race and economic differences in our society that both reflect the received wisdom of the day and form the opinions that will be shared in the classroom tomorrow. They will not be challenged by these men and women: after all, this is the textbook. Yet Dr. Boone points out that even in this latest edition there are already facts and figures that are obsolete. "We live in a world that's changing too fast for them to keep up with."

This seminar seems like a summation of something. Dr. Boone mentions the implications for schools of the larger birth rate among the poor: society may become oriented toward the lower class and the schools more devoted to serving the handicapped of all kinds. Legislation has already, he tells them, been proposed for enrolling children in school as early as three years of age. Day care programs in the public school setting are clearly on the way, with legislation already on the books. School will be the child's home away from home. A special-education teacher says, "Good. We're getting to them earlier and you can do more for them if you get them young."

She seems to be illustrating what he means when he says, "As the percentage of minorities grows and conflicts over matters like language in the schools proliferate, schools will be the institutions expected to solve all society's problems. They always have been. And schools always agree to this."

"Classroom teachers have no say about that. We're victims," says one of them. Boone smiles, agrees that "we serve at the pleasure of politicians." The discussion moves to the high and growing proportion of the nation's children enrolled in metropolitan-area schools, the abandonment of the inner cities to the poor and immigrants. "What is happening in society should be in the background of your thinking about educational policy, about what you do." They talk about cultural pluralism and current claims for group recognition of an official kind, institutionalized rather than informal as in the past, when the public school was expected to assimilate all comers to the larger society "and the private sphere did the special ethnic thing. Take nonstandard language," he says. "We got off on some real rabbit trails on that one. So many of the changes we see just depend on who has the button."

"Why are you here?" he asks them. For some it's simply a matter of earning higher pay, others mention status ("respect"), some are climbing the career ladder. Five of the nine graduate students in the seminar are mothers. One of them says, "It's a luxury today to be a mother, but it's a necessity to be a worker."

I'm invited to comment at the end, and I ask if I may put a few questions of my own. They readily agree. I ask them to tell me what they think school is for.

The answers at first run to piety: "To develop self-esteem"; "To prepare them to cope with the future"; "To acquire work skills." One young woman offers, tentatively, "To impart knowledge of the culture." She adds, "Of our values. For them to feel that learning is important, school is a warm place to be."

They all agree that teachers should not bring politics into the classroom "except for democracy and equality." They are equally in agreement about sex education. "It's necessary." "It's our responsibility as educators." "It should be there from kindergarten up to twelfth grade, whatever they need to know about sex—but teaching morals is the parents' job."

A quiet woman who looks around forty and hasn't said much leans forward and animatedly cuts to her point: "I teach in a rural county over the state line in Kentucky and I have twelve-year-olds in my classes having kids. You wouldn't believe the incidence of child abuse. And when a girl is sexually abused, it's her father, or her brother, or her uncle, or her mother's boy friend. Who's there at home going to teach these kids how to protect themselves, what it's all about, if we don't?" Then she leans back, looking tired, and says, "I've been teaching fifteen years, and I'm already teaching the children of the first children I taught."

A young man says, "We're really in crisis management. We have to have AIDS education—there's no other way. We've been teaching it in the schools since it's been mandated—for a year now." How does he feel about the added responsibility? He shrugs. "Somebody has to do the job."

The other male in the class adds, "You don't think about the politics of it. You just think about surviving from eight to three."

Boone is playing with a piece of chalk, leaning back in his chair.

He says in his slow drawl, "It's like the little boy picking up starfish on the beach and throwing them back in the water. Someone says he can never throw all of them back, so why bother? What difference does it make? And his answer is, 'It makes a difference to this one.'"

4

Peabody College

The Undergraduate Model

Peabody might be the Platonic Ideal of a college. On the green and pleasant campus of Nashville's Vanderbilt University, with which it merged only a decade ago, its handsome brick buildings set well apart on spacious lawns with overarching trees, it boasts a selective student body, high standards, and a national reputation unusual for a teacher training institution—even a private one. One of its professors told me what Peabody tries to do is "provide models for how you do school."

Its students are the better and brighter ones who can meet its admissions standards, which are higher than those of other regional or state schools, public or private. They are also a more representative national sample geographically. It is a place perceived as, in Michelin terms, worth the trip.

The college offers a master's degree and a doctorate in education, but it is best known for representing the cutting edge of undergraduate teacher education. "We graduate few teachers," says the dean, a leading figure on the national education scene. "We don't expect to change the world by the number of teachers we throw out there, but we can do things others can model. Our faculty has a light teaching load; we're research intensive and oriented toward learning technology. We believe what we have to impart is not teaching skills

56

but how to think about being a teacher. We want our students to *reflect* on the answers—not just learn that peer tutoring is an effective strategy, for example, but why, when, and especially how."

The college is a center for research on mental retardation and other aspects of development, biomedical and psychological, related to education, much of it funded by the National Institutes of Health. Because it is a research center, it attracts scholars who in turn add to its prestige.

"As teacher educators," says the dean, "we're in a bind. We can't escape the expectation that we will yield up from this womb precocious teachers ready—with a little help from peers and mentors—to deliver to the school system. If we do not meet that test of relevance, teacher educators are not thought to be doing our job."

The dean is a major spokesman for undergraduate teaching programs, for "getting them early." As such, he disagrees with the authors of the Holmes Report, the graduate school administrators who prescribe a four-year liberal arts background for prospective teachers with education as a postgraduate professional course of study—like law or medicine.

As I settle myself in his book-lined office on the pleasant common and listen to this civilized and soft-spoken educator, it seems easy to be persuaded of the value of his approach. Talking about these matters here in this burnished wood-panelled office with the sun coming in through windows overlooking the peaceful green campus has a different feeling from talking about them with classroom teachers in rural Kentucky or the North country or the Bronx.

"Teachers," he says, "are always telling us that their preservice training is inadequate, that they learned what matters on the job, from experience, from their colleagues, from trial and error. Isn't that bizarre for a profession?" He thinks there is no "transfer" of what is learned in a liberal arts program to what is needed in terms of teaching strategies, which must be incorporated from the beginning into the education of those who would be teachers.

"There are these three things that have to be taken into account," the dean says. "The need to make a respectable profession of teaching, the need to meet the demands of the state legislature, and the fact that teachers can only learn on the job. Theory and liberal arts just lie there like a dead cadaver. Like medical students, they have to learn on a living body." They have to serve an apprenticeship.

"In order to prepare people to learn how to teach we have to relate theory and what is learned in the liberal arts to classroom management. That learning won't just pop up at us at the right time. We need the software to bring it out of memory so we can use it.

"Secondly, we need an institutional bridge between learning and doing. The school system has to join the university. We're beginning such a program here between Vanderbilt and the Nashville schools. The idea is similar to that of a teaching hospital. It means putting teacher education in the school *and* the university and overstaffing the schools with those who can provide a bridge between them, teach the new teachers. Now you can only do this if the culture supports it.

"Our students today are better, we're leveling up." He says the often-quoted statistics on the low SAT scores of teachers are misleading. Those are the scores of high school students who say they *plan* to go into teaching; so they don't represent the ones who actually go into education. Another factor that he says has contributed to smarter education students is prevalent market conditions, which means higher salaries. A third factor is what he calls the Peace Corps effect—the altruism of many young people.

The dean is working on plans for a National Institute of Urban Education, to be concerned with such things as "the qualitative differences of teaching in the inner cities and how schools can facilitate helping these children through such strategies as problem-solving skills and reading. We are moving into the twenty-first century, the information age, and we must know how to utilize information." Thus what you need to teach is not history and literature, but "how to think."

I would see his ideas in action in a little while, in a class on teaching mathematics in elementary school and later in the Learning Technology Center.

Crossing the manicured lawns I pass young women who bring to mind the old-fashioned word "coed." They have a shiny, well-cared-for, self-confident look, the glowing skin and hair of young people who have eaten well and spent time in the sun. Their genteel southern accents sound different from the rural ones I've been hearing. And there are a few young men among the students of education—if not many, more than there used to be. Like the young women, they are open, direct, and sincere. They hold doors open and say "yes, ma'am." They take seats clustered together at the rows of tables in the classroom, two or three young men together here and there among the women, who include some older students, already parents.

The class on the Foundations of Mathematics for Elementary School Teachers is a good example of what the dean was describing. It is both intellectually rigorous and practically useful to a degree unique in my experience of such classes. I had been in classes in which theory was explained—Piaget's schema, for instance, of developmental stages—but not related in a specific way to the teaching situations in which it might need to be used. And I had been in classes in which students were told how to present certain problems and how to deal with their students' responses—but not the principles that would explain the why behind the how. Here, the class is told, the idea is to understand the nature of mathematics and the nature of the learner and relate them to "instructional format"—what materials to use and how to explain them.

Articulate and well organized—she has developed this course and has been teaching it for years—Professor Farber, as I'll call her, began with how math differs from other subjects and why it has to be taught differently. She talked about the great need for problem-solving skills today in the face of the information explosion; technology quickly becomes obsolete and it is impossible to predict what students will need in the future—what problems will face them and what technologies will be available to them. What they will need is an understanding of how to think about problem solving. The task of the teacher then becomes constructing a lesson with that aim. Understanding mathematics, she explained, depends on how well you can translate between the representational systems of the real world, of concrete models, of pictures and diagrams, of mathematical symbols and of spoken language. The fact that children can perform at one level doesn't mean they understand what they are doing. They have to be able to translate from one situation to another—say from real-world situations into symbols and back.

What does the nature of mathematics have to do with the teaching of mathematics? Here is where developmental psychologists like Piaget and Bruner, whose work these students have already been introduced to in other courses, were brought in. If a child is at what Piaget calls the concrete operational stage, she told them, the teacher should not be using symbols. Elsewhere in my journey, courses in the teaching of elementary math had dealt with how to teach it but had not made clear why.

On the subject of how people learn, Dr. Farber described the information process model in which brain components correspond to computer parts. In this view, we must establish links that allow us to use what we've stored. The view is of a structure that allows you to file information and access it, storing a limited amount in short-term memory and calling it up when needed. The implication of the model for teaching is that it is less important to teach arbitrary facts than an understanding of the structure, the relationships of facts.

Now these ideas were illustrated by a videotape of a student teacher giving a first-grade lesson on subtraction. ("If I take away one of these teddy bears. . .") Dr. Farber stopped the tape repeatedly to show what was taking place in the classroom: how the lesson illustrated the points she had been making, and how ideas about the nature of math and the capabilities of children at this stage of their development should influence what is taught and how it is taught. It was as though we were all in the first-grade classroom, with the magic of being able to stop time and go back to see what happened when this little girl didn't make the connection at first and how the teacher was able to make it clear to her.

It is the first time I have felt this positive about a methods course in education. It is the first time I have seen one this good.

Later, in the Learning Technology Center, I am introduced to the use of video in instruction as well as teacher education. The aim seems to be to provide an interesting environment for the student of the TV generation to work in. I am given a demonstration of a videodisk lesson. The class watches a dramatization on the screen (like watching a videotape on a VCR). In this case it's a drama featuring a young man with a boat on which he makes a trip, buys gas, meets a girl, loses his compass, has to figure out where he is and what time it is, buys another boat from the girl, has to negotiate the price—a whole series of practical problems involving reasoning and computation.

I am told by a member of the Center's staff that the rationale for a taped enactment instead of having the same problems presented in a book is that "problems don't occur as a set of problems in a book. They occur in the context of real-life situations. In the real world things are not focused for you, not filtered. You sort things out. The simulation presents the students with a problem as they would encounter it in the real world." That one went by a little fast for me—a simulation? the real world?—but the technology was indeed impressive and made it easy for the teacher to structure a lesson involving the events depicted. In case she had any difficulty doing so, a study guide would suggest a lesson plan, offer sample questions and answers, and give the exact points on the disk at which certain information could be found—what time it was when our hero left the dock, how much change he had left over after he had paid for the gas, how far he had traveled by sundown—in order to solve such problems as whether he had enough left to buy the second boat, whether he had enough gas to make it back home.

The laser technology made it possible for the teacher to move the tape immediately to the exact frame on which her study guide indicated the information the students wanted could be found, so that they could consider how to solve the problem. I was shown a videotape of a teacher using a videodisc—the one I'd just seen part of—in a class. She posed a question and the class discussed what they would need to know to answer it. She then referred to her list of frames, activated the search mechanism, and was able to move back and forth instantaneously from one part of the disk to another, as one would flip pages, while the students gathered the information they needed and solved the problems.

The center is funded in part by the university, in part by government and foundation grants, and is currently developing the use of this technology, which it calls "anchored instruction," for use in the schools. Some of the selling points demonstrated in its "case studies" have a familiar ring: the tapes promote cultural diversity by enabling students from heterogeneous backgrounds to see contrasts among different people being depicted, different modes of behavior, different ways of solving problems. They are "effective supplementary tools" for the teacher with thirty kids in her classroom, especially when some of them are "special ed" students (who bring with them "special ed" funds, which can be used for the purchase of "special resource materials"). They can also be used to provide enrichment for the talented.

In short, we have here a potential mini-industry backed up by research on learning at the university that is producing packages of classroom materials different in form from textbooks but with the same potential for defining what will be talked about and taught. The sample I saw was a math lesson, perfectly neutral. But possibilities suggest themselves. I cannot help feeling that this project is a case of "publishing" having to do at least as much with inter- and intra-university prestige as with turning out effective teachers for the schools of the nation. I had found the use of video a boon in the context of showing teachers what goes on in an actual classroom, but they are already grown up, know how to read, and have different goals as teachers from those of the children as learners.

A class on social studies for young children is meeting for the second time this semester. The professor begins with an assignment for the students in the class: "It's Parents Night at your school. The parents want to know what's going on, what social studies are all about, what advantage it's going to be to their children. Prepare a presentation." The selling of social studies in a consumer-service-oriented system.

These pretty girls, shiny-haired and smooth-skinned, well-fed and well-dressed (but not too, for that would not be the right style) are empty vessels. They will leave here with a point of view about social studies and take it with them into the schools where they will teach and most likely not reexamine it again. (One of them asks about the assignment, an oral presentation, "Can we have something written down on a piece of paper or are we supposed to like learn it?")

The professor, a gracious white-haired lady in a print dress and jacket, reminds them that every subject teacher has to think about what she would do for a child with, for instance, a sight loss. Then she asks them to begin by responding to the question, "What does social studies mean to you? What do you think it is or should be?"

Some of the answers: "It starts with learning about yourself"; "Getting along with other people"; "The differences between people, where they live, their vocations"; "It can be anything about people and their relationships"; "It's to help you realize yourself as part of a world community"; "To understand that you are responsible for what goes on in the world." I wonder what this young woman means by responsibility, what she has ever been responsible for, what she will actually do with her life in the years to come, and marvel (not for the first time) at the confident sense of omnipotence with which the young are willing to consider taking on the world before they have even learned to cope with a small part of it. The litany is going on: "You are a citizen of the world"; "How you can affect what goes on in the world."

The professor has given out, among other readings, a Xerox of an article by Diane Ravitch entitled "Tot Sociology," a criticism of the social studies curriculum and a plea for history, biography, story and myth, and for the study of what used to be called civics. "I want you to be familiar with the other side too," she says. A student points out that several pages of the article are missing in the copies the professor has handed out.

One student says she agrees with the idea that grade-school children ought to be given a sense of their own culture, "A way of looking at maps and history that explains the past. The content matters. If they don't learn it now . . ." She trails off. The atmosphere is not inviting. No one else chimes in. The professor says, "As long as it's not just facts, dates. As long as it's dealing with concepts. How nations do problem solving."

Continuing around the room, another student says, "Social studies doesn't have to be about people, it can be about the environment. What you can do about conservation, pollution." Another adds, "What you can do as a person for society." A third says, "It's about political and economic systems." The girl on her left groans. "We did that in high school. Current events. We were supposed to bring in articles from the paper. I was always saying, 'Mom, I gotta cut this out.' I never understood what they were about." Laughter of recognition, and another young woman adds, "Remember memorizing states and their capitals, presidents, the Preamble to the Constitution?" (Loud groans and more laughter.) "It comes in handy playing Trivial Pursuit, knowing the state flags."

These are the best and the brightest of the undergraduate education-school world. They are intelligent, if measurable capacity and inferred potential is what is meant. But they themselves are uneducated, naive. Or unspoiled—it depends on one's point of view. Certainly they are different from undergraduates at the Ivy League schools, who may not have a superior mentality but certainly have a more sophisticated vocabulary, that of the "culturally literate." What they use it for is another matter. But it seems to me the young woman who defended "the content" was on to something. What these young women haven't learned won't be passed on to their future pupils. The last word on defining social studies belongs to the last student at the end of the table, who says, "It was just kinda the general thing we were studying—the world."

We move on to method. Projects should be done in class in a cooperative way, working together, not assigned to be done at home. "It's too individualistic; it's unfair, some parents help." One of the students remembers learning about the Civil War in the eighth grade. "We dressed up as slaves 'n' all. It was kinda fun, real neat." Other suggestions: "We can use simulations to give them the concept of what it was like in a far-off time and place like the frontier. Do role playing, make time lines, bring in artifacts." No one suggests assigning books about these far-off times and places.

Late in the afternoon I joined a group of beginning student teachers, all juniors, in a seminar with one of their supervisors. Also joining them were some veterans—seniors who had come to tell them what it was like at the front. One battle-scarred young man, his appealing but rather crooked smile seeming to temper his evident enthusiasm with a bit of rue, was leaning forward earnestly when I came in, describing life in the trenches to the new recruits. He was objecting to having to follow an instruction plan set by the district "bureaucrats" to implement state regulations.

"They actually check up on you. You're teaching a class and you've finally got them involved and this woman walks in with a clipboard and makes notes and wants to see if you're giving the tests." Another one of the seniors tells them, "It's two different worlds out there, the inner-city schools like Napier and the suburban ones. Some of the Napier kindergarteners come to school with no coats or shoes on. Their mothers don't care. . . . We became too involved, trying to be their mothers. We got stressed out. You just can't work in all the neat things you learn here." Still another: "Some of the older teachers, they'll learn a lot of things off of you. They've spent ten years in a rut."

All of these young people look tired. Under every chair is a bag or briefcase overflowing with books. Their slightly unkempt look doesn't suggest sloveliness so much as busyness—too much to do to think about things like dress and hairstyles. They balance cardboard cups of Coke or coffee with some fast-food item—a bag of chips, half a sandwich—in this version of the business lunch. At four o'clock it's the first break they've had in their teaching day.

They complain that there's no money in the metro (downtown) schools, no "manipulatives." You have to use your own money, in addition to your ingenuity, to provide the things you want to use. "All these ed classes—your student teaching experience is your best training. There's no way to prepare you for what's out there, for the fact that these kids have had experiences that you haven't had. To the older teachers there's one right and one wrong way to do things. To me what teaching is all about is that there are more ways to do things and what matters is do you get there at the end."

Wearily, another young woman pushes a lock of hair out of her face as she adds, "You can't always implement what you were taught here. You don't have the materials. The requirements are that you teach verbs, pronouns, that you use these particular examples, that you give a test at a particular time when everybody else is giving it." They all agree—they want to "veer off," do "something wonderful."

One of the juniors says, "My cooperating teacher went here.

She does not teach the way she was taught to teach here because if you do, you mess up the system. But I resolved myself to the fact that I'm going to teach creatively, the holistic way, not from the basal."

The supervisor says, "The issue in like teacher education today" (and I realize that "like" is here to stay) "is that the real world is fragmented but we have a skill-based curriculum. That imposes constraints on your chances for eliciting creativity. You must make professional decisions about how you want to develop the learning process for your kids."

The young man who'd been talking when I came in describes the "CCRP"—a booklet of tests of reading skills—and the "MPI"—its math equivalent—and the supervisor nods and sighs. "You take away your beliefs from your university teaching about encouraging creativity and then you encounter these ritual behaviors. You have to find a compromise."

One of the new student teachers says, "We don't spend enough time in the schoolroom. We should be there all day in order to see what the teacher has to do—for instance, how she handles transition times. You know—fifty creative ways to line up kids—before you begin your student teaching." Some like the idea, suggested by their supervisor, of an internship. "We're exploring the idea. It would be like medicine. You'd have a variety of experiences, learn the nature of the profession before you take on all the responsibility." Others balk at the idea of a five-year program with a postbaccalaureate year. They're anxious to get out into the field—or onto the battleground, as the young man puts it, telling them they'll change their minds later.

The supervisor turned to me as they were about to end the meeting and asked if I had any comments, any questions. I asked, "What attracts you most about being a teacher?" One of the seniors, the young woman who had talked about "what's out there," seemed to be speaking for all of them. "The kids. School may be the biggest positive force in their lives. Education can move them out of that life. School is a place for education, where you can give them the tools to learn. You have to take on the responsibility. If you don't, it won't get done."

She wasn't thinking about changing "society." Just children.

Over coffee, after class, I asked Burt, the one young man in the group, why he'd chosen to become a teacher. To be a role model, he said, for children without fathers. Karen said she's always been "high on teaching." They were interested in the idea of the book I was writing, and one of them suggested I ought to call it, Teaching About Being Taught. Lucy said kids today watched too much TV—she felt she had, herself—and she wanted to show them "print has something in store for them." She thought it was important to see the parents, hoped she could find a way to get them involved. Being interactive was the main thing with the elementary classroom, she thought. Burt agreed, but added, "In secondary"—he's planning to teach high school—"you have to know content."

These are the students who at another time—and as it sometimes seems to someone my age, in another country (as L. P. Hartley put it in *The Go-Between:* "The past is a foreign country: they do things differently there")—went into teaching as a kind of social service, as something to do until they got married. Now they are committed to teaching as a profession or at least think of it as a job opportunity leading to a lifelong career. This is the observation of Bill Jeffries (I'll call him), the professor of social studies education who drove me to the middle school where Peabody students would observe classes for a project on society, school, and the teacher. "It's not enough to have knowledge of content, not enough to love kids. You have to have certain skills to teach. In this project they learn from their observations that there's more to teaching. They ask, How do teachers do it all?"

The professor I'll call Bill Jeffries, who served in the Peace Corps in the 1970s, describes his students as middle-class, loving kids, and "committed to breaking the bonds of cultural deprivation. They don't believe that circumstances should dictate outcome. They have high expectations for themselves and for their students." He thinks the two kinds of teachers who are no good for inner-city schools are the incompetent and the "missionary," whose paternalistic attitude implies low expectations.

We talked on the way to the middle school where his student teachers would spend the day. I knew it had been one of the worst schools in the city. Jeffries—for all his commitment, his idealism, his Peace Corps outlook—had once said, he told me, that he would absolutely not send any of his student teachers into the building. Now he sent as many as possible. Some forty of them, in small groups, were visiting today, notebooks in hand, walking through the quiet hallways, standing in the back of busy classrooms. Between classes they passed adolescent boys and girls, mostly black, some Hispanic, a minority white, talking, laughing, moving purposefully from one room to another. They seemed lively enough—a little playful jostling, someone grabbing another kid's hat and holding it behind his back—but the underlying sense was of an orderly place.

The school had been "turned around" by the principal—a short stocky man, informally dressed, whose ruddy face, easy manner, and regional accent could have belonged to a "good old boy" from almost anywhere in the South—and his assistant principal, a pleasant-faced, well-dressed black woman of middle age and bourgeois demeanor. They were an icon of the new South, a couple who might have been invented for a network TV series. They obviously liked and respected each other and told their story in tandem, occasionally interrupting each other with mutual praise and private jokes, like people who have been on a trip together and have shared impressions of the landscape and their fellow travelers. "I'm on a roll," he said at one point. "I'd need another half hour just to answer that question." Betty Arthur, the assistant principal laughed, "He always needs another half hour to answer a question about our school."

Ben Monday, the pseudonymous principal, has strong feelings about the institution of the middle school and "the learning strategies appropriate to it. The junior high becomes a mini–high school, and that's no good at all. There's too much social pressure to grow up too soon."

He described the middle school as child-centered, flexible, and team oriented. "Our teachers have to be surrogate parents, advocates, counselors, advisors for the fifteen kids in their home room. They have to be caring, deal with the disabled, teach English and math as well as Family Life and STD . . ." I looked questioning. "Socially transmitted diseases." A moment's pause. "Somebody has to do it. They aren't going to get it at home.

"We have to help build their self-esteem. It's not so important to stress quantum mechanics or algebra. They need to see a lot of different things other than math and science, which they learn to hate at an early age, so they'll be attracted to school, feel it's a welcoming place. We have programs in art, music, shop, a school band. Our teachers are involved in all of that. They're the reason for our success—a band of committed teachers working together, with high standards and high expectations." (Arthur, smiling: "He built that team.") "Our kids make it. They know what we expect of them and they stretch. They respect us, each other, themselves."

Thinking about the job description he'd just given, I asked Monday what his teachers earned. "A starting teacher in the system today gets $18,200—and it gradually increases to a little more than double that amount after twenty-five years." He read my expression, sat back, rolling a pencil in his hand, and said, "I have to moonlight in order to support my family, send my kids to college. I make about $50,000 a year at this job. I have a brother in New York who's with an investment banking house. He moves paper, writes bond issues. He takes home $400,000 at the end of an average year."

Vanderbilt students have the fresh-faced preppie look of the models in upscale clothing catalogues like Land's End. They are not in rebellion against their families or their society but they do want to "make a difference." They are expected to demonstrate social concern, but not to be "smaltzy" about it, as one student put it to me. Coming to Nashville directly from the East Coast and the Ivy League, I was startled to see young men in uniform on campus, marching in what looked like close order drill. Out in America, ROTC lives, along with respect for many things that, like the military, are viewed askance in the coastal cultures. Also, the young here seem to be still young. They lack the angst as well as the anger of their counterparts better known to the media. Waiting to meet someone in the Student Union building I chanced on the only philosophical question raised with any urgency by a student in my hearing: "Would you *spray* peanut butter on a piece of bread? I'd spray peanut butter on a cracker, but on a piece of *bread?*"

Before leaving Vanderbilt, I talked about some of the current issues in education with a professor who'd started life in the East and lived and taught in the South for a number of years. "Professionalism is about power," she said. "The federal government makes rules and the state legislature passes laws intended to make everyone do the same thing. Teachers are on the bottom, with administrators in the middle. But teachers do make decisions in the classroom, about time, curriculum, access, from moment to moment every hour of the school day. They're street-level bureaucrats. When they get together, they swap war stories. Right now there's this horrendous freight train coming down the track—the public law on mainstreaming the handicapped—adding pressure and stress to a situation that's already pressured and stressed." She paused, then added, "No child is safe as long as the legislature is in session.

" 'Free, appropriate, in the least restrictive environment' means putting the LDs, the 'learning disabled,' in regular school classes, but we are running out of money while the referrals, the enrollments have doubled. . . .

"Teachers are coming back for an M.A., a Ph.D. They're going to leave the public school classroom for private schools and colleges because of this situation. Advocacy for the handicapped has become a way for someone to develop their own constituency. It's subverting the original intent of the legislation."

As I continued on my journey through the ed school world, I would have ample opportunities to see what she meant.

PART THREE

The Midwest

5

Michigan State University

Professionalism, Power, and Practice

The institution most closely identified with the effort to "professionalize" teaching by making it a postgraduate field of study like law,
medicine, business, or engineering is the College of Education at
Michigan State University. Its dean heads the Holmes Group of
elite graduate schools of education that issued the 1986 report "Tomorrow's Teachers," calling for abolishing undergraduate education
degrees altogether and requiring education students to possess four-
year bachelor's degrees in a subject area before embarking on a
year of graduate study in a professional school and an internship
doing supervised teaching.

The college's descriptive literature is as impressive as its national
reputation. Both exemplify the current rhetoric of the ed school
establishment, and I was curious about the reality I would find there.
I was learning that the descriptions of programs and courses are
one thing. What actually transpires in the classroom is often something else.

I was introduced to the MSU philosophy by the faculty member
who heads the Department of Teacher Education and whom I'll
call Professor Taylor. She described herself as "part of a small but
sturdy band that began to rethink things here about twenty years
ago, when no one here thought much about the question of how

people learn. Methods were not connected to subject matter or to school and society. It was a status quo model. We have moved from that to a creative student-teaching program, the use of concepts in the classroom, a process model of assessment, goal-setting, strategies, and evaluation.

"Over the years, we developed a model professional school as a learning community in which teacher candidates, teachers, and teacher educators share their different kinds of expertise in dealing with the problems of teaching and learning in the classroom—learning from each other. Scholars and practitioners informing each other in a cooperative venture."

More specifically, the college offers, in addition to the standard program, four "thematic" ones that Dr. Taylor described for me. "In the standard program you present a sequence of related courses— it's the traditional approach, the cafeteria approach. The Academic Learning program emphasizes content in science, math, English. You start by asking what is worth knowing and what meaning that has for the tasks in that study area. What do you want the beginning teacher to know? The conceptual foundation. In the Heterogeneous Classrooms program you concentrate not on the subject matter but on the child's background and ask what the implications of individual differences are for instruction. The emphasis is on equity and on special students. In the Learning Community program you ask what are the practices in schools that work against development, such as tracking as opposed to multilevel groups. It emphasizes group responsibility." (Later I would hear an anecdote about an MSU alumna so committed to the principles of community learning and so against competition of any kind in her class that her pupils were not allowed to participate in events like the sack race on the school's field day.)

By now Dr. Taylor had come to the jewel in the crown of the college's special curriculum, the Multiple Perspectives program, in which, she explained, "the emphasis is on interactive decision making and an ethical commitment to equity . . . on creating a positive learning environment in order to foster personal development and social responsibility. It starts with the routines of teaching and encourages student teachers to reflect on what they do.

"The student makes a commitment to one program he or she chooses, which is to say a philosophical position, which becomes the context emphasized, the in-depth approach, but throughout there is exposure to the other approaches as well, and always field work throughout the program. You are always asking, Why did I do it this way, how else might I do it, how should I do it next time? Eventually, we would like the Multiple Perspectives approach to replace all the others."

One thing that struck me as I listened to all this was how little it had to do with ideas and how much with socialization. I had heard next to nothing about what it was children would learn in the heterogenous learning community with its multiple perspectives. Even the Academic Learning program was described as "the conceptual foundation." Of what, I wondered?

Dr. Taylor went on, as though responding to my unspoken question. "The aim is to foster personal and social responsibility, to learn to work with others in egalitarian ways, respecting diversity and integrating everyone for the future of our country. Self-confidence, positive self-image, respecting others from all cultural backgrounds. There has to be an emphasis on acquiring new information, not just absorbing the old, not a body of content, of facts. Teaching is not telling. Knowledge is remade in someone's head, it has to connect with what's there in the learner, what he brings from his culture. We've moved into the knowledge age. It calls for certain skills. If people don't learn them it creates terrible problems for society— drug use, violence, homelessness. What is needed is a greater support system—social service agencies together with the schools."

Leaning forward, Dr. Taylor went on intently. "What we need is enough money to achieve a smaller student–teacher ratio. With thirty kids in a class there's only so much you can do. The young teacher is well aware of the child's need, of what his deficits are, what kind of help to give him, but there's only so much one person can do. Other kids can help in a multilevel classroom, but money pays for aides, resources to provide the help that's needed to create a network dedicated to educating the young from preschool on, with whatever special work they need. Business and industry can contribute along with the federal government. Our student teachers have a dedicated professor who knows what to do but you can do it better if your student teacher—pupil ratio is fifteen, not thirty-five; you can make more personal interventions if you have some paraprofessionals, secretaries to take over some of the paper work, make materials." (As always, when the talk came down to the actualities of classroom practice, it began to make sense.)

"Teachers need to feel some power in the classroom," she went on, and told me about her own daughter, a young teacher making $20,000 a year who had used $2,200 of her own money to buy materials and books for her class and had taken on an extra job in a teacher center in order to get a discount on teaching materials.

Most MSU students, Dr. Taylor told me, are middle-class white women from within the state, most of them from suburbs and small towns within 100 miles of the campus. About 5 percent are classified as minority; about the same percentage of the students are men. All of them start in education as college juniors majoring in their subject field and taking some pre-education courses "in which they are acquainted with ideas and concepts and do field studies. As seniors they are screened for the MA program. They do a summer internship, practice teaching, and a year-long internship beyond their course work. It adds up to approximately two years beyond the B.A."

The aim of all this is "to develop an educational leadership. All will have master's degrees. They will be career teachers, not just working at a job until they get married but for all of their lives. A principal should be an educator, not just an administrator. If teaching is to be a professional career it must prepare you for professionalism."

Dr. Taylor described experiments in Dade County, Florida, and in Flint, Michigan, where "they are conducting demonstrations of the radical reorganization of the school structure. It's not just a matter of raising teachers' salaries but of forming councils of professionals and parents to make major decisions on curriculum and courses, to decide how they should use their available resources. This kind of thing works best in small towns. These schools are professional development communities. They have reorganized high schools so they consist of cohorts of students with teachers who deliver all the core courses to that group for four years. The students acquire an identifiable group image. They know each other; they feel they belong. They have a sense of ownership instead of alienation."

I was impressed with what I had heard about equity, community, decision making, and social responsibility, and also aware of how much influence what went on here had on others in the field. I wondered how these ideas translated into classroom reality, both here where teachers were trained and out there where they went to teach the young. Every year, Dr. Taylor had told me, the MSU College of Education places some six hundred student teachers in the local public schools. That afternoon, I had an opportunity to see some of them in action.

Together with a member of the Heterogenous Classrooms program faculty, I visited an elementary school in which a group of MSU students were student teaching. They go to the school as a group, work in different classrooms, have a common supervisor who observes them at work and comments on their performance. All of them seemed eager to get their lessons across to the children. Some were having an easier time of it than others, but that seemed to be more a function of personality—how lively, how shy—than in any obvious way related to "instructional models." Some of these student teachers, I learned, had already had teaching experience in church-related programs in inner cities or in missionary programs.

In this school there were a number of Asian pupils. "They do well," my guide said. "They know you're supposed to pay attention to the teacher, they sit quietly and seem to absorb things even before they've learned English." While we were there, several of the children were taken out for bilingual instruction. It was part of the constant comings and goings in the classroom—children being taken out for bilingual or special ed classes. There are, I was told, some two hundred transitions in the typical inner-city classroom day, which for some of these children begins with breakfast. When they first come in, the teacher may be checking math books, taking attendance. At 9:15 she says, "Good morning!" All these other things have been going on already but now school is starting.

Michael is taken apart for individual help by the teacher's aide. Michael, my guide tells me, is "one of the many children we're seeing these days who were born to drug-addicted mothers." With all this going on all day the teacher seems to have little time "to reflect on what she's doing."

At another elementary school in a poor neighborhood later that day some kindergarten girls and boys were drawing on large sheets of paper spread out on the floor while a teacher moved among them answering questions and offering suggestions. Others were being read to by a student teacher while another group worked on a puzzle. In one class some children were making paper patterns with a student teacher while the cooperating teacher worked on the "F" sound with two little girls who were having trouble recognizing letters. In a fourth-grade class a fortyish black teacher who obviously had his class in the palm of his hand used my unexpected visit spontaneously to teach manners and a bit of group esprit. I was introduced to the class mascots, two exotic birds named Lady Day and Coltrane, by lively youngsters whose hands shot up to be first to describe their class's progress so far that semester.

(It's impossible not to be touched, amused, fascinated by the children in any elementary classroom. I couldn't help wishing I had nothing to do beyond reporting on them and no world to describe but theirs. It would not only be more enjoyable but would, I suspected, certainly be a more popular report than one such as this on the training of their teachers. Months later, such a book was published, to enviable critical acclaim. A heartwarming anecdotal record of the daily doings of vulnerable little children and their spunky teacher, it made readers feel good and provided much lively copy for reviewers. But what good did it do, I asked myself, in what way did it contribute to rethinking anything that needed changing? Sour grapes? I had to ask myself that—and go on with my own reporting.)

After the tour of the school, a visit with the principal. He's proud of his school, and pleased by our enthusiasm for what we've seen there but deadly serious when he talks about what he thinks is wrong. "Our main problem," he says slowly and deliberately, "is decision making about funding. We're a business run by a political organization—lay boards of education with a constituency—and as long as that's true we're doomed to mediocrity. Unsound business practices are bound to result when governance is in the hands of interest groups. Imagine General Motors running that way in terms of accountability. What we need is not in-service programs but continuing project development—staff development, which involves planning, support services, having teachers making decisions." I can't argue with him about staff development, which, translated, means that teachers should be encouraged to go on learning more. But does the school/business analogy really hold up, and aren't unionized teachers just as much of an "interest group" as parents and taxpayers?

The next day I sat in on a class on the Exceptional Child in the Regular Classroom. Taught by a professor I'll call Sloan, it was an education in itself. Professor Sloan, who seemed at first glance too young to have written as much as he had on the subject, began talking about the children classified as learning disabled.

"There has been a 365 percent increase in LDs, the mildest level. It's leveled off because the government stopped paying. There's great variability in who we are talking about—is it a kid who can't read or do math or is it one who is failing social studies? It started out as a program to provide special help for a small group—now it's up to 3.4 million. The government has pulled out, that pot of money hasn't been increasing. We have to ask, Are the ones with the worst disabilities being served? There are no exit criteria established for these kids—they're lifers. They never go back to general education. It's a McDonald's ethic—more people are served every year. The special ed people want to keep them there."

A pair of interpreters stand at the front of the class signing for a deaf student. They alternate—it looks difficult, a strenuous exercise to keep up with his pace simultaneously. A student asks about mainstreaming—does it hurt the rest of the class? No, Professor Sloan says, it's an opportunity for them to meet other kinds of people and learn to interact with them. No one seems to question learning to interact with other kinds of people as schooling's aim.

"Who," the professor asks, "is learning disabled? The school imposes the label. The aim is to reduce the child's difficulty in adapting to society. But there are," he tells them, "two problems. First, the category is too inclusive. Are they all really disabled—or are some of these children instructional casualties? Secondly, to be eligible for services the child has to be classified—referred and evaluated. And unfortunately, the system doesn't work, it's not very accurate. It costs three to four thousand dollars to declare a child eligible, and afterward we can't distinguish the LDs from others. We have only a 50 percent success rate in telling the difference—about as good as tossing a coin. The tests are inconclusive and the main purpose they serve is to support the testing industry.

"We should reallocate from diagnostic to instructional services. If we are talking about the mildly handicapped, as distinct from the sensory impaired or physically disabled, there is nothing special that we do."

As for the policy of mainstreaming, he asks, "Can we really do this—teach heterogenous groups of kids in the classroom?" His answer is, "Yes—to a limited extent. And we get better at it by trying. You folks will make it happen," he tells the class, "it's not going to happen at the university level." And then he tells them, "There are things you can use to integrate some of the kids some of the time."

He suggests a few practical things for these future teachers to keep in mind. "Learning or failure," he tells them, "is a function of the interaction between students and their learning environments—how they're taught. It doesn't matter whether we label them low-IQ, cognitive dysfunction, developmentally delayed, or what. What matters is what we do, what tasks we ask them to do. And by observing the interactions between those things, we can find environmental contributors to learning or failure. For instance, with kids who can't read on grade level, how much time they spend reading may be more significant than what Mommy did about the

potty or what their cognitive functions are like. If they only spend
six minutes a day reading, you can't expect them to get good at it.
Get them more actively involved, spending more time reading. What
we do can effect change in what they do. We can't change their
home life, take them out of poverty, increase their parents' involvement. But we can change a child's performance by changing some
of these environmental factors.

"Effective instruction for the mildly handicapped"—he writes
three words on the blackboard while explaining—(1) *activate* the
learner. They should be doing something, not screwing off. Instead
of just sitting there they should be reading, discussing. (2) maintain
high *success*, so they get the feeling they're doing the right thing.
(3) they need enough opportunities to *practice* important skills, academic and social. What they spend their time doing has to be what
we really want them to learn how to do. These goals of having
them be active, successful, and doing something important can, to
some extent, be done in the general classroom." On the one hand,
what all this adds up to is the good old traditional formula for
teaching any child—keep them busy practicing what they're supposed
to be learning. On the other hand, I am grateful for his unpretentious
common sense.

Some of these LD children will be taught by the regular teacher,
mainstreamed. Some, he tells them, will be in a special ed teacher's
special classes. He offers some tips: ". . . physical arrangement of
the classroom . . . learning areas . . . easy flow of traffic . . . minimum distractions . . . easy to supervise." This turns out to mean
desks separated by rows, facing the chalk board, and away from
the window.

"The low-achieving kids should be as close to the teacher and
as apart from each other as possible. Rewards should be learning
related—you earn the privilege of sitting in the reading tub, and
you can only stay there as long as you are reading. The amount of
time you'll have to spend correcting materials (math, spelling) will
get you, whether it's during or after school. Kids learn a lot from
other kids and you can use managers to check other kids' work.
Get them to work cooperatively, assist each other, bring things in
and share them. When you get out there and you're trying to handle
a million things simultaneously . . ."

Before the class ends, a teaching assistant offers "a list of positive
verbal responses you can say to kids."

That evening in the restaurant of the university's conference and visitor's center, which I'd been told was staffed by students of the university's Hotel and Restaurant Institute, I asked my waiter, a friendly young man, whether he was enrolled in the Institute. It turned out that he was a student in the College of Education. Interested, I asked what had attracted him to the idea of teaching and his answer was, "I was afraid I wouldn't have enough money to go to grad school and my mom said, Get a skill, and well, what else can you do but this? I wasn't sure how it would work out, but I've kinda gotten to like it. It was a nice surprise." What did he plan to teach? "Social studies in high school—or English." He had chosen the Academic Learning program—"where you teach the same thing to the whole class. I forget what the Multiple Perspectives is."

In the class on Social Studies in the Elementary Curriculum, the assignment is to prepare a lesson on a topic dealt with in the sixth-grade social studies curriculum and then prepare a module in an additional two pages showing how they would adapt it for special education students. Today a course in social studies—or anything else—has to include how to teach it to "special" children.

"This is the law, PL 94–142," the professor I'll call Shaw tells the class, "that strikes fear into the hearts of the most stalwart" because of the "least restrictive" provision. "Michigan put teeth into that law," he tells them. "It's one of the toughest states on equality of educational opportunity for the handicapped. Special ed teachers will be taking mainstreamed kids out of your classroom to the resource room and will advise those of you who are regular teachers. But EH kids," referring to those classified as emotionally handicapped, "are a threat, let's face it. Prepare your module with that EH kid in mind.

" 'Exceptional' covers a lot of ground, from severely handicapped to gifted. What they have in common is something that prevents them from learning at the same rate as other kids. They may be hearing, visually, mentally, or emotionally impaired."

He passes out copies of paragraphs from textbooks of four major textbook publishers—Allyn & Bacon; Scott, Foresman; D. C. Heath; and Silver, Burdett. All are from chapters on Canada, and all are on the sixth-grade reading level, although they are designed for use in high school.

"I want to give you some warning signals about the limitations of textbooks," Professor Shaw says. "How they address important problems, like acid rain." Asked what they think of a factual textbook paragraph, the students offer comments like, "Sounds like an electric

power company wrote it"; "It doesn't point out the social significance"; "There's a lot of things ruining the environment . . . they
could have said more about the effects on buildings, people, food
crops." The professor says, "We don't experience the acid rain problem here so we don't conceive it as a significant problem. In International Falls, Minnesota, and upper Vermont, in the path of the
winds that bring pollutants up there, they are more alert. It's an
ecological disaster. The passage ignores that. Nothing in this paragraph would get kids concerned." Of another textbook paragraph:
"If there's a nuclear war some of those nukes will drop before they
reach the U.S. That's why nuclear proposals that have come out
of the Reagan administration bother Canadians." This is material
for discussion with a class that can't read above the sixth-grade level,
that knows nothing of the history of the post-World War II period,
to say nothing of the events preceding that war, the war itself, or
the political and social developments of the preceding couple of
centuries. "These books have profound limitations," the professor
says. I certainly agree, but we have different limitations in mind.

Of a paragraph that speaks of the Inuit people "learning our
way of life," he says, "There is an implied value judgment that
they were primitive, backward. Most of you know something about
the Eskimos. The Inuit were in many ways just as sophisticated in
their life styles as we are. It's an ethnocentric putdown. The truth
is that the government rounded them up and took a census and
gave them medical attention and schools and everything was going
to be hunky-dory. It's understandable the long-smouldering resentment these people feel. The textbooks that are put in your hands
are full of misconceptions you have to identify and correct in your
modules."

The class then turns to an examination of some poster-size photo-
graphs to be used in role-playing exercises, in which the children
decide what's going on in the picture and then act out the situation
with various outcomes they decide on. The aim is "to afford children
an opportunity to grapple with a problem situation and to resolve
it." Primary school students—kindergarten, first-, second-, and third-
graders—are to be encouraged in "sharing experience and generaliz-
ing about a few well-chosen questions." The aim is "to get kids
thinking about themselves."

Making sure they do not miss the point, the professor goes on,
"That's the aim of social studies, or social science, if you prefer
the term. Its aim is for children to learn about themselves." And
role playing is "a way of dealing with interpersonal relations. They'll
learn more from role playing than listening to you talk." Almost

an hour goes by dealing with how to use pictures in role-playing exercises, how to help children "test their own sense of reality" in the discussion that follows the enactment.

I expected to have reached what sounded like the very summit of the graduate ed school experience the day I sat in on the Action Research Seminar for secondary teacher candidates on "Choosing a Research Problem."

The fifteen student teachers are one of the "cohorts" in the Multiple Perspectives program, the "meta-theme program" dealing with teacher decision making in terms of academic disciplines, social community, and "appreciation for the diverse learners that exist in a diverse society"—the themes of the other three programs.

This impressive description left me unprepared for the actuality of the class, which begins with an overhead projection of a vast outline made up largely of phrases like "engaged-interactive." The professor moves along the outline, repeating out loud what is there for the eye to see—"contributive strategies to norms of interaction" and "impact on learning context of second-order learning strategies," which seem to mean (one can't be quite sure) bringing things out into the open and clarifying what you think so it can be examined and tested. With each phrase he reads, he turns and looks at the class significantly. I am reminded of nothing so much as the class at SUNY that acted out its scenario of progressive "existentialist" education. Only, of course, on a "higher" level.

"Asking for a research report on your student teaching," the professor tells the class, finally turning off the projector, "is our way of helping you to become reflective teachers." Asked for some ideas for research projects, one young woman offers, "How I am interacting with them to help them work together well to create a cooperative learning environment." Other students follow suit: ". . . to be able to work together . . . self-concepts . . . to become a group . . . using Cohen's materials . . . Stafford's stages."

A few have questions about their classroom experiences: "Maybe it was me, maybe it was them—do I require students to answer questions or just encourage them to formulate their own?" Many of these young faces look bored. "Conceptualization" of teaching seems to be the name of the game. One young woman has her eyes closed; others, sitting back in their chairs with their sneakers up on the conference table, occasionally whisper to each other. Even the one with the problem under discussion—how to instill community feeling in her class—seems to be getting more muddled.

They're all carrying a heavy load of courses and practice teaching long hours at the same time. The girl next to me says, "I know what *my* problem is. My problem is I'm not getting enough sleep." She laughs. Meanwhile, another student is describing her idea for a research problem: "My students have low self-esteem. They've had little positive feedback. I plan to see, if they get positive reinforcement instead of negative, does it have a positive effect on their learning."

They know all the "right" words—"not motivated to learn . . . inhibition to writing . . . reluctant to answer." They talk about the problem of "too much negative feedback." How far away all this is from any body of learning, all this talk about the nature of the learning process, the relation of the learner to the learning community. What about *what* is being learned? For the moment it seems forgotten in the emphasis on the low-achieving problem student. Here the teacher's task is once again being defined as "changing their attitude towards themselves." The professor is asking them to consider "what instrumentation . . . what functionalities" can contribute to that end.

Finally, the inevitable breaking up into small groups—in this case, of threes. I join the threesome closest to me, which includes Sheila, the young woman who made the joke about sleep. She comments to no one in particular, "We're all interested in how to teach it, not making up a problem about it. It's the kid's problem!" It's her style—she's tough, funny, and—by virtue of her working-class background—guilt free. She isn't necessarily buying all of this. She says she thinks she'll do a project on students' expectations. I ask her what she thinks they should be. She looks surprised. "What I think they *should be*?" She thinks a minute. "I want them to say, 'I want to learn history.'" She smiles the smile of one who knows she has just said something outrageous.

The second young woman, trying out her idea for a research project on the other two, says she thinks she'll use a scenario from a values textbook, set a problem such as, "You're the President and France invades a country in South America. What do you do? That'd be a lot more fun than just doing the Monroe Doctrine."

The young man, Doug, says he has a real problem. He went around his classroom making sure every group understood the assignment he'd just given, and when he came to a group of four black students, one of them said, "We can't do this. We're black." He understood them to mean they couldn't do it *because* they were black—that they weren't up to it. Sheila looks at him inquiringly. He says, "My temperature really went up. I felt awful. About the stereotyping. I mean mine." Sheila smiles. "What a copout. Don't you think they were riding you? Being hostile, maybe?" Doug looks a little sheepish. He thinks he'll study the problem in the classroom as a microcosm of the larger problem: Are we one society or many subsocieties. Ultimately, he thinks, we need global studies. "We've got to get different cultural backgrounds interacting in a unicultural classroom, white and black." Teachers should interact in decision making with students, who should play a role in planning their learning. He'll try to think of a way to get that into a research model.

At another elementary school where MSU student teachers work, the principal gives us a tour of the building. The place is quiet, attractive, with freshly painted pastel walls and deep-colored, new-looking carpeting. Children's art work hangs everywhere, along with maps, posters, and a heavy concentration of pyramids, hieroglyphs, mummy cases, and other evidence of the fourth-grade project on Egypt. The classrooms are uncrowded and well furnished. I have been told this is an "underutilized" school, which means the demographics of the area have changed since it was built to hold 600 students; the present census is 290. There is a lot of space. There is also an atmosphere of order I'm not used to seeing in schools. It's not passivity or rigid control I sense, but something positive. Calm. The principal is talking about team teaching and differential staffing. He tells us that when the funds were available, "We cashed in one teacher for four teacher's aides. Our kids got used to having several additional people in the classroom, so it was an easy matter to introduce the student teachers from MSU." Now they have an ongoing program in which the student teachers, their supervisors from the university, and the school's cooperating teachers work together.

We stop in at one of the classrooms where a student teacher is giving a fourth-grade social studies lesson about the assembly line, something familiar to many of these children. The student teacher is from the Cooperative Learning program. She appoints a recorder and a facilitator, whose job is to read the directions for the activity to the group. She tells them they are going to make something—a small model of some kind—"first by yourself, and then as a group, to see which is easier."

In another classroom, the student teacher has written on the blackboard the two words "Conservation" and "Development." She tells the class the people who are for conservation want to keep the forests for later; the development people want to use the forests now. "Which seems more important to you?"

An older teacher tells me she is particularly interested in children's literature. She shows me the catalogue of a book club from which she orders every month, "so we keep up with the new things coming out." Looking through it I recognize some old friends among the books—*The Yearling, The Mixed-Up Files of Mrs. Basil E. Frankweiler, Beezus and Ramona, Charlotte's Web*—but many more recently published "young adult" books in a distinctly commercial package of offerings. I wonder who runs this book club and how many teachers let it determine what their pupils will be offered to read.

What is impressive at this school is the involvement of so many people in these children's day. There are teachers, instructional aides, and student teachers from the university program. In one large room, formed by removing a wall between what had originally been two classrooms, six adults are working with sixty-one children, a ratio of about one to ten, although they are available where needed— sometimes with a small group, sometimes a larger one, sometimes an individual child. Everyone seems busy, everyone looks interested. It's a far cry from many of the inner-city schools only a few miles away, this display of purpose, order, and pleasure—and this spaciousness.

The principal invites us to have coffee with him in his office and we visitors are given an explanation of the MSU program by a Multiple Perspectives faculty member. (He tells us he once worked for a large accounting firm which provided him with professional management development training. He talks about "turning out a quality product." It is not clear whether he is referring to teachers or pupils.)

"The idea of the programs is for the education student to be part of a cohort. They remain together and work as a group instead of competing for a few prizes. It's a collaborative approach to professional behavior." He adds, "There are not many models for that in our society.

"It's a professional preparation program that involves a real sacrifice in terms of time and effort, not just another major. You can't skip classes or sleep late." The future teachers, he explains, have to be prepared to deal with the situation that's coming their way: The school day is being extended—preschool, after-school programs for latchkey children. "Soon they'll be dropped off at seven A.M. and picked up at six P.M. There's less and less parent involvement as increasing numbers of parents both work."

It's hard to see how the "meta-theme conceptual" framework relates to such problems.

Probably the best thing about teacher education at MSU is something it shares with the program at Peabody, as different as they are in their particulars as well as in their underlying philosophies. In both cases they get the student teachers into the classroom early on and encourage them to think about what they do there. The worst thing is something it shares with too many other teacher-training institutions—the substitution of indoctrination for education.

6

Eastern Michigan
University

Special Students and the Bias Business

Eastern Michigan University looks a lot more like the Plattsburgh campus of SUNY than its next-door neighbor the University of Michigan at Ann Arbor. Like Plattsburgh, it began life as a state normal school, the first such teacher-training college west of the Alleghenies, as its catalogue and other promotional literature points out. That beginning persists in a somewhat plain and poor-relation aspect when compared to the richer charms of Ann Arbor. A marker at the entrance to the unprepossessing campus notes the founding of Michigan State Normal School in 1849 with the aim of providing instruction "in the art of teaching and in all the various branches that pertain to a good common school education." A nearby plaque bears the date 1865 and honors "students who died at the front in the War of the Revolution."

EMU is the largest producer of teachers in the country.

The dean is a gentleman, kind and concerned, who has come through the troubles that beset the institutions of the higher learning in the 1960s and 1970s, and whose first concern about EMU, in answer to my questions when we met, was that it had so few minority students. It was a situation he considered the most important problem of the moment and which he was hoping to change. We agreed that my schedule would include talks with members of the faculty and administration currently involved in efforts to increase minority enrollment and to smooth the way for minority students once enrolled; arrangements would be made for me to meet some of the minority students already matriculated. Meanwhile, curious about how teachers of teachers felt about the issue of sex education in the classroom, I chose to start my first day at EMU in a class on Health Education in the Elementary Grades, a required course for all elementary certification students.

Arriving early, I met the chairman of the physical education department, who looked and sounded more like a teacher of history, which indeed he had once been, than the stereotype of a jock I might have expected. Silver-haired, pipe-smoking, formal in dress and manner, he had strong opinions about the current requirements of the state that "health education" be incorporated into the subject matter—into the teaching of history, geography, language arts, math—starting from kindergarten through twelfth grade.

"The teacher has to work it into all her lessons. Classroom teachers are so weighted down with responsibilities they can't do the things they're supposed to." He told me about a rural school district in the throes of modernization. "Twenty years ago they were truck farmers. Now the community is changing. The associate superintendent in charge of curriculum says his problems are insurmountable. We're at the mercy of bandwagon jumpers in their desire to be responsive to the culture. Political pressure groups are like a crying baby; we'll do anything to stop them from crying. The result is we're not teaching what we ought to be. We put driver education in the curriculum and at the same time we teach less math and science. The insurance companies lobby for legislation that puts driver education in the schools—just one example of the influence of pressure groups on the state's education laws.

"In the days of Henry Ford and of Horace Mann we prepared young men by means of vocational education. Today we don't need toolmakers, we need computer programmers, but we're graduating young people who can't even make change. Too many of them can't even get up in the morning to go to work to turn hamburgers over.

"The problem isn't going to be solved just by raising teachers' salaries. Washington, D.C. has the highest pay scale for teachers in the country, yet the district also has the highest dropout rate. So paying teachers more doesn't in itself improve the situation. . . .

"I'm not interested in seeing teachers arrange their students' chairs in circles. What matters is do they have a subject matter content to teach. Discussion with kids in the first weeks of a course is ludicrous. They have no understanding or acquaintance with the meaning of an industrial civilization, of what preceded it, they play around with concepts like fairness—they don't begin to understand the meaning of fairness. . . .

"We're too worried about methods and not enough about what we use them for. The best way to learn is still to listen to a learned person who uses reasoned logic and will expect you to demonstrate understanding." This is heresy in the ed school world of today and he knows it.

"Unions have given teachers a false protection. They protect the weaker members of the faculty. In Detroit, there's a private challenge to public education. Sixty-five percent of blacks in Catholic schools are not Catholics. They're there because the parents feel the education is better. We may see the demise of the public schools because parents see their kids are not learning."

The Health Education class is simple and obvious. Keep a flashlight in your desk for emergencies like power failure, don't wear red under fluorescent lighting. The five men and eighteen women, presumably grownups—one of them mentions that she is the mother of four—have been given an outline of the material covered, yet they all take notes as they listen. A whole hour of this—the subject is classroom lighting—and yet the teacher somehow holds their attention. She's forceful, funny, a little mocking of the material even as she explains, gives examples. On a scale of one to ten, the course is a 1 as subject matter, a 10 as a demonstration of method.

After class, I learn that I've come during the part of the course that precedes the later treatment of sex and AIDS education—"reproductive health," it is called. "Sex," the teacher comments, "is threatening to parents." She tries to keep the emphasis on reproductive biology, not interpersonal relations, thinks the Michigan Model, a K through 7 comprehensive health curriculum that mandates teaching about AIDS in elementary school and has been adopted by 400 districts in the state, is "exciting." You have to make the assumption today, she tells me, that a fourteen-year-old is sexually active. "And so many of their problems are due to misconceptions." She smiles at the pun, intended or not. "Some girls believe they can only get pregnant on January 14, March 14—'the middle day of the month.' Or that you can't get pregnant in the first year of sexual activity. If you just tell them that's wrong, you're 'moralizing.' That's no good. You have to explain.

"But," she continues, "the qualities of the people who teach this two-semester-hour, twenty-clock-hour required course differ widely. One male student teacher said, 'I don't care if they take my job away, I'm not going to talk about menstruation to sixth-grade girls.'

"The section of the course that deals with reproduction is called Figuring Out What's Best For Me, not Sex. The focus is on decision making, overcoming barriers to using contraceptives." On her desk stands what looks like a taper left over from some candlelit dinner party. It is a dildo, she tells me matter-of-factly, used to demonstrate the use of condoms. No, she never would have expected, at the beginning of her teaching career, to be doing this. "But I'm teaching them"—the education students, about to become teachers—"what *they* need to know, not what they will teach kids in their classrooms."

In the mid-1960s, before coming here, she taught health education to Mexican-American girls from sixteen to twenty-one in a program sponsored by UCLA. "I knew the textbook, not the street. I had to use street language, so I tried making a dirty words list, but the words changed to fast my list was always obsolete. We talked about abstinence, tried taking a moral position. But that's really the job of the parents, and they're not doing it. . . .

"Even in middle-class schools you find teachers and parents have stopped supporting each other. The parents feel guilty about not fulfilling their parental responsibilities and they attack the teachers as their response to the accusation that they give no help with homework, don't turn off the TV, aren't even there a lot of the time. . . .

"Some of the suburban kids have so much money. . . . A teacher I know set a fine of a dollar for every time a kid misused grammar. At the end they were going to use the money for a pizza party. Some of the kids just started putting in five dollars, ten dollars, paying their fines in advance. These kids have four pairs of Reeboks, a VCR, computer video games. . . . They don't see the place of school in their lives. They've already got everything.

"And the teacher's attitude is, I give up. Don't fight it. We're just coming out of a period of oversupply, and many teachers, particularly older ones, feel their jobs are tenuous. They're insecure. A friend of mine, out of a sense of responsibility to her students, taught during a strike. They called her a scab. Now she's afraid her job is threatened.

"We feel no real sense of empowerment in our jobs. We're invited to a conference and then when it's over the deans and department heads tell us it was only advisory—they'll make the final decisions.

"Young teachers today are just not well educated enough to do the job we're asking of them. I look at them and I think, How are you going to manage? They're ignorant, naive, they have low abilities. Let's face it, education is what you go into if you can't get into anything else. I had a student, a very nice young man, who liked people and got along well with kids but just could not write. His mother called me to complain because he was failing and I asked her, 'Does he really belong in education? In that field, our tools are reading and writing.' And she said, 'But if he's not a teacher, he'll have to go and work on the line.' So there you have it. We're the next to the bottom rung."

That same morning, dispirited by what I'd just heard, I took my seat in a section of a secondary methods course on Teaching Social Studies expecting the worse. What I got instead was a taste of education, something I'd almost given up expecting to find.

"We're discussing background . . . theories . . . bias" was what I heard as I took my notebook and pen out. The text on the armrests of the chairs around me was *The Western Intellectual Tradition: From Leonardo to Hegel*, written by J. Bronowski and Bruce Mazlish some thirty years ago and revised about fifteen years ago. As I looked around the room it seemed to me the students were more alert, more focused, than the elementary group I'd seen earlier. As the hour proceeded, their comments and questions made it clear they were more intelligent, more articulate. There were many more men— thirteen in the class of twenty—and two middle-aged women along with five younger ones.

I wouldn't have been able to predict the direction the class would take from the way it began. "Bias," the dark-haired, bearded, casually dressed professor was saying, "means something has to be left out for some purpose. Take the title of this book. It leaves out Eastern thought and how the West drew on it, and parts of non-Christian Western Europe, and even then it's just a history of thought. And even in those four hundred years it covers, it leaves out women. It was written in the fifties and our frame of reference has changed. The civil rights and women's movements, the awareness of minorities, had not hit the scene yet. Our consciousness has been raised since then. History meant to these authors a male orientation. If you were to use this book—not as a text, of course, but even as a source book—you would have to recognize the bias in the book and do some digging around to include women in those four hundred years. No women intellectuals in that period? What about the patrons in Italian noble families? You'd point out the Jewish importance at the roots of Christianity. . . ." And somehow, having said what had to be said about the role of minorities, we have elided into talking about civilization, the expanding world.

There is discussion of the move from the medieval religious society in Western Europe to the secular, to nationalism, exploration and colonization, the development of mercantile capitalism, the industrial and commercial revolution. Questioning, summarizing, the professor, a former high school teacher of history, suggests how these student teachers might present or highlight an idea, an example. How could they help their students relate the Renaissance to what came before and after? ("Let's pursue Leonardo. How does he represent one of those characteristics we associate with the Renaissance?") What's an effective way to bring in documents? To bring in references to other cultures that are significant? ("In Confucian times we find . . .")

I left the class exhilarated. The level of interest shown by these teaching students (self-selected, to be sure; this was not a required course) was like a reminder of something forgotten. As I walked across the campus thinking about some of the things I had heard it occurred to me that students would need to master basic skills in grade school if they were going to be able to follow and understand in high school a book like the one we had been discussing. If you have spent all your time learning to adjust, you don't have the vocabulary or the habits of mind to call on. Perhaps the students in this class and others like them would be the new monks, keeping learning alive in a new kind of academic dark age.

The class in Social Aspects of Teaching, a course required of all certification students, consisted entirely of women. Four of them were mothers preparing to go back to work now that their children were in school, and the other dozen or so ranged from a couple who might have been taken for not-very-bright high school students to a few who were self-possessed, attentive, and articulate. Responses not surprisingly ranged from the vague and meandering beside the point to focused and germane to the issue, which on this day was the Hidden Curriculum. The capital letters were there in the emphasis given the words by the professor, a young woman whose somewhat bohemian dress, a long skirt and an oversized dark sweater embroidered with what looked like a South American Indian motif, contrasted with the standard jeans and corduroys, bulky sweaters, and down vests of her students. A young woman with a blank face chewed gum next to an alert-looking bespectacled student of about thirty writing in a looseleaf notebook. They were a blue-collar group, as their occasional references to their own lives made clear (a husband on the line, a father out of work, the first of her family to go to college).

We got right down to business with a distinction between the functionalists, who say the hidden curriculum (we are not debating its existence) is necessary, integrative, helps fit individual's into society's needs, and the conflict theorists, who say the hidden curriculum is what those in power, "capitalists," want, that it serves the interests of one socioeconomic group over the interests of others. The professor then offers a definition of ideology: "a shared system of beliefs of a dominant class or culture." She gives a few examples: fundamentalists; history that leaves out the part played by women; a biography of Andrew Carnegie that leaves out the negative parts. "It's not the whole story. It says if you work hard you too can succeed, but we can step back and say that belief is operating in someone's interest." When you realize it's an ideology, she says, you can start to criticize it.

Watch out, she tells them, for ideological bias in social science textbooks. They can be "vehicles for leaving things out and a person who doesn't know that doesn't question it, doesn't ask whose interest it is in." Example: the ideology defining the place of women in the nineteenth century. Men benefited. She asks for other examples of beliefs grounded in social structure.

The *A* student, the one who always has the answer and does most of the talking ("Can I hear from someone besides Amy?" the professor asks plaintively at one point), has her hand up. "Going to the doctor," she says. "That's an ideology. It benefits the group of doctors at the expense of native healers and herbalists, people who practice holistic medicine." The others are catching on. "Prescriptions," says a young woman with a vast cloud of blond hair. "The IUD benefits the prescription companies [sic] at the expense of women." The professor nods. "As a culture we've become the medical model." A heavyset sallow young woman offers: "The power people who own the textbook companies—" she pauses, looking at the professor, then says, "the capitalists—they want us to think unions are bad." The professor nods again, encouraging. "The people doing the selecting," she says, "the district school boards, don't take into account lower-class culture."

A young woman who has been quiet up to now raises her hand, asks, "As a teacher, aren't you supposed to teach what's in the curriculum? That's your job? You can't just . . ." She's not getting encouragement from the front of the room. She trails off.

"I wouldn't be teaching you to question the texts you give your students," says the professor, "if I didn't want you to read the material you give your students critically and find ways of supplementing it, correcting it." She moves on to a discussion of an article from the *Harvard Educational Review* called "Tootle: A Parable of Schooling and Destiny," copies of which she has given all the students to read. In it, a university professor analyzes the text of a Little Golden Book, first published in 1945 and by now a classic of children's literature, that tells the story of what happens when a young locomotive goes off the track, fails to follow the rules of the school for engines. In the end Tootle learns there is nothing but trouble for locomotives that go off their tracks and when he becomes a famous Flyer he advises the young locomotives, "Work hard. . . . Always remember to Stop for a Red Flag Waving. But most of all, Stay on the Rails No Matter What."

In eighteen pages, the story is exhaustively analyzed as a "picture of society . . . meritocratic . . . a class system" which "works because responsible authorities make decisions and because everyone else follows rules." There's a good bit about "the State . . . conspiracy . . . surveillance" and Tootle as "a worker, not a decision maker" who has to "stay in his place without question" and not "presume to choose his own course or destiny," rewarded in the end for conforming to the manipulators.

It is not clear whether the author of the article would ban *Tootle*, rewrite it, or provide each three-year-old with a study guide. It is also not clear from anything this earnest young professor tells her class of unsophisticated young women—and they would have no other way of knowing this—that the article itself represents a particular ideology, the Marxist "revisionist" school many of whose members are the authors cited in its scholarly footnotes.

"*Tootle* didn't seem to me," says one of the students, but she isn't good at argument. ". . . to be about all that," she finishes lamely.

Another, one of the older women, says, "What would a six-year-old get out of it? I read it to my kid. 'Work hard in school'—isn't that what we all want?"

The professor pounces. "What does that sound like? Anyone?"

Amy's got it. "Meritocracy! And if it doesn't work, if you don't succeed, you think, What's wrong with me? Because it doesn't always work."

GAIL: After the war, World War II, that was important then. I know, my folks . . . you had to work hard, rebuild.

PROFESSOR: The ideology of "work hard and you'll make it" covers
up a whole set of social, structural issues. We have to question
it, find other ways of thinking about working in our society,
organizing our culture.

AMY: We're giving kids these messages in these texts, in books
like *Tootle* that reinforce the culture. That if you work hard
you'll get someplace.

PROFESSOR: If it were Communism or Nazism we would notice
the ideology, because that's a set of beliefs we've rejected.

JEANNE: But like in education, we have to conform to the
system.

PROFESSOR: Do you really want to teach if that's so? I wouldn't.
Let me ask, this institution, do you think of it as liberal or
conservative?

LISA: Well, compared to the small business college I went to before . . .

PROFESSOR: I'm given a set of goals, I'm observed, but do you
think I teach the same way as everyone else?

JEANNE: Those are just general guidelines they give you.

AUDREY: You can't change the real world out there. You have to
function in it. You've always got a boss telling you what to
do—the principal or parents or the school board . . .

PROFESSOR (emotional): Why are you all so hostile? I feel your
hostility when I suggest you ask these questions.

AMY (coming to her rescue): We're powerless. It's a closed system.

PROFESSOR: Aha! (That was her cue, and now she hands out copies
of a passage from a 1973 book called *Pedagogy of the Oppressed*
by Paulo Freire which reads in part):

> Education either functions as an instrument which is used
> to facilitate the integration of the younger generation into the
> logic of the present system and bring about conformity to it,
> or it becomes the "practice of freedom"—the means by which
> men and women . . . discover how to participate in the transfor-
> mation of their world.

PROFESSOR: Where do you stand on one or the other of these?

JEANNE: We can't bring about change.

CAROL: How do we know change will be improvement?

ANGIE: Thinking for yourselves is what will bring about change.

GAIL: American culture has no problem with change, it's changing
before our eyes! My grandparents in the old country—the culture was passed on from generation to generation. Change is
okay with industry, inventions, but the culture is going to de-
struct it's going so fast.

JEANNE: You have to have rules and regulations. If everyone is
free to be what you want to be, everyone does his own thing—

PROFESSOR: Is that freedom?

GAIL: We *have* freedom. In the East Bloc countries there's censorship, you stand in line all day. We can choose between the conglomerate or the corner store. Every American citizen has the right to say I don't agree with this rule and I want it changed.

CAROL (to the professor): You always throw meritocracy at us. What's the alternative?

PROFESSOR: It doesn't exist and won't if we always say we can't do anything about it.

CAROL: It depends on what you want out of life, what you're going for. What's wrong with working hard in order to eat, give your kids better things? Success for one isn't necessarily the same for others.

PROFESSOR (demonstrably patient): What's wrong with having a hierarchy?

CAROL: I'm middle class. I'm working hard to finish school and succeed as an educator. That's my choice. Others make their own choice.

PROFESSOR: Schools reproduce particular social hierarchies, the class system. Teachers make choices according to particular ideological systems. What happens when they reject the standards, the norms of society?

CAROL: That's what they choose.

PROFESSOR: If you say that, it's an insult. You're blaming the victim.

ALISON: The poor don't have equality of opportunity.

PROFESSOR: Aha!

ALISON: They're tracked.

PROFESSOR (folding her arms): So what do we do as teachers?

AMY: Break the cycle. From first grade on, give them the message. You *are* smart, you *can* achieve. You take their background into account when you're grading . . . mixed ability groupings . . .

The rest is lost in the general hubbub of chairs being pushed back, coats and books gathered up. Class is over for today.

After class I thanked the professor for letting me visit. She looked unhappy. "I don't know what's with this group," she said. "They're so hostile to me. I have two sections of this course and I think I'm the same but the other group is so much more . . ." She didn't finish. I didn't think I'd ever see her again and I broke my silence to say, "I don't think they're hostile. Maybe they're just older, and with their life experience they're secure in their middle-class values and don't think this is a closed society." She still didn't look happy. "Do you?" I asked.

She looked at me with some surprise. "Of course!" she said.

The gentlemanly, easygoing, liberal dean invited me to a meeting of the University Council on Teacher Education. The endless consideration of minute questions about descriptions of major and minor course requirements in the current catalogue left no time for discussion of other items on the agenda such as a proposal for a bilingual/multicultural group minor, an overview of enrollment data, or a report on career services. I learned nothing about those things but I did learn that whatever else one might fault the administration for, it had to be said that no decision was lightly taken. At the end of two hours a motion was tabled because the endless ruminative discussion had failed either to enlighten or convince anyone about something that no one was sure was very important anyway.

I left the meeting with Dolores Wagner, as I'll call her, the handsome, gracious director of admissions, a fiftyish black woman who seemed to know more about every detail that had come up in the boardroom than anyone else there. We talked about a number of things on the way to her office, where we had coffee and continued our conversation, which ranged informally over the ed school scene. Among her comments:

"Our education students are older these days, around twenty-six or twenty-seven when they're seniors, five to seven years older than they used to be. About one-quarter of them already have degrees and come here for their education courses and certification. About three-quarters are female. Last year [1987] less than fifty black teachers were certified by the state—including elementary, secondary, and special education. Only thirteen of them were male. Historically, three-quarters of black teachers came from black colleges like Howard, Fisk, Spelman. Today the teaching profession is drawing on a smaller proportion of a smaller pool." (Because, although she doesn't say so, with affirmative action programs and the outlawing of segregation and changing attitudes in society, more options are open to black students.)

"What do we need to do to produce more black teachers? The first step is to identify potentially qualified minority students and prepare them, something the cafeteria-style high school doesn't do. We should recruit them from the start, strengthening them in math, seeing that they take courses in algebra and geometry. They're coming ill-equipped from high school, never having used their potential. At the same time, colleges of education have increased their standards. I told my son Robert when he said he wanted to go to medical school that it wasn't enough just to take eighteen credits. He was up there with *everybody's* Robert.

"When our students come, they should get realistic counseling about what they need, what they should take. And of course they need scholarships, not just loans. At present only between 4 and 5 percent of our education students are blacks; the figure for the university as a whole is closer to eight percent.

"We might attract more minority students if we made it clear it was all right for them to go into teaching for four or five years, the way women formerly did, and then go on to something else.

"Blacks," she insists, "can never assimilate in this society. We'll always be a separate culture. There is an invisible ceiling for blacks in terms of how far they can go." Dr. Wagner is director of admissions here, her husband is a midlevel corporate executive, her children are college-educated professionals. Her parents were professionals, her father a lawyer, her mother a teacher. She and her family live in an upper-middle-class suburb in a university community known for the excellence of its public schools. She tells me that her daughter wanted to go east to an Ivy League school "and room with her best friend, Debbie Blumenthal," but she insisted that she go to a black college. "I told her, you need to get some soul, know who you are as a black." When I expressed surprise that middle-class blacks would repudiate the goal of one integrated society, she told me all her friends, no matter how successful, feel that way.

A class on the Exceptional Student in the Regular Classroom required for all certification students is held in a large lecture hall in which about 150 students are seated in rows that rise like those of an operating theater. The professor looks up at them, says, "I've got fifty minutes to teach you all you ever wanted to know. . . .

"When you get these kids in your class you're going to wonder what to do—so *don't* sell the textbook. It has some good practical tests." And practical is what she aims to be, steering them through the shoals of definition and practice.

She starts with "learning disabled," explains that it involves a discrepancy between ability and achievement, refers to the child who has a normal IQ but is more than two years behind grade level and whose performance is erratic, varying from subject to subject. These children, whom a teacher can expect to find in any regular classroom since the "mainstreaming" legislation took effect in the mid-1970s, may not be able to read, to recognize words or even to pay attention, usually have poor motor coordination and impulse control, and often "shout, cry, or pick on other kids." They are "not stupid," she tells the class, "they just have problems learning." Since they have "specific problems with processing information in traditional ways," the classroom teacher will have to have a repertoire of other methods for dealing with them in addition to those required for teaching children who fall within the normal range of abilities and behaviors.

She shows them a film "to show you some of the kinds of kids you might see in your classroom—some of the warning signs, what to look for," but cautions them, "Don't ever label a kid or you'll end up in court. Refer him. He'll be tested by a team and diagnosed. An individual educational plan will be drawn up."

The faces I see around me register more apathy and boredom than any sign of being daunted by the prospect of what will be expected of them (one young man is asleep, one is reading the campus newspaper, a young woman is leafing through the pages of a date book). The professor continues to provide "tips" in a manner both cheerful and matter-of-fact. She belongs to that army of optimists ready to go forth and do battle wherever ordered. She describes the whole-word approach to reading, suggests sight will work better than sound, says, "Tell them to spell it, not sound it out. Watch 'em, they will. Eventually they'll trust you and they'll learn to read."

If I thought I had tasted variety in the courses I'd already sampled, the class on Children's Literature proved something else again. The cheerful, rotund professor seemed intent on getting her students to pass the upcoming exam they would have to take. The entire hour was devoted to tips on how to take the exam: how to answer true/false questions, how to study ("Don't read the books, read your notes"), how to organize the titles in categories so as to remember them ("Make a list with the name of the story on one side, some characteristic on the other, then cover up one side and check yourself"), and a reminder that they should memorize the names of the authors as well as the titles of the Newbery Medal winners. Just recognizing, summarizing: "It would take you forever to reread and remember the books." We are talking about *children's* books, some of them picture books.

She reads them a sample question—"In which of the following tales does the protagonist not succeed"—and then explains to these college students what "protagonist" means. When she turns to the subject of Hans Christian Andersen I expect some consideration of what it *means* that Andersen's tales are "individualized, autobiographical, not generic folk tales" (a statement to be noted down and memorized). Instead of assuming they have read the tale and discussing it, she will read parts of it to them. But before that she summarizes it. ("There's no formulas in it," this teacher of literature remarks.) They take notes. And, finally, she offers some comment on the tale she has summarized and read them in part—"The Ugly Duckling." Andersen himself, we are told, identified with the ugly duckling. And like the duckling turned swan, when he became successful he "never questioned the system, never tried to better the lot of the others, the lower classes, once he'd made it."

It was at a combination Chinese restaurant and coffee shop across the street from the campus that I learned what was being done to recruit prospective teachers, and particularly minority (which for the most part means black) students. Among those who were lunching with me was the head of a program funded by the federal Office of Educational Research and Improvement (OERI) to encourage the development of "reflective thinking" on the part of education students before they begin their teaching careers. The student participants are introduced to current research on teaching and learning, enrolled in certain required courses (among them, Social Aspects of Education, in which I had learned so much about the "hidden curriculum"), and assigned activities to carry out in cooperating classrooms in local public school districts (e.g., "studying the ethnic makeup of the community, interpreting student test scores, and so on"). They spend a half-day each week during a semester at a school, observing and discussing teaching methods and finally teaching a week-long unit they've designed. They keep a journal on this week of teaching, and at the end of it they give a test of their own devising.

Also present was the head of a model urban teacher education program designed in response to new State Board of Education certification rules requiring all prospective teachers to have "preparation in dealing with culturally diverse groups." The aim of the program is recruiting—and keeping—teachers for urban schools "from diverse racial, socioeconomic and nontraditional backgrounds who possess rich life experiences for the teaching profession," by "increasing opportunities for minority and economically disadvantaged students." A nearby community college will offer preparation for transfer into the university's teacher education program, "with particular emphasis on the critical areas of mathematics and the sciences," to be followed by field experience in local school districts with the help of mentor teachers. The program is intentionally based close to where the prospective students live, offers paid internships in their junior and senior years, ongoing help in everyday classroom activities such as taking attendance, tutoring, and grading from experienced teachers (offering "multiple opportunities for bonding to occur") and administrators, as well as "a cohort of classmates who will coalesce into a support group."

Over a midwestern Far Eastern lunch that seemed to echo the concern with cultural diversity, the program heads, an assistant, and a student teacher shared their thoughts along with their Cantonese vegetables. Some of their comments on the current crisis in American education and their own projects:

- We need to develop with school people a common core of what students ought to know and be able to do, what associated field experience they need, "so classroom teachers and education faculty are singing off the same song sheet."
- The kids are different now, it's not just what I hear from burnt-out teachers. Special education has gone beyond the original intent. Once you label a kid he can never break the barrier of that label afterward.
- In the university budget, teacher education has been treated as an academic subject rather than a clinical one like nursing, and there's no money from the state for field experience. Our project is located in the community college so students don't have to leave their neighborhoods, and they're paid for their field experience so they won't have to work at McDonald's in order to go to school.
- Who's going into teaching today? Some of the young are interested in teaching but many of the older people have no place else to go or are just looking for a second income. Teaching is looked on as just another occupation. That's why the teaching leadership is concerned with professionalism, with issues of autonomy and empowerment. What's happened is that teachers' concern for service has been replaced by a concern with power.
- What is schooling for? School has always been about character development. But the indicator of it is academic performance. It's also supposed to be a preparation for lifelong learning—teach one how to think, how to solve problems, to look critically at ideas.

(Is the professor in the course on Social Aspects of Teaching doing that? When I raised the question, not mentioning the professor's name, knowing there were other people teaching the course as well, there was general grimacing, rolling of eyes and obvious meeting of minds across the table. One person groaned. They knew who I meant. Her ideas and methods did not seem to have met with universal approval. The usual dichotomy, I supposed, between academic radicals and practical reformers.)

Impressed by the projects I'd heard described, I wondered if the subsidized programs with their paid internships ought not to require some give-back of service in the form of a specified commitment of time to be spent teaching in the urban schools after graduation. As it happened, I would have reason to ponder that question again when many of the themes that had announced themselves during the classes and conversations of recent days came together in a meeting with some students.

The promised meeting with black students took place on my last afternoon on the campus. Dolores Wagner brought me to the door of the conference room, introduced me to the six young people already seated in comfortable leather chairs around the walnut table, and withdrew. I told them why I was there—to learn something about the experiences and thoughts of future teachers for a book I was writing—and asked them to introduce themselves. They went around the table: Laura, Ben, Patricia, Helena, John, and Richard.

Laura, perhaps because she went first, revealed little except her name and her desire to be a teacher because she liked children. She seemed shy, and rather than make her uncomfortable, I passed on to Ben. Easy, voluble, he talked about his large family, in which he'd been ninth of eleven children, about his love of sports, and about his decision to go into teaching in order to provide a role model for inner-city black boys who hadn't had "my advantages," by which I took him to mean his intact family. He said he'd been lonely at college at first—"not many other black faces around"—until he'd seen Richard in the science building ("We were the only two," he said. "They discourage blacks") and struck up a conversation. He smiled across the table at Richard, who nodded acknowledgment but didn't smile. Richard sat back in his chair as though to put some distance between himself and the rest of us, and his expression remained—well, I didn't want to sound like the professor who found her class "hostile," but there was an impassive if not actually surly aspect to Richard's demeanor. I gathered from Ben's remarks that they had become a twosome since then.

Patricia was poised, well dressed in what seemed more of a career than a student mode, and told me that she was here because of a teacher she'd had in high school. "I never had any encouragement at home or in school, and then when I was a junior and I was thinking about college, this teacher said to me, 'Forget it. You'll never make it to college. Don't waste your time. You're cute,' she said, 'look for a husband, get a job. Forget about college.' That did it. I decided from that day I would make something of myself, become a teacher like her—a better one than her—and when I graduate I'm going back there with my diploma and show her." We all smiled, sharing vicariously in her revenge fantasy. It struck me that I'd heard worse reasons for career choices.

Helena came from a solid middle-class background, the child of a retail store manager and a nurse, and reminded me of her counterparts in the student bodies of Ivy League schools whom I knew—the children of my friends. She was sure of herself and her many opinions. With her shining face, her hair drawn back in a severe pony tail and her large horn-rims, she could have been cast as the brainy girl in the movies of a generation ago who takes off her glasses to hear the hero say, "Why, you're beautiful!" Her anti-authority stance seemed less like radical rebellion than a rite of passage common to the children of the bourgeoisie. She was "becoming her own person." Helena talked seriously and with enthusiasm about doing research on "black children's learning styles." She was convinced they were different, and "we should value and exploit that difference. "Black children," she asserted, "learn better in groups—community learning—than from the teacher up front and books. We lose the black male in school by the time he's three years old. Black males are more aggressive," she added, and the other girls, both more conventional and quiet than Helena, nodded, met each other's eyes, laughed.

Gentle and soft-spoken, John had an impressive history to present. I found myself leaning forward to catch his words, soon understanding why. John had been "given up" as uneducable because of multiple sensory handicaps as a young child, and only the perseverance of a dedicated mother had kept him in school and found him there when the law mandated schooling for children like him. He was understandably in favor of the legislation and touchingly eager to do for other children what had been done for him, although, he felt, not as well as it might have been. He spoke of a lingering sense of shame in his days as the only "different" child in his class, both in terms of race and physical deficits, and for him the operative word in the new scheme of things was "entitled." I would have found it impossible to argue with John about the effects of mainstreaming even if this had been the occasion for doing so, which, to my relief, it was not. His own achievement in overcoming his handicaps certainly put him on the high moral ground, and, even aside from questions of tact, other considerations seemed out of place there.

I was beginning to feel a certain disquiet about the discrepancy between the outlook of these young people and my own, and I made a mental note to think at a later time about the cause. Their experiences, their attitudes? I didn't think it was their age or race per se. And then I turned to Richard, who remained tilting back in his chair, in a position I tried not to perceive as insolent, with one suede boot on the chair beside him, arms crossed over his fisherman's knit sweater. One thing was clear about Richard. He was angry.

The others had introduced themselves by name and added whatever personal details about family and background they chose before answering the question of why they had decided to go into teaching. Richard skipped the personal part and came right to the main point. He was going into teaching "for personal reasons, to learn, to travel." He wanted to go to Africa, specifically to East Africa, when he graduated. He felt he belonged there, not here. "They teach us about Napoleon and his wars with the English. They don't tell us about the black emperor of Haiti who beat him. We're learning the dominant white culture. We need to learn to think critically, to ask why am I learning this, whose interests does it serve?" This was beginning to sound familiar. "I've had one teacher here," he went on, "who really opened things up for me. She gave us things to read. Have you ever heard of Paulo Freire?" I said I had.

Then I asked him whether, when he finished the program and graduated, he planned to teach the children of the neighborhood he'd grown up in. He shook his head contemptuously. He wouldn't go into the schools here "and be part of the oppressive system for assimilating us into the existing power structure. You have no power in the classroom. I don't want to give this garbage to kids in the ghetto. They make you teach them what serves the ends of the power structure." He paused for a moment, leaning back in his stylish clothes on the comfortable chair in this nicely decorated room provided along with so much else of the community's resources in the form of stipends, counseling, and other kinds of consideration, and said, "I've been oppressed too long."

While Richard was talking, the door had opened and four students appeared. They stopped, reluctant to interrupt, and then tip-

toed into the room, taking seats along the wall beyond the table
where we sat. They were all white and, somehow, looked pale, hesi-
tant, and out of place. One was a young man. They smiled at everyone, and one of the young women, a tall blond who seemed to
stoop slightly even when sitting down, explained apologetically that
they had been invited to meet with the visiting writer but evidently
someone had gotten the time wrong. Explanations and apologies
all around, and we went on almost as though these intruders—for
this was how they seemed to have been cast and how they seemed
to play their roles—were not there. Uncertain of how to draw them
into the circle, I let it go. I was the senior person in the room, but
a certain palpable tension had defeated any impulse I might have
had to take charge of the situation.

Ben was talking now. About how the curriculum was all based
on the white culture. "Take the class in black literature . . ." Surprised to hear the reference to such a course in view of what he
had just said, I asked where this course was given. In the English
Department. "We, Richard and me, were the only two black faces.
The teacher asked how many of you have read a book by a black
author or can name a black author. We were the only two who
raised our hands. But look how many *white* authors *we've* read!"

Behind him, the tall blond girl leaned forward, took advantage
of the momentary pause to say, "I just want you all to know how
glad we are you're here. We really want to learn about your culture."
Wry smiles, pained silence. She sat back. Confused or crestfallen, I
couldn't tell.

Later, I asked Dolores Wagner about Richard. She "found" him,
she told me with some pride. He'd had two years of college when
he applied to the education program. "He had good grades but a
weak autobiography. I advised him, gave him some pointers about
writing and other things, told him, 'Come to me when you've got
the credits and I promise you a good student-teaching place.' When
he came back, I told him, 'I've found you a good one.'"

Her motives may be laudable, but what about the social costs
of recruitment, remediation, counseling, scholarships—the whole
package—if students like Richard don't stay in the teaching force?
Who pays?

The answer is, taxpayers from across the social spectrum, including the working poor on whom the heaviest burden falls. But the
faith in social engineering combined with the sense of entitlement
makes this a question that is never even asked.

PART FOUR

The West Coast

7

The University of California at Los Angeles

Language, Literature, and Learning

Everybody's an expert on schools. The driver of the shuttle bus that took me from the Los Angeles airport to the UCLA guest house asked whether I was a visiting professor. When I told him I was a visiting writer, he wanted to know what I was writing about and when I told him my subject was education, he nodded approvingly, as if to say there was a lot to be written on that subject, and said, "Now if the Western countries would just treat teachers a little more like they do in other cultures . . ." When he looked to me for some reaction, I smiled noncommittally. I couldn't imagine what other cultures he was talking about, but it was late, I was tired, and I was saving my reactions for the next day, my first on the UCLA campus.

The education school of the University of California at Los Angeles began life as a normal school and its original purpose of training elementary school teachers left it a legacy of emphasis on practical training that distinguished it early on from its sister campuses like Berkeley, which emphasized theoretical research. UCLA's reputation puts it, along with Michigan State and a handful of other graduate schools of education in public universities, at the forefront both in research and in professional training while it remains practice-based and involved with the public schools of the surrounding community, a huge metropolis with a various and changing population. Such is the received wisdom in "the field."

The UCLA campus is luxuriantly green, dotted with sculpture gardens, terraces reminiscent of Europe's outdoor cafes, and sleekly modern halls of learning next to older, vaguely Moorish, ornamented brick buildings. The outdoor tables and chairs, like the lawns and the steps of the buildings, are full of young people who seem to have found Eden. If there are intense intellectuals or malcontents here, as there must be—certainly a few?—they must be inside. I see no sign of them. But perhaps it's because when they come out they melt into these relaxed figures sitting in the sun in their shorts with piles of books beside them and an air of contentment that seems to come with the soft air perfumed with whatever it is that's in bloom just now. This morning in New York it was snowing. I wonder how anyone manages to work in this climate. Perhaps indoors.

On my way to a course in the education department I stop in the hall outside two classrooms. From one comes the sound of words by now long familiar: "the learning process . . . social values . . . cultural cognitive interface . . ." I peek inside at the faces. Some of them look blank, some intent, some as though they wish that they were elsewhere. Next door, an English-accented voice is talking about "the delta mean equation" and I see a man writing a long equation on the board as he says "in theory we would expect . . . but in the real world . . . analysis of the conditions of the experiment shows transfer reaction at each electrolyte interface." The room is utterly quiet except for his voice and the sound of the chalk on the blackboard, the scratch of pens on paper. Every eye, I see, is following his chalk. Almost every face, I notice, is oriental. Reluctantly, I move away and into the other room, which is, alas, my destination this morning.

The Graduate School of Education grants higher degrees to future scholars of education who will fill professorial chairs and obtain research grants at other universities or administer schools or state and local boards, committees, panels—the education leadership cadres. It also trains about 170 elementary and secondary teachers each year in its Teacher Education programs. These are college graduates with a B.A. in some academic discipline who spend a fifth year in teacher training, à la the Holmes Report model, although perhaps not with all of its specifics. Still, they have presumably mastered some subject. It is expected that they will learn what they need to about teaching it to the young—about instructional strategies, classroom management, and other aspects of the routines of teaching—in the three academic quarters it will take about a third of them to meet the state's requirements for teaching credentials or the full year it will take the other two-thirds of them to earn an M.A. along with their credentials.

Unlike students in programs elsewhere, none of this group will have majored in elementary education, but in history, English, mathematics, and science, as well as psychology, sociology, and the other social sciences. And while the California State University system as a whole provides—"cranks out" is the expression used by an instructor here at UCLA—not only most of the state's teachers but *10 percent* of the entire nation's teachers, this small group of fifth year students stands apart from that system. Tuition here is more expensive, entrance standards are higher. All education students in California are graduate students, but some are more graduate than others. Those studying at branches of the University of California, which include Berkeley and UCLA, are among the top-ranking one-third of high school graduates in the state.

Their year is spent observing and participating in classrooms, where, as one of the program's field coordinators puts it, "They learn basic logistics and gain some experience with children in a variety of grades and with a variety of socioeconomic and ethnic groups." They also carry a heavy course load that includes educational psychology, principles and methods of instruction, cultural and cross-cultural foundations, special education, and curricular decision making, along with laboratory courses in math, reading, bilingual methodology. Almost all of them are women, one to ten being the average ratio of male to female. Several are mothers coming back to pick up their teaching credentials now that their own children are in school; others are refugees from the business world like the one from law who felt her career was, as she put it, "not what I was looking for." Her field instructor says, "She's seen the outside world, she's not just drifting into teaching because she can't think of anything else to do. Students like her are committed. They're idealistic. We try to feed their fires."

And yet, a recruitment brochure for the program sends a message in reverse. It asks:

What do all these positions have in common: Marketing for the New York Times, Technical Training Coordination for Bell Telephone, Industrial Pension Consulting, Real-Time Programming for Communication Networks?

They are all careers for teachers who have moved successfully from their classrooms into business and industry.

Such a pitch seems to be the ed school's own acknowledgment of what its critics have said all along: The best and the brightest go elsewhere, if not after higher forms of knowledge then after higher salaries and higher prestige.

It has been estimated that there are as many as one hundred different language groups within the Los Angeles Unified School District boundaries. The largest of these is the Spanish-speaking community. Although generally lumped together under the heading of "Hispanic," this group consists of many subgroups—Mexican-Americans, emigrants from Colombia, Nicaragua, and other Central and South American countries, Cubans, Puerto Ricans—and within each of these, both newcomers and second- or third-generation Californians, disorganized members of the welfare class as well as stable middle-class families. It should come as no surprise that not all of them agree—despite what the generally self-appointed spokesmen for "the Hispanic community" say—about the issue of bilingual education. Some are for it, some are against it, some—the least in touch with their children's schools and with the culture in general—are unaware of the issue.

In recent years the politics of race has been extended to ethnic groups and pitted those who would take advantage of the openness of the American system, which is what brought them here to begin with, against those who would use ethnicity as a power base for special group entitlements. While many Hispanic immigrants have their eye on the possibilities of material self-betterment by means of hard work and education leading to entrance into the economy, their leaders would prefer separateness to assimilation. That way lies power for them.

Nowhere is this clearer than in the movement to provide bilingual education in the public schools. Since the passage of the original Bilingual Education Act in 1968, which provided $7.5 million for programs to provide instruction for Spanish-speaking children in their native language while they learned English, appropriations for all federal bilingual programs has grown more than tenfold.

The original intent of these programs was to help non-English-speaking children keep from falling behind in reading, math, and their other subjects while they learned English, when they would move into regular classrooms.

With the arrival of millions of Latin American and other immigrants in the ensuing decades, both federal and state programs (which now amount to about three times the federal total, or more than $2 billion) not only grew to accommodate these new new clients for bilingual education but saw a shift from their original purpose of enabling children to move into the English-speaking mainstream. Some Hispanic leaders saw them as instruments of political power that would help create a bilingual society like that of Canada, in which a language group would become a distinct voting bloc.

Generations of immigrant children have learned English as the first step up the economic ladder to the better life they came here to seek. Along the way, they have inevitably lost some aspects of their old culture while keeping others alive in the family and in religious and fraternal organizations. No one ever suggested it was the responsibility of the government to do so for them. What the government offered them was an opportunity to be educated in the larger society so that they might eventually enter it. It would have seemed like a deprivation to be taught in their native language. It would inevitably have slowed their assimilation, relegating them to unskilled jobs at low wages with little chance for advancement and leaving them the pawns of their political leaders in a self-perpetuating patronage system.

Today in the Los Angeles Unified School District, some schools teach children exclusively in their native language for the first three grades of elementary school, not introducing English until the fourth grade. In all other schools, bilingual instruction is required whenever there are ten or more pupils in an elementary-school class (fifteen or more in a high school class) who speak the same language and have little or no English.

With children from Samoa and Laos, Armenia and Mexico, Korea and Haiti in the same school, there are seldom enough certified teachers for all of the language groups. Teacher's aides, who may speak the language but many of whom have no education themselves beyond high school, fill the gap. Sometimes children with a somewhat better grasp of English translate for the others. In classes that do have a bilingual teacher, everything must be repeated in both languages, which means that only half as much can be covered in any class period. With the further complication of busing, many children

who might be far ahead in reading or able to deal with more demanding homework assignments are held back waiting for the non-English-
speakers to catch up. And their number is growing daily.

I came to California opposed to bilingual education. What sense,
I reasoned, did it make to educate children in any language but
the one of the country and culture in which they would have to
make their way as adults? The United States is an English-speaking
country and its citizens need to speak, read, and write English in
order to get along in it, to hold down jobs and to communicate
with their fellow citizens and understand their ways. I had become
convinced over the past few years that the bilingual movement was
more in the interests of a small group of lobbyists presuming to
speak for the parents in whose name it would control billions of
dollars in federal funds than the real interests of those parents or
their children.

In talking with student teachers and looking around at children
in their classrooms, I found that neither the problem nor the solution
seemed quite what they had before I came here. If the problem
appeared to be more intractable, more different than I had realized
from that of other immigrant groups in other times, the bilingual
solution came to seem more likely, if used in the right way, as a
transition to English—an important caveat—to foster learning, both
of English and of other subjects.

At UCLA I sat in on a class in Teaching Bilingual Reading
given by the principal of a Los Angeles school with a heavy concentration of Spanish-speaking children, herself of Mexican-American
background. A cheerful, voluble woman of ample proportions and
boundless enthusiasm, Mrs. Garcia, as I'll call her, had invited one
of the teachers from her school—"Mrs. Rivera"—to demonstrate
to the class of about a dozen student teachers how she teaches the
writing process to children for whom English is a second language.

The skirt of her bright red dress and the swirl of her shoulder-
length black hair as she turned to write things on the board made
Mrs. Rivera seem to be constantly in motion. Since she was also
pretty, and eager to share her successful experiences with these
relative novices, watching her and listening to her was a pleasure.
Like actors, teachers gain something when they have this kind of
personal appeal; it becomes part of their gift. So inviting was she
that she could barely keep up with the clamor of questions that
followed on her asking if they had any. They wanted to know how
you could correct the children without hurting their feelings, how
to teach them to "self-correct" without making it a chore, how to

keep them feeling "up" when they saw the more able getting ahead of them, how to keep everybody with different abilities writing, how to get them to like to write, to want to write—"how to excite them," as a particularly earnest young woman put it, "about the language experience."

"If you change their writing style," said another, "it's just not them. What's the bottom line," she wanted to know, "for acceptable work to send home?"

The rest of the two hours was spent in dealing with their questions, which she had written up on the board, the answers weaving into a set of suggestions, consistent if not really systematic, for drawing Spanish-speaking children into English expression. The themes were encouraging pride in their work, maintaining a warm print-rich environment (lots of pictures and posters, book illustrations, children's own poems and letters and drawings), keeping an individual folder with examples of their work at various stages so they and their parents could see progress and variety, introducing journal writing, with daily time set aside for it, and—the only time I had heard this said in months of visiting classes devoted to the educating of young children—"reading lovely things," or, as it was put in slightly more formal educationese: "modeling good writing."

One of the student teachers told of asking her fifth-grade class to write about their wishes. A girl who had never contributed before wrote a sentence about wishing for a "corvet." "I didn't correct the spelling, I just wrote on her paper that I had the same wish. She wanted it with one *t* and I wanted it with two *t*'s, but the idea was that I understood her. She loved it, and after that she couldn't write enough for me."

"She'll spell it the way you did," Mrs. Garcia assured her, beaming. I wasn't sure quite how or why, but I was caught up in the enthusiasm, ready to believe in magic. These students were serious, intelligent, witty—a most unusual commodity, I was finding, in education students—and more wide awake than any of their peers I'd met so far.

Mrs. Rivera talked about the importance of the teacher reading aloud at every level, about constant word play. "These are students whose first language is not English and you're asking them to write in English. Use the sounds of words in games during that two minutes when you're lining up. Think of it like Michelangelo, who said he chipped away at the block of marble until he found the statue within it. You're giving them the words."

This, I thought, is real teaching. Tips for taking kids step by step from here to there, with no agenda other than learning to love and do writing in English. It made one want to teach, where most education classes tend to move one away from any such feeling.

She talked about providing models for writing, bringing in literature and showing them form, but most of all, "Get their ideas on paper. Focus on the ideas, not the spelling or punctuation or sentence structure." The method, according to Mrs. Rivera, was based on what writers do—on "the writing process."

This seemed more useful to prospective teachers than all the abstract theory about cognitive development, all the educational methods research courses I had sat in on. What was useful in them for the classroom teacher could all be condensed into a single-semester course, supplemented by the understanding of different methods to be gained working with teachers like Mrs. Garcia and Mrs. Rivera. A combination of what they referred to as modeling, and explanations drawn from vividly recounted experience. It really came down to individuals. Teachers had to be, like these two, performers, whether in a motherly (like Mrs. Garcia's) or some other style.

Mrs. Rivera had gotten to the question about sending imperfect or unfinished work home. She had a suggestion for that—a rubber stamp that read: "Draft. Child's own work. Enjoy. Appreciate." Spelling and grammar are not isolated, she told them. They're taught in the writing process. Not because of the "feel good" philosophy, not with self-esteem as the goal in itself, but because they were more effectively learned that way.

They talked about children who were FEPs and LEPs—fluent English proficient and limited English proficient. About grouping the children so the FEPs in the class could help the LEPs, show them how to do things. One student teacher objected, "Some kids don't want another kid to show them. They say, 'I want *you* to do it'!" Another asks, "What's wrong with pointing out errors, giving the kid the responsibility to correct his mistakes?" "For LEPs," Mrs. Garcia says, "the important thing is to create a positive atmosphere for writing, to let the child know you think he can do it and to show pleasure when he does. I'd rather have a kid who *owns* these mistakes than one who spells it right this time and will never do it again and you'll go on making red marks."

(Whether or not joy in the writing process can by itself lead to correct spelling—a doubtful proposition—I am suddenly struck by the fact that in this classroom I've heard fewer "likes" than anywhere I've been so far.)

After class I help Mrs. Garcia take down the large sheets of paper on which questions and answers overflowing from the black-board have been written, and gather the pages of children's work—funny poems, touching letters to their teachers, little stories, two-line descriptions—that were shown on the overhead projector, some half in Spanish, half in English, some partially corrected by fellow pupils, some before-and-after examples of English words and sentences gradually taking over from Spanish. I ask her what she has to say in answer to the sober arguments against bilingual education with which I had arrived. Plenty, it turned out, and in a less benign tone than I had heard her use until now.

These children, she believed, were different from other generations of immigrants from other places in other times. Their parents were often illiterate themselves, did not place great emphasis on schooling or great value on education; and society offered fewer kinds of prospects today for those who did not acquire it. There was no frontier any more. Many of these children had only a shaky foundation in Spanish; they did not come from a language-rich environment. You built on what they had, using what they already knew, or you would turn them off, and eventually out. They would never get into the system. She knew. And she spoke bitterly of prejudice and discrimination encountered in her own childhood and of the one adult who comes riding over the horizon in all such anecdotal histories—sometimes a teacher, sometimes a relative. In her case, a grandfather.

I could not get over the impression that underneath all that love for the children she identified with was a deep anger at the rest of us.

A class in Teaching Poetry. I find myself again in one of those group encounter sessions where students are asked to "share anything you think about the word poetry." Again, no one expects the professor of literature—even children's literature—to know more than her students and have something more valuable to impart to them than what they can "share" with each other. They witness each other's feelings about their bad experiences having to analyze poems when they were in school. "Longfellow, Tennyson, ugh!" One of them says, more in puzzlement than in anger, "I thought I'd learn something about teaching poetry here today." They all laugh good-naturedly.

The professor believes that "the process of creating is far more important for children than learning *about* poetry. That nineteenth-century stuff—images, metaphors, symbols—that's not our philosophy any more. It's the language of the streets, the modern black poets. Not lofty, high, elevated language but *fun*, a discovery process." She cautioned against correcting spelling, punctuation, capitalization. "Don't worry about those things. It's more important to create than follow rules."

She suggests having the children make anthologies of the poems they like, including their own, and suggests some most children will like—A. A. Milne, Shel Silverstein. "There's even some that are easier than those."

This class meets in a room in the model elementary school, and we can hear the voices of children playing outside in the yard. Watching them smile, I think that these girls and women, more literate, better educated than most ed school students, are still mothers manqué and that teaching children has always been considered an appropriate career until having children of one's own. The very brightest are never going to go into teaching on this level, but early elementary doesn't need the brightest. We can settle for the best—in terms of character. Perhaps there should be different requirements and different training for elementary and secondary teachers. College preparation requires more intellectual ability, a more complex foundation in mathematics, science, as well as literature and history. Perhaps the motto for teachers of the very young ought to be the same as that for physicians: "Above all do no harm."

Yet what are we to think of a professor of literature who tells her prospective teacher students that Southern California kids playing with their electronic games and listening to their Walkmans don't need obsolete skills, they need to be put in touch with their feelings? "The use of poetic tools—analyzing forms—comes way down on my list."

But in teaching, as in any job market, emerging conditions dictate where the demand will be. In teaching, the "hot" areas are expected to be bilingual education, English as a second language, and special education. Prospective teachers are encouraged to specialize in those, which may in time create a special interest lobby within the profession, whether or not they have proved effective additions to the schooling repertoire. Poetry itself must be way down on everybody's list.

8

California State University at Northridge

School Politics and School Practice

California is second only to New York in its number of institutions of higher learning, with more than 300 colleges and universities spread throughout the state. Private institutions vary from the most elite like Stanford down through small local colleges, religious as well as secular. The public institutions include universities like Berkeley at the apex of the University of California system, with high admissions standards and distinguished research and teaching faculties, as well as a second-tier system, less selective, which brought together what were once the California state colleges—some of them originally normal schools—in what is now designated the California State University. The Cal State system is enormous, with some 330,000 students enrolled on its nineteen campuses in 1990.

The CSU campus at Northridge is one of the largest, with an enrollment of around 30,000 students. It was here I came from UCLA, from a campus of the more selective system to one more representative of the average student in more mundane surroundings. On my first morning at Northridge I crossed a campus indistinguishable, except for the California weather and the flora that seem to erupt in it everywhere, from almost any state campus anywhere else in the country. Architecture on the cheap, nothing like UCLA's backdrop of imposing buildings, sculpture gardens, and cafe umbrellas.

The ten young women in the class were talking when I came in, standing around in little knots of three and four. The group nearest the seat I took were talking about the kids in the schools where they were practice teaching. One of them slipped in an anecdote about a friend in a class for incorrigible boys. "They burned down the bathroom," she said. "So he assigned them a writing topic on 'Why Did We Burn Down the Bathroom?' " The professor, overhearing as he comes in, gives a hearty laugh and says, "Good!" He's tieless, in jeans, balding and bearded. He takes a seat in front of the class, one foot resting on the opposite knee, relaxed and casual, gesturing with his hands as he talks.

He's going to show them a tape, he tells them, of a program on dropouts that had been presented a couple of years earlier on the local educational TV channel. It was filmed at and around Venice High School, a part of the Los Angeles Unified School District with an ethnically diverse and socioeconomically varied population—low-income families, including some from the projects, and more affluent families from the marina. He tells them they'll see individual dropouts as well as teachers, counselors, police personnel, attendance officers, and parents. "Pay attention to the interaction between those adults and the adolescents," he tells them. "See what works and what doesn't in terms of the ideologies we've discussed. We call these kids dropouts, but ask yourselves if they aren't really pushouts."

With that prologue, he turns off the lights and starts the video. A genial on-screen host named Warren Olney informs us that 40 percent of students in the L.A. Unified School District dropped out that year, that the figure statewide was 30 percent. We would now meet some of them.

In the dark it was hard to take notes, and the drama was absorbing enough to discourage the attempt. But caught up as I was in the stories of the boys and girls on the tape, I did manage to note the recommendation that the state should provide more funding for more counselors, and the conclusion that we—"society"—were to blame for the increase in the dropout rate following the passage of California's notorious Proposition 13 and the subsequent budget cuts. Along the way to that wrap-up I was especially struck by the voice-over of a teacher commenting on a black girl who had done well in elementary school and been one of the speakers at her graduation, only to fail miserably in junior high, drop out of school, and spend her time on the streets, "hanging out" and getting high. "In elementary school lots of people hold your hand," the teacher said. "In junior high a lot of kids fall apart. There's no one to hold your hand."

I was also impressed with a black judge who dealt severely with truants brought before him, insisting that they go to school or go to jail. He lectured them sternly, telling them they were throwing away their chances for a decent life, and lectured his audience just as sternly, insisting that "we" had to spend the money necessary "to prepare them for adulthood."

When the lights went on again the discussion began, at first—as is often the case—with personal anecdotes of doubtful relevance. One of the students, a mother herself, thought the problem in schools was competition and it was on that that she blamed the problems her daughter had in school. "As soon as they put her in the blue reading group, even though they didn't *say* it was the lower one, it affected like her self-esteem."

The professor interrupted to call attention to the relationship one of the boys—who hung in until graduation in order to stay on the swimming team—had with the team coach. He was obviously suggesting the coach–team member relationship as a paradigm for the teacher–pupil one. From there on the discussion moved quickly. One exchange stood out:

STUDENT: It's easy for the coach to relate to a kid but if you're a history teacher your job is to teach them history. They have to understand.

PROFESSOR: Remember Goodlad's *A Place Called School* [a book that criticizes the passivity and regimentation of the typical schoolday routine]. The coach puts a value on them, catches a problem when the kid isn't a good student, so the kid stays. . . . Not like the history teacher who says [in the film] that he "can't be an entertainer all the time." You have to see students as people with feelings, not just history learners.

STUDENT #2: The average kid gets lost in the system, not noticed like the problem kids who get marked, signaled, pulled out for special attention, whether or not they accept it. The majority are just ignored.

PROFESSOR: A class should be like a team—interdependent, working to achieve a common goal. Instead, the classroom consists of separate individuals, not working together, just passive recipients, competing. Exploitation . . . a zero sum activity . . . competition . . . After Proposition 13, art and music programs were cut—all those things like band, choir, orchestra, dance, drama that involve the group as a team working together and provide the adult with another relationship with the kid, a closer relationship that gives the kid a motivation to stay.

STUDENT #3: But it's a *personal choice* to drop out. The kid has no sense of the future. What can the school do? It seemed to me everyone at the school was trying.

PROFESSOR: Isn't "choice" within a context? They're depressed. . . . The choice of your child and mine to go to college is made in a context of family expectations. (He is smiling fixedly, but clearly he finds it uphill work arguing with this young woman as she persists.)

STUDENT #3: But isn't it a matter of what context she chooses to put herself in? The home or the street? After all, her grandmother wanted her to stay in school, told her she'd be ruining her life if she didn't finish.

PROFESSOR: Who do you think is the hero of that whole program? Not the teachers, the attendance officer, but that grandmother. She gave her whole life—raised her daughter, then her granddaughter, now her granddaughter's baby.

STUDENT #1: Why didn't the grandmother teach her daughter to take care of the baby?

STUDENT #3: My mother wouldn't have raised my baby. She'd have helped me raise it, but she'd have insisted I take charge.

PROFESSOR: There's a conflict between the culture of poverty, the street culture, and the culture of the school. You can't say one is right and one is wrong, they're just different cultures and you mustn't judge. They are just two different ways of structuring life.

STUDENT #1: Another *choice*. The kid who got arrested and went to Phoenix House and *stayed* in the program when some of the others didn't. The girl that's on the streets—they offered her a place in the job training program.

STUDENT #4: Have *you* ever been in one of them places? (This is the one black girl in the class.)

PROFESSOR: Bonnie hit it right on the head!

BONNIE: It's just drill, drill, drill. All they do is point out all your little mistakes. I know. I been there. I walked out. It wasn't going to help me none.

PROFESSOR: . . . importance of small groups, special attention. Notice how she's okay as long as the counselor is eliciting her view, but when he tries to give her advice, tell her what's what, she shuts down, same as with her mother. It sets up a superior–subordinate relationship.

STUDENT #4: What parent wouldn't feel that way?

(Here again, as at Eastern Michigan University, we have the situation of the radical professor/conservative students. Unlike their counterparts in the upper-middle-class world of the Ivy League schools, these students have not been predisposed either by parental liberalism or a sense of guilty privilege to any radical outlook. He can't catch hold of them, with the exception of Bonnie, who's already way ahead of him.)

STUDENT #3: The problem is there's no family unit.
PROFESSOR: What do you mean? (He's indignant.)
STUDENT #3: Where's the mother and father?
PROFESSOR: The grandmother . . .
BONNIE: In black culture, that's acceptable. It's from slave days, when families were separated. That's *our* family unit.
STUDENT #1: That's not the no— (She can't get the word out, can't say "normal" in this setting, brave as she is. She pauses.) Not stable. Children are experiencing change from the original family unit. It's conditional, the family in our society today. And what teachers are expected to do is provide the nurturing that parents are naturally supposed to do.
PROFESSOR: This is a time of change and transition. The arrangements and structure of child rearing, what we call "family," comes in all forms now. Only a small minority fit the standard two-parents, two-children pattern. The trouble is there are no social supports for single parents. We even have to educate parents to be parents. In other times, throughout history, they learned it in the group context, just by living. Our present social arrangements—fragmentation, alienation, individuation—are symptomatic of the crisis in our society. We're learning from one another that different experiences have different meanings to us. The girl that did well in elementary school and then dropped out in junior high—we expect that in three months a child can make an adjustment from elementary school—remember that patronizing bit in the film about "hand holding"?—to junior high, a dominant-culture school where you have different teachers every hour, large classes. The middle-class kid gets support from the family at home—unless it's a chaotic one, which increasing numbers are—but the lower-class kid gets pushed out.
Maybe we really want to lose them. We're talking about reproduction of the social structure. Junior highs have been losing students for decades. (There are sounds of protest among the students. He raises his hands as though to hold them at bay.)

It's not your and my conscious intent, not on an individual level, but when we keep doing the same thing over and over again that is presumably contrary to our intent . . .

STUDENT #3: The school or the district don't want that dropout rate. It's a reflection on *themselves*.

BONNIE (scornfully): They don't care about dropouts!

PROFESSOR: (Now he is in his element.) The role of the school is to reproduce society. It's a meritocratic ideology, a hierarchical order where success means being at the top and failure is to be on the bottom. It's a zero sum game concept of success. Schools are part of that and not acknowledging that junior high pushes them out is part of that process.

BONNIE: We need to pay more attention to the problems of kids in junior high. Their bodies are changing—

PROFESSOR: (Bonnie's bag of opinions obviously includes a variety of subjects, but he is not interested in moving off the political turf just now, and interrupts her.) Yes. But also we need to pay attention to what we carry within us as part of that collective whole that makes us fail to acknowledge this and do something about it.

STUDENT #1: The judge made them responsible for their own actions. Not like the grandmother. She didn't help her daughter be responsible for her own actions.

PROFESSOR: What about the alternative of going to school or going to jail?

STUDENT #5: Maybe if we put 'em in jail we could educate 'em. (This releases a burst of laughter from everyone.)

STUDENT #3: Disciplinary techniques have been repudiated by our society along with the idea that people are responsible for the consequences of their actions. You have to learn that as little children.

PROFESSOR: (They are talking past each other; he chooses to ignore her. The class is almost over and he winds up for his peroration.): If you put every truant in kiddie jail for thirty days the costs would be monumental, almost as much as sending them to an Ivy League college. We're saying there's insufficient money to create opportunities for adults and kids to relate to each other. What we have to do is restructure our funding system for competing needs that have to come out of a limited pot. Dropouts today find themselves in a different world from those of forty years ago. Then they could work in the steel mills, it was an expanding economy, the requirements for jobs were different. But if you're pushed out of school in today's economy the structure of employment is altogether different. The job market is in low-level service jobs. The individual is being made responsible for wider social conditions over which he has no control.

In a course on Education in American Society I was reminded again of the mission of the schools to take in the handicapped of all kinds and to deal with their needs. A deaf student followed the classroom discussion by watching a young woman signing; occasionally he would nod off and she would relax, watching him and picking up again when he woke up. Another student was confined to a wheelchair. The subject was a different kind of handicap, defined by the professor as "social class as the basis for ideas, motivation, and action."

He was a spellbinding talker, with a *shtik,* as he would put it, to rival that of any standup comic. For most of the hour he roamed through anecdotes and opinions, pausing only to hear from those who persisted in volunteering from the audience (which is what the class had become), usually to confirm something he had said with an anecdotal experience of their own, once or twice to ask a question. Only at the end did I realize that his entertaining presentation had not been as haphazard as it had seemed at the time; it had a unifying theme.

Professor Worth, as I'll call him, talked about how social class operates in California today, naming the various regions around Los Angeles and defining the common values and attitudes of upper down to lower class in terms of such status symbols as the kinds of cars they drove. He wanted to show, he said, why busing was absolutely necessary. Its purpose was to enable lower-class children to assimilate attitudes from their classmates starting as early as possible—in preschool via Head Start programs, in the schools from kindergarten through third grade. "Who you sit next to is what counts."

The lower-lower class, he told them, is the class of despair. They are not involved with society, don't know how to deal with the system and its bureaucracy. They are "people-haters, self-haters," oriented toward kin rather than anyone outside their extended families. They are highly transient. "You'll have some of them from the ages of six to about fifteen and a half. Their records get lost because they move around so much. They're a floating mass, many of whom get involved in crime and become institutionalized prisoners for most of their lives." He was talking, he explained, about the *campesinos,* the pickers with a rural background who come into the cities, never learn to understand the world beyond their families. And the families fall apart in the cities. Their "social disorganization" involves incest and drug abuse. "We don't know how to cope with them. We've given up on them. Traditionally, school has been the way out, the ladder to mobility—but not for them. The dropout rate is phenomenal. The children are often brutalized, abused sexually. They are property. We have no way to get at them now that most of the social programs are defunct. We have them only in the early grades; we lose them by sixth or seventh grade, when they leave school." In the Reagan years, he told them, "We seem to have lost our social concern. We've given up. All we have left is just a finger in the dike."

The ones they would be involved with, he told them, were the upper-lower class, the working poor. He gave a long and entertaining disquisition on Archie Bunker's move from the working class to the middle class in the course of the "All in the Family" television series, talked about how the idea of a union, of collective bargaining, gives power to the working class, the "camper class." Here he rehearsed the exquisite distinctions between recreational vehicles, trucks, trailers, vans of various kinds. Cars and guns, he maintained, compensated working-class men for the loss to their sense of masculinity when working-class women went to work during World War II and stayed on in the labor force after the war. This need for a masculine image to identify with was, he suggested, brilliantly captured by the "Marlboro Man" advertising campaign, and that kind of "tapping into what motivates people" ought to be used in teaching, in textbooks.

One of the students wanted to know, "How can we use the Marlboro trick to teach U.S. government?" The answer: Understand working-class social organization, which is based on decision making by a leader, unlike the middle-class idea of democratic decision making. "It's another world. Relationships between boys and girls, family and teacher, have to take into account the macho male ego." Professor Worth found it particularly ridiculous, by way of example, to include in the curriculum for these children such books as *The Great Gatsby*. "You have to find ones that fit their world view. They have a different view of reality. We should be giving them books like *Chronicle of a Death Foretold*. They understand that world—about having to defend one's manhood, about revenge and getting even. The idea of machismo makes the world go round."

At along about this point I began to wonder if Professor Worth, who obviously prided himself on his understanding of poor Hispanic children and their culture, had ever realized how patronizing he was and how little good his double standard would do these students in the long run. Up to now, seduced by his capacity to amuse, I'd not seen that his was the kind of liberalism that makes special rules for "minority" groups, excuses them from the norms of civil behavior—or, to put it another way, says that they can't be expected to behave like the rest of us. "It's impossible to get the idea of democracy across to them. The Latinos steal the classroom furniture. They just take the tables and chairs home with them." And I wondered, If one supposedly studies literature to open new worlds, and if middle-class American children could appreciate Garcia Márquez, why shouldn't lower-middle-class Hispanic children, by the same token, be expected to appreciate Fitzgerald?

Professor Worth seemed to feel that Hispanic children could never make it on their own. "They have to go to school with Anglo kids, sit next to them in order to internalize mainstream values." They would never appreciate Mark Twain, but would like Poe, with his mysterious stories and the repetitious beat of his poetry.

Several members of the class were older than the college students planning to become teachers. They were working class themselves, and had done other things in life and now decided that they wanted to try teaching. About the younger ones, Worth said to me after class, "They don't know what else to do." Too many of them, he felt, were going in for "touchy-feely ed psych," which would do "these kids" no good. And he was convinced that one would "*have* to speak Spanish" in order to teach them. "Spanish only, nothing but Spanish instruction, from kindergarten to third grade. They'll pick up English along the way, they're always hearing it in the playground, on the TV. They *want* to learn English, it's going to happen. Meanwhile, you teach them classroom Spanish—close the door, open the book, shut up, bring your parents, put down the gun . . ." Of course, he is only joking . . .

Another class on the same subject, Education in American Society, was completely different. These students were all teaching at present. Some had been teaching for longer than others, and when the professor opened by asking if there were "any war stories," one of the young men doing practice teaching offered the information, gleaned from the papers, that one of the Northwest states—he thought it was one of the Dakotas—was looking for a hangman and that the salary offered was considerably higher than that of a teacher.

The class got under way with the distribution of a "Statement of Philosophy of Education," on which the students were invited to comment. The statement began, "While reasonable efforts will be made to meet all the needs of children, consistent with our democratic heritage and ideals, the primary responsibility of the schools is the intellectual development of its pupils." Clearly, the statement was intended as a starting point for the discussion to follow, which was led off by a middle-aged woman. "This statement makes me uncomfortable," she said. "Part of our *democratic heritage*"—she emphasized the words with heavy irony—"is the imperialistic thing. What if I teach about those things, the down side? It's like when I read the Preamble to the Constitution, it gives me a little shiver." Other students referred to "the hidden curriculum," to "empowerment" and "decision making." But this professor—Dodson, I'll call him—wasn't interested in holding an encounter group.He was interested in teaching these prospective teachers how philosophical beliefs influence educational policy. For him it was not a matter of being familiar with names and having a slogan to match them with, and he didn't expect his students to read Plato, either. But he would use Plato's scheme as an example of what he did want them to see: how conceptions of reality, knowledge, value, and human nature lead to conceptions of the good society and the good person, which in turn suggest purposes for education and lead to beliefs about practical schooling matters—school practice and school policy.

On the board went "Metaphysical (beyond evidence)" and "Ideas, forms are the true reality, not matter, change," and he began to talk about the Platonic universe in which the world of ideas is the real world. (I asked him later why he was telling them all this instead of having them read *The Republic* and then discuss it. He said, pace Mortimer Adler, that it was not Plato's ideas per se he wanted them to learn, but to see the connection between basic philosophical assumptions and classroom practice.) Some of the students were yawning, fidgeting, while he wrote on the board, "Soul," and underneath the headings "reason, will, appetite." When he interpreted these as referring to the philosopher-kings, the "executives" ("people who like to manage companies, push people around, get things done"), and "producers," they woke up.

Stimulated to talk about things they'd already learned, they mentioned Hobbes and Hamilton, someone called Plato a fascist, someone else said, "You don't have to be a Republican . . . ," and they began to see how testing and tracking, college prep advanced placement courses vs. vocational courses, actually grew out of a set of beliefs and not out of the devil's imagination. They are all self-described liberals, all against tracking. The received wisdom is expressed by one student: "Jose is a slow learner? In sixth grade? How does the teacher know? It's so sad."

The downside of this kind of discussion is how all the ideas are recast in modern terms: "totalitarian," "what about the objectivity of those doing the evaluation?" But at least he is bringing them to see that in Plato's view education was for citizenship, for the good society, and that everything follows from that, as distinct from another idea of the purpose of education, such as self-realization, or keeping up with Japan, or even achieving social equality, all of which will produce other curricula, other strategies. The difference in underlying values will even determine such things as who should decide on curriculum—professional experts or local school boards.

"Plato in L.A." would be followed next week, the professor announced, by a consideration of Rousseau and A. S. Neill, when a very different set of underlying values would be shown to determine what should be taught and how.

Tying all this together, he made a little statement at the end of class for them to take away with them and think about. The biggest problems in American schools, he said, are that they are expected to be all things to everyone, that they don't prepare anyone for anything, that they are too responsive to fads such as new ways to teach mathematics or social studies, and, in addition, the influence television has on the students. He suggested they should be giving thought to the role of education in the future of the country, that in order to have a productive economy we would have to think of the young as capital, an investment. Hard to believe this was the same course I had watched being taught by his tieless, blue-jeaned colleague a little earlier.

Hard put not to squirm with boredom and embarassment, I next sat through four hours in which three "teams" of three students each presented reports on evaluation, accountability, and the heredity/environment question. In a seeming parody of a thesis defense, they stood and simply took turns reading out loud from thirty- and forty-page reports as though auditioning for a part in some play. They demonstrated that they could read, and that they had good word-processing equipment. Indeed, the computer graphics were impressive.

These papers were only a rehearsal for the thesis they will produce to earn their master's degrees. One of the students, disgruntled and unkempt, in the clothing and hair style that used to be called "hippie" and still makes a kind of anti-authority statement on some campuses, told the class, "They hired an M.A. in lit instead of me, but an M.A. is no guarantee you know how to teach, whereas I can go into a classroom and I know how to deal with kids."

9

❧ —————— ❧

California State University at Long Beach

Methods and Minorities

At another campus of the Cal State system, the California State University at Long Beach, I arrived early at the class in Sociological Foundations of Education. It was held in a building that reminded me of a barracks, in a room too small for the number of chairs, whose armrests were scratched and dented and did not all fold up the way they should. Looking for one that worked so that I could take notes, I moved close to two young women talking animatedly. One of them was telling the other about a Tupperware party she was planning and recommending one of the plastic containers as "great for putting your leftover pizza in." Their clothes, like their conversation, like the room they were in, were a distinct contrast with those at the more prestigious institutions that trained "leadership cadres" for the educational world. These, too, are working-class women and young men. And again, some of the women already have families of their own.

A tall, rather ungainly young man comes in and sits down near the two I've been listening to, dropping his bulging book bag and slumping into his seat. He looks exhausted. Most of them, I learn

131

later, have worked all day before coming to this evening class. Some haven't had time to eat and bring bags of chips and cans of soda, take out a carton of yogurt or a banana. They are graduate students, with five or six years of teaching behind them, here for the M.A. or administrative credentials.

The two women ask him how it's going and he smiles and says things are better. Has he decided to stay? Yes. I introduce myself and ask what they're talking about and they tell me that he's been teaching in a high school in Watts, a class that has already had four different teachers in the current school year, and that last week he'd said he was ready to walk out, quit the school if not the profession. He told about kids who wouldn't stay in their seats, roamed the room, left if they felt like it, were insolent, afraid of nothing, respectful of no one—except the drug dealers. Some wore beepers in school in case of a deal. When he asked one boy who told him he was dropping out what he expected to do next year, the answer was, "Sell drugs."

Still, he'd tried some of the things they'd talked about in this class last week, and he felt he was getting through to them. Things had improved a little and as of now he had decided to stay with it, keep trying. Other students had been drifting in all along, and they all seemed interested in the problem, praised him for his decision, wished him luck.

I asked the little group of three if they ever had a breakthrough, felt they had touched their students? Oh, yes, one of the young women said. The other day a pupil had brought in a newspaper and announced, "Look, I found a metaphor." The other two nodded when she said, "That's what teaching is all about."

When the professor entered, she welcomed me to the class after first making sure that I was not there representing Accuracy in Academia, a conservative group that she said had been infiltrating classes on the campus lately. She then explained to the room at large that her concern was global, international, multicultural education and that the schools had to come to grips with ethnic pluralism and the problems of children with learning disabilities, drug abuse, and no parents at home, as well as average class sizes of thirty-two in the primary grades and thirty-five in the upper elementary grades, when they should be no more than twenty. She summarized the educational philosophies they had to consider: Plato ("prescriptive"), Aristotle ("environmental molding"), Rousseau ("extreme freedom: Summerhill"), Spenser ("Darwinism, survival of the fittest"), Dewey ("practical, learning by doing"), Hutchins, Adler, Bestor ("back to basics, conservatism").

The students had read a page or two of each of the authors in question in a textbook published by an alternative press and designed to present the work of revisionists of the Left who might not appear in the more standard texts and anthologies. The professor's comments made it clear that the bad words were "conservative," "structured," and "merit." Particular scorn was reserved for the New York State Regents exam as an example of elitism, and the greatest current problem in public education the threat of religion invading the classroom. Today, more than ever, she said, there was a need for values clarification in the classroom, and the class would be viewing a film on the Values Clarification Curriculum based on the work of Lawrence Kohlberg and others. The film was made in 1975 and I had seen it before. The "values" involved were distinctly radical. I decided to give the film a miss and use the time to visit another class, returning for the discussion period that would follow the showing of the film.

When I returned, one of the students was complaining that "this business of small groups, we're most of the time just rambling, shooting the breeze." He didn't think they could learn enough from each other in that kind of discussion. The professor's anti-authority stance evidently extended to her own authority, and while she smiled, she did not seem moved. She thanked him for sharing his thoughts and suggested breaking into small groups for discussion.

The group I joined consisted of a dark, intense, strikingly handsome man I guessed to be around thirty (I'll call him Pablo); a young woman who was also Hispanic; a Cambodian woman, slight and self-effacing; and a white woman, probably in her late twenties. Within moments they had drifted from the subject of values clarification to concerns of more pressing immediacy to them. The Hispanic teacher talked about the difficulty of preparing lesson plans every day for the different kinds of children in her class. She had different grade levels in reading and math, different levels of understanding of English, perceptually handicapped and emotionally disturbed children, all in the same class. How many times and in how many places by now had I heard this story?

Lenore, the white teacher, had seven languages in one class. She counted them on her fingers: Laotian, Spanish, Cambodian, Vietnamese, English, Samoan, Thai. "We're expected to cater to their cultures," she said. "You're not supposed to send a note home to Cambodian parents. It's considered demeaning. Well, if they're going to stay here they better learn to fit in. We should be sensitive to their cultures but introduce them to our ways and our language."

Pablo had another point of view. In other countries, he said, being bilingual is the mark of an educated person. He felt all children should be trained in basic skills in their native culture and language. Maria asked, "How am I going to teach them *anything* when they're pulled out all day—for ESL, for reading. They'll miss the things I want to teach them. I can't start a science project because I can't seem to find a time when the whole class is in the room." Pablo said that the so-called bilingual program was really a monolingual one. "They are taught in English, and it's reinforced in Spanish by an aide who may be an uneducated person herself. The idea of a bilingual program is that the Spanish fades off."

Lenore shook her head. "These children are not being served," she said to Pablo. He reminded me that when there are more than ten children in a class who speak Spanish (or any other language other than English), the law mandates a bilingual program—that is, instruction in their language. But there are not enough teachers to go around, so the parents sign waivers ("It's sign or bus, and these parents do not want their children going out of the neighborhood") and their children receive instruction in English with support from an aide.

Lenore thought the system was terrible. "I can't reinforce the core curriculum. I can't get support from the family if an aide has to speak to them for me. You lose something in translation." Pablo said, "Use parents as aides!" He had the kind of warmth and enthusiasm that made his recommendations contagious. Things that had never sounded to me like good ideas sounded plausible coming from him. And he had an endless store of anecdotes about Barrio life.

"If I tell a kid, 'Don't be a cholo'—a gang member," he explained for my benefit— " 'it's stupid,' then the father comes to school and he's got cholo tatoos all over him up to here and he says to me, 'I hear you said . . .' " He laughed his infectious laugh and shrugged. Pablo thought it was natural for young men to band together, and said smilingly that the Sons of Liberty were a gang, Patrick Henry was a gang member.

"What we ought to do," said Maria, "is have health spas where they could work out, learn to prize their bodies instead of filling them full of drugs." She agreed with the others that the idea was probably unrealistic, "but how about businesses and fraternal groups sponsoring clubs, with uniforms and everything, for them to belong to instead of gangs?" They nodded, smiled, shrugged. The talk shifted to sex education, which Lenore referred to as "showing 'em how to do it." Maria said it should start earlier, and the rest agree with her.

In a course in the teaching of "language arts," the professor, who had taken a great deal of care with her appearance—elaborately coifed and strikingly made up, in a tight-fitting bright print dress and spike heels—was demonstrating "modeling behavior," as she put it, showing her students "how to use questioning to keep your students' attention." What she was telling them was reproduced on word-processed sheets handed out to everyone and written down again by Lance and Shelly, Kit and Pat. In all versions, the subject matter consisted largely of terms like "bouncing off," "feedback," "auding." Everything of value in this course—including what's in the textbook—could be presented and absorbed in a lecture/discussion of an hour or two, and then put to use in a practicum in the time saved.

Modeling away, the professor asks concernedly, "Kit, how do you feel about what Shelley just said?" To which Kit replies, "She validated my content." And the professor goes on, "You must ask, what am I as a facilitator of learning, doing here . . . according to Bloom's taxonomy . . . synthesizing, analyzing, evaluating . . ."

The message: Encourage discussion among the students; do not make yourself, the "facilitator of learning," into the center of learning; enable the students to learn from each other. "More important than content or thinking is the students' feelings. You are not there to feed them information but to be sensitive to their need for positive reinforcement, for self-esteem."

To a question from one of the students about "burnout," the professor responds that idealism isn't enough; everyone has a need for support; you can't win 'em all. "You can't develop their self-concept, you can only provide the atmosphere for it. You can validate, encourage, suggest a way of doing something where the student could possibly be successful—but only *they* can do the learning." The students are busy writing down what has appeared on the blackboard. "Written communication is a real-life way of thinking things through: clarifying, exploring, growing."

The professor talks to them as she wishes them to talk to their children. "Thank you for sharing that with us." She cautions them, college graduates, to "listen and think and inform yourself before you write."

By eight or nine years of age, around third grade, the professor tells them, most children are stifled in their creativity by teachers who say, "I'm the expert, you do it my way." What we have here is part of the antinomian legacy of the 1960s, in which education was supposed to move away from the teacher as authority to the student as experiencer. Shades of A. S. Neill's *Summerhill* and its ideological offspring, the works of such radical writers on school reform as Paul Goodman, Ivan Illich, Jonathan Kozol, and Herbert Kohl. What matters, she tells them, is not "the mechanics of how the students say it, but thoughts in progress." Marcy has her hand up. "Is thoughts in progress on paper or just in your head?" she wants to know.

Even mathematics, supposedly a "value free" discipline in the curriculum, has become a battleground between those who would emphasize mastery through repetition of certain basic facts and rules and those who would instead emphasize concepts and general principles. There is also argument over the proper place of calculators and computers in the classroom.

Such considerations, however, seemed far removed from the classroom where an elderly professor, a textbook author and presumably a veteran of many curriculum wars, talked to his class of three dozen—all but two of them white women—about teaching mathematics in inner-city schools. He emphasized the usefulness of "manipulatives" like sticks of different sizes to make the base-ten system clear. "You need a lot of tongue depressors," he told them, "in a class for the disadvantaged." He showed them how to paste lima beans or stick paper dots on the ten stick as an alternative, acknowledging that the schools would often have few materials and "you'll have to make your own." Blocks were best, but they were expensive. He illustrated ways of using visual materials to translate base ten values into place value concepts, ways of incorporating calculators and computers, when available, for reinforcement.

He was in favor of the self-contained class with children at various levels ("ability grouping benefits the gifted only") but recognized the demands it makes on the teacher to be able to deal with them all and "give 'em all lots of support. If you want to do multiplication and they're still counting on their fingers you'll have to go back to the beginning." He talked about how words could obfuscate or clarify number operations ("you're not borrowing anything from anybody, you're regrouping, renaming, or overloading the place"), which would have to be reinforced by repetition (otherwise known as "drill") and in the same breath about how manipulatives and visuals could aid in "understanding, not just memorizing."

When the class was over and the students—who had been quietly attentive throughout, taking notes and referring now and then to a textbook or asking a question—got up and stretched and reached for coats and book bags, it struck me that what I had feared would be a dull hour had held my attention throughout. And I realized why. It wasn't charisma. If this professor reminded me of anyone it was Harry Truman. Nor was the subject one likely to generate excitement, in me at least. It was because this class was actually useful to the relatively inexperienced teacher. It was practical. His eclectic approach, combining drill with theory, was what his experience had taught him would work. And the kind of support he was concerned with teaching them to offer was support for their students' understanding of certain kinds of symbolic operations and relationships, not for their "self-image."

When I came into the class on Social Studies in the Elementary School, the pretty young instructor was saying, "Hunger kills. These are scary statistics. I would have you share this with your kids."

She was demonstrating the use of a unit intended for sixth graders called "The Descent into Hunger." Looking at the material I was handed, I saw "GOAL: Through the vivid description in the reading entitled 'Descent Into Hunger,' students will begin to more fully understand the plight of poor and hungry in developing countries. They will recognize the connection between poverty and hunger. Then, they will attempt to communicate in a letter format what form of help they would like to receive if they were in a developing country." Under OBJECTIVES, I read, "Students will contrast their lives with the poor in developing countries." The section headed INSTRUCTIONAL SEQUENCE offered suggestions for ways in which, instead of studying hunger "in a manner which makes it seem rather distant and abstract," the teacher could "make it seem more real and terrible."

Under PROCESS QUESTIONS were "How does your life contrast with the life of the poor? . . . What do you think is the primary cause of hunger in the world? . . . How does this information affect you?" OUTPUT QUESTIONS included "Imagine you are poor in a developing hungry [sic]. Write a letter to the students of Bonita Canyon concerning how you wish to be helped." FOLLOW-UP ACTIVITIES suggested the teacher "Have the students read the 'Hunger U.S.A.' article so that they will not forget that hunger and poverty are problems in the United States as well as in the rest of the world." The teacher should then "ask the students to suppose that their family has only $300 per month on which to live. Have them prepare a budget for how that money would be spent. . . . They should consider the changes they would have to make in their lives to adjust to a low income." Then they should "conduct a phone interview to determine the requirements for receiving welfare and food stamps in California. Discuss how some people might not qualify even though the need is great."

The text for this lesson stated that "most hunger and starvation is due to poverty and inequality" and that "extremes of wealth and poverty" are "much worse" in "the developing countries." In order "to give you a better idea of what the life of the poor is like in a developing country," an article by Robert Heilbroner originally published in 1963 described invading the house of an imaginary American family and stripping it of its furniture ("Everything will have to go . . . beds . . . chairs . . . television . . . We will leave the family with a few old blankets, a kitchen table, and maybe a wooden chair.") Next the clothes. Each family member is allowed to keep his or her oldest garment. "We will permit a pair of shoes for the head of the family, but none for the wife or children." And so on. "A few moldy potatoes, already in the garbage can . . . will provide much of tomorrow night's meal." Everything else in the kitchen, all of the fresh food, must be taken away. The water is shut off, the electricity cut off, the house itself taken away and the family moved to the tool shed. "It is crowded, but still much better than the shacks where people live in Hong Kong." The entire suburb is transformed to a shantytown. But, the children are assured, they are still better off than the people in Calcutta who live in the streets. "And still, we have not yet reduced our American family to the level at which life is lived in the greatest part of the globe." Still to go: fire and police services, hospitals and doctors, family income. ("The children . . . may be employed as are children in Hyderabad, Pakistan" or, "if they cannot find work . . . they can scavenge as do the children in Iran who, in times of hunger, search for undigested oats in the droppings of horses.")

Nothing, to be sure, was said during this class about what makes it possible for Americans to enjoy a higher standard of living than people "in the greatest part of the globe." The aim seemed to be simply to make American sixth-graders—children about eleven years old—feel guilty for what they and their parents have, and to frighten them ("make it seem more real and terrible") by means of an exercise which "brought our typical American family [they know this means them] down to the very bottom of the human scale."

The graceful young instructor in her flowery summer dress and expensive-looking sandals emphasized, for those who might somehow have missed the point, the aim of the "Descent Into Hunger" lesson. "It strips the middle-class family of all its resources and puts them on the street so they will identify with the plight of the poor and hungry in developing countries." She tells the teachers to ask, "Is the problem of the poor and hungry their problem, or should the world get involved." She also tells them, "You may be disappointed with your kids. They may chat while you're trying to get into this." She tells them that a child in her class, asked how her life contrasted with that of the poor, said, "I have a bathroom and they don't." And how she pointed out that the suburban American middle-class bathroom was "a decorator-color shrine to our body functions."

The main idea to get across, she told them, was that the major reason for hunger was inequality, the unequal distribution of resources between the haves and the have-nots. And she suggested, "Establish a rapport, ask them with tenderness. I would tell them, 'You're in a position where you might be able to be part of the solution.'" She added, sorrowfully, "The children of Irvine don't experience homeless people." It was important, she said, to ask the children, "Do you think it's something you need to get involved in?" And equally important to pursue the follow-up activities, such as learning what it takes to get food stamps. "For my school it's a very appropriate activity because they haven't a clue." One of the student teachers commented, "With inner city kids, though, this might give them a complex."

The instructor moved on to "another valuable lesson in Global Education for third- to sixth-graders" based on *The Butter Battle Book* by Dr. Seuss, a story in which the conflict between the Yooks and the Zooks is a matter of preferring butter side up or butter side down. "They see how silly the superpowers' competition in the arms race is." The Thinking Lesson Plan offers these Expansion Ideas: "Does this story remind you of anything that is happening in the real world we live in now? Why? (How are they similar?) If you could talk personally to President Reagan, what suggestion/recommendation would you make to him about this issue?"

"It works for every year," the instructor assured the class. "It's peace education. I would read it to them. They love it. I tell them to listen like they were in second grade again, so they don't listen in a sixth-grade way." So much for fostering "critical thinking."

Class was over, but before leaving everyone received one more handout, a sheet headed "Accepting/Acknowledging Students' Responses Without Using Value Words." The list included *Um-hmm, That's a thought, That's one possibility, That's one idea, That's another way to look at it, I hear you,* and eleven other ways not to tell a student the answer was not right or—dare one even suggest it?—was wrong.

PART FIVE

The Northwest

10

❦ —— ❧

The University of Washington

Educating for Citizenship and Educating for Skills

The professor is European. A softspoken man with a warm smile, he came of age in the post-World War II years in central Europe and became an anti-Stalinist for the same reasons that brought him to this country and made him want to be a teacher here. His students at the University of Washington remind me of those I saw at UCLA. They are for the most part tan, fit, cheerful young women (and a sprinkling of men) with the untroubled collegiate air that goes with the handsome brick buildings and wide avenues lined by cherry trees on this campus. At its edges are well-tended lawns in front of fraternity houses and a village-like neighborhood of fast-food, book, and offbeat clothing shops.

On this beautiful spring day the cherry trees are all in full bloom and so are the students strolling under them, showing off lithe limbs in shorts and brightly striped tee shirts, or sitting on the emerald green lawns with books nobody but the Asian students seem to be reading. A few are with babies or small children, books alongside bottles in the strollers. Snatches of overheard conversations range from the godlike jocks sunbathing on the fraternity-house porch inviting someone to a beer party to a young man and woman on the steps of the art building comparing results of a science exam. A chorale wafts from the open leaded windows of the music building.

There are fewer of these golden youth in the education building. These are not the campus heros and heroines, not the best dressed or the most attractive or, one guesses, the most gifted. There are a few Hispanics, some foreign students, including one of the few black faces, a student from the Sudan, and, as ever, several older women returning to teaching from the world of family or business. The usual picture of the ed school subset in the college or university.

Professor Farkas, as I'll call him, begins the class on teaching history in the elementary grades with the observation that Americans are not in the habit of thinking much about what's going on in the world and the suggestion that they start with some discussion of today's news. Students respond with comments about events in Yugoslavia that lead to some observations about the historical background—Tito, the various ethnic groups within the country—and Professor Farkas's comment that we might have created an economic showcase there and how and why. Another student brings up the troubles in Namibia. Another wonders what will happen if the Vietnamese actually leave Cambodia. It's clear they've all taken the trouble to look at the newspapers, listen to the news to bring something with them for an exchange with this amiable man. And it is also clear that what he is after is their acquiring the habit of being informed, not any ideological agenda.

As the class moves on, he demonstrates the uses of information. They have all been assigned to survey the elementary social studies classes in which they practice teach or, for those not teaching at the moment, some of the textbooks currently in use, to compare them in terms of scope and sequence. "Compare and contrast . . ."

Interesting differences emerge. Some teachers and some textbooks focus on "learning about, information, describing" and others on "improving, changing, solving problems" such as transportation, pollution. The observations have the air of discoveries. They are learning to think about what they are doing in the classroom. They note that the American Book Company text stresses civic responsibility, while the Silver Burdett one, published in 1979, emphasizes how to change things, and that this is less true of the 1982 edition, which leans more toward background. Professor Farkas doesn't take sides here, makes no political judgement as to which is preferable.

His message: "Make sure you know what you are doing and have good reasons for your choice."

He asks them about similarities and differences in the programs they find for each grade and about their criteria for topics they themselves would choose for each. Kindergarten is almost universally concerned with "me," they find: myself, family, community, world around us—what is known as the "expanding horizons" approach. "Social issues" are now part of the first-grade curriculum: drugs, alcohol abuse, AIDS. Some districts mandate the teaching of such topics before anything is learned about the nature of one's own city, one's own country. "Changes in the nature of family structure" are thought to be "connected with a sense of self" from kindergarten on. Professor Farkas encourages them to "bring out contemporary issues so the children can practice problem solving and decision making in their lives." One of the students says, "But this is only kindergarten and first grade!" He smiles, tells her not to underestimate children.

In second grade they find the curriculum organized around the concept of communities, from the neighborhood to "the global community." The community may be in Africa or in Korea. Professor Farkas is not passing judgment on this one. "I want you to be inner-directed teachers," he tells them. "You're professional people. You should have your own criteria, your own reasons for doing what you do. That doesn't mean ignoring what others say. Listen to advice. But put it together in your own frame of conceptualization."

Third grade goes on with communities, with a commonly found emphasis on the influence of the natural environment—deserts, plains, shores—and how the resulting form of specialization—such as farms or cities—affects peoples' lives. Conservation becomes a topic in Silver Burdett's textbook, not in American Book Company's or Follett's. Again he asks them about copyright dates and points out that books published in the 1970s tend to emphasize process, not content, and that by the 1980s the pendulum has swung back toward more content. One of the students says, "I had the seventy-nine edition in school. We didn't learn anything. All that about decision making, problem solving. We got no history, no geography."

Professor Farkas nods, says the ideal would be background knowledge and presentation of issues for practice in decision making. One student thinks there ought to be more "government and citizenship." Another is critical of the move away from "how to change things." Another says, "Well, if the book gives the information, we can supply the issues. We decide what to do with the material."

Fourth grade deals with the varied environments of natural regions—forest, mountain, coast. Illustrating how they can adapt the material, "Get your issues in," Professor Farkas suggests bringing up the recent oil spill off Alaska in connection with coastal regions.

Someone suggests adding culture to climate and terrain. Still no history. We are up to fourth grade, our pupils nine or ten years old, and nothing in the curriculum so far has acquainted them with events or lives of the past, with chronology, biography, story or myth, heros or heroines, triumphs or disasters. History and all that it has encompassed has been set aside for social issues. It would seem they are meant to put all "communities," like all regions, climates, terrains, and other phenomena, on an equal footing, to "solve problems" and "decide issues" without making judgments.

In fifth grade, U.S. history finally puts in an appearance. In this year the teacher is expected to cover all periods from colonization to the present, with due emphasis on native American studies, the roles of blacks and women, and attention to the contributions of whatever ethnic groups are able to bring pressure to bear on a particular state's textbook adoption committee. Chances are that if the state is California or Texas the effort will have nationwide results, since these two largest purchasers of textbooks effectively tell publishers what to include in the books that the rest of the states will have a chance to choose from.

But teachers don't always depend on the textbook, it seems. Many make their own curriculum. One of the students says that although the school in which he is teaching uses the Ginn text, which emphasizes economics and agriculture, especially in dealing with the Civil War years, the teacher he is assisting teaches political and military events, emphasizing racial prejudice and civil rights. Another student points out that the same text deals with the United States in terms of how it relates to other regions of the Western Hemisphere. She thinks there ought to be more about the history of "the United States itself as a community. How the railroads unified it, things like that." Another adds, "We ought to study the country, or the state, with a chronological approach. They need that historical background."

Professor Farkas tells them there is "ninety-five percent unanimity across the country" on the U.S. history curriculum including chronological history and geography from the age of exploration through colonization through westward expansion.

Having dealt with Latin America in the fifth grade (United States history in terms of how the U.S. relates to other regions in the Western Hemisphere, which sounds a little like dealing with U.S.

history without concentrating unduly on the history of the U.S., as though that would be impolite), sixth grade moves on to "the world," and specifically to the Eastern Hemisphere. Early civilizations—the Greek and Roman—and the middle ages in Western Europe may be considered part of the world, but for purposes of the sixth-grade curriculum they must make room for the East, Asia, Africa, and the South Pacific. This usually takes the form of units on the Soviet Union, China, various African nations, and Australia. Professor Farkas sees the problem here. "Democracy didn't start with the Declaration of Independence, it started two thousand years ago with the Greeks. If we are concerned about issues, we have to consider them in their historical context, how they came about. How the Magna Carta led to our system today."

Summarizing the national trends in curriculum, Professor Farkas offers some advice: On the kindergarten-primary grades "expanding horizons" program, otherwise known as "me and my family," he tells them not to be limited by geography, to use the program as an organizer but to reach out for examples and issues. "Some of these ideas were conceived and put into practice years ago. There have been enormous changes since then in communication and transportation. We've come farther than anyone then could have conceived."

In sixth grade, where the requirement is to deal with "the world," the question is, but how? Of three textbooks currently in use, one deals only with Canada and Latin America, one with the Eastern Hemisphere, and one with "everything but the U.S." He wants them to realize they will have something to say about what they choose to teach. And he wants them to give some thought to the choices they make. Beyond that, he does not proselytize. He tells them to avoid biases and inaccurate superficialities. And as the class comes to a close he gives them their next assignment. He wants them to choose a topic for their grade level and go to the library and look up books on that topic by social scientists.

"Not children's textbooks. We want to correct those. I want you to go into schools and move the state of practice to the state of the art in the various disciplines. So see what social scientists today are saying, what the up-to-date knowledge of your topic is, the concepts, the generalizations. Look at some of the textbooks used in university courses to see how the basic issues are defined, to get an idea of how to give depth to your topic. They will have bibliographies that will direct you to primary texts, articles in the professional literature."

"State of the art" social-science literature, especially as found in textbooks, may not be the most substantial key to the treatment of issues and ideas, but they are being encouraged at least to think about what it is they are doing.

Professor Klein has an image problem as a professor. She does not seem professorial. She is—no other word will do—cute. Perhaps that's one of the things that makes her effective. Like most good teachers, she has a recognizable style of her own—in her case, the style is feisty and bouncy. I would recognize her if I saw her on a subway platform, say, years from now.

Professor Klein sets the mood for the Seminar in Elementary Education by laughingly apologizing for her somewhat disheveled entry. She has just come from school, where her class was dissecting frogs, and one of them split "and got all over me," necessitating cleanup efforts that have made her a few minutes late and somewhat out of breath. This is her cue to say that dissecting frogs is an activity that inspires most beginning science students to groans and comments like "ugh" and "gross" (delivered with such recognizable authenticity that everyone in the class laughs appreciatively) but that almost always can shift to comments like, "Look at that ovaduct!" (Again, laughter.) Professor Klein is making a point about the value of the hands-on approach in teaching science. That's clear enough. What is less clear but no less true is that she is demonstrating a point about teaching as an attention-getting activity. She certainly has mine, and looking around I guess she has everyone else's too.

The culture of the classroom, the ambience in a school, she tells them, makes a big difference, and she asks them to try to think back to their own days in fourth or fifth grade, that stage at which the nurturing atmosphere is withdrawn and study skills more or less suddenly emphasized, and to share their memories with each other. After that, she asks them, "What does it feel like in the room you teach in? Describe the culture of your classroom. Is it communal, studious? What does it seem to you is being perceived as important in there?"

Both questions release a flood of responses of a surprising variety. For the first time since beginning my ed school odyssey I hear a young teacher mention Latin and French as languages to be taught in public schools. Another, a vague young woman of a type not uncommon in undergraduate education programs, whose devotion to children sometimes suggests a convenient avoidance of the demands of more adult pursuits and more adult relationships, talks about the importance of the posters and the baby animals in her

room, about sitting on the floor with "my kids and our bunnies."
Another describes her classroom as "active, kid-directed." An older
woman, shy at first, becomes emotional as she tells of her early
years teaching in a small town on the Mexican border. "We didn't
have any equipment, any of the things you're talking about, because
it would always be stolen. Every weekend the building would be
broken into and anything they could move they would take. Monday
morning all the children would help clean up the broken glass from
the windows where it was broken into. As much as we could we
would take home with us at night. They were the most wonderful,
those children . . ." She is unable to continue for a moment, then
tells us that she left to raise a family and is now continuing her
education so she can "go back to them. I always knew I wanted
that."

This room is alive with the stories they all have to tell about
what has brought them here. Professor Klein points out some of
the common subtexts and says they must pay equal attention to
the goals of personal development and to academic achievement.

A student responds that teaching is mainly communicating with
people, and that academics is a part of that. Another talks about
"self-concept," says feeling good about themselves and performance
are connected, praises cooperative learning techniques. Another
takes the floor to say, "How do you teach kids who come to school
without breakfast, sometimes without shoes or a coat, whose parents
aren't even home all the time and certainly don't come to school,
kids who come with bruises on them, who move every two weeks
when the rent comes due and their files can't even catch up with
them? These are two different worlds, the lower class and the suburban, and they need entirely different kinds of academic and nonaca-
demic things. The more diverse the population becomes, the more
broadly we have to teach." This stimulates a rush of discussion about
what schools used to be like—transmitters of the common culture,
implementers of the acquisition of basic skills—and what they have
become—agencies for social change, solvers of society's problems.

A sleek woman who manages to look elegant in a plain shirt
and slacks speaks up. "I'm forty-seven years old," she says, "and
I've had it all. I had a highly paid position with Boeing, raised a
couple of kids, but, believe me, making money can be—just empty.
Now I'm in a classroom and I'm staggered by the power I have."
Another student seems staggered not by a sense of empowerment
but by responsibilities. She enumerates some of them: She must
teach the basic curriculum to children of widely varying abilities,

some of them intellectually unfit or emotionally aberrant. She must communicate with indifferent or hostile parents, grade papers and tests after hours, arrange her teaching schedule to dovetail with those of the special-program teachers, work in instruction on drugs and sexually transmitted diseases.

These complaints have the ritual character of a support group. They are getting things off their chests, but in the end they will do what's asked of them. It's part of the job. No one here would even consider, let alone bring up in public, the idea of splitting off the teaching from the social work and providing different things to different children with different needs. That would be "tracking," and the very word is like a bell. It is racist, elitist, unacceptable in a democracy. Any discrimination in the sense of acknowledgment of existing differences is automatically equated with discrimination in the invidious sense of unequal and unfair treatment. No one can with impunity raise the question of whether doing things differently might be more effective, might better serve the needs of the disadvantaged.

Professor Klein says, "We've lost the other educating institutions in our society—families, churches, training of the young in the workplace. I'm not sure the schools have the power to restructure society." One of the students says, "TV, not us, is the educator." Another says, "The parents ask you all these things—what do I do about my kid—and you're just this young teacher. What do you tell them— Gosh, I don't know, I just got out of college?"

The talk turns to teacher's unions and Professor Klein asks how they think about the NEA and the AFT. One student says unions have dealt a blow to the image and status of teachers, make them seem unprofessional, "like we were blue-collar workers." Another disagrees. "We can't just be passive mothering types." A student who had objected to individual state education budgets as "unfair" nods emphatically and says, "I went into teaching with noble intentions." Her voice dripping with sarcasm she recites, ticking off on her fingers, "The educational process. The welfare of the child. The child is my client. I'm going to make their lives better." She pauses. "But who is my client? Is it the child? Or is it the parents, the government, society, business? Who?" Another one says, "It's hard to think of the child as your client when he has a gun in his hand."

The witnessing goes on as they continue around the U-shaped table saying in turn why they decided to become teachers: I love kids. It's gratifying. I always enjoyed teaching. I want to bring all those things I've done to focus on something that matters. I never thought of doing anything else. I didn't want a paper-pushing suit job. I thought kids deserved better. I want to make a difference. I'm fascinated with kids and learning. I want to go back and be a role model and show those kids they could do it . . .

"We need parental support to be respected," someone says, somewhat apologetically. "The parents aren't there for anything," one of the others says. "If they were we wouldn't have this new curriculum—our sexual disease thing." To which Professor Klein responds, "We have to do these ancillary things to get at the academics, in order to be able to teach basic skills." Some of them agree. They think kids are getting better, are being socialized by the teaching about drugs and sex. Professor Klein nods, ties it all up:

"Get your influence, the classroom culture that you create, to move beyond the classroom door." She'll give them an example of what she means, something she saw in a first-grade class this week that actually made her weep—"and I don't cry easily." The first-graders "studied" the Exxon Valdez oil spill off the Alaskan coast, were told about the effects on marine and wild life and asked to write their feelings as though they were little animals caught in the spill. They wrote things like, "I'm scared . . . It's so dark . . . When will I find something to eat . . ." There is an audible taking in of breath. Some of the students smile, shake their heads. "You see," she says, "teachers can manipulate the youth culture to good ends."

The class in Secondary Social Studies was involved in a demonstration of student team learning, the agenda for which was written on the board by the instructor as he explained it to the class of future high school teachers. They would divide into expert groups, each of them responsible for mastering a part of the material; there would be team coaching, in which the other group members would be taught the material; there would follow a formative quiz (for feedback, check for understanding), a reward, a discussion; and, finally, there would be a briefing before a summative quiz (the real thing, before moving along to the next subject). To help form team identity, each team was to choose a name for itself. Somewhat self-consciously, the class settled on names of local sports teams for their groups. I joined the Pilots, feeling, I imagined, about as silly as they did.

It's typical of ed school teaching, this emphasis on a method, a gimmick, and having the student teachers take the part of children—in this class, of high school students—in order to learn how to do the obvious. In this case, the material to be learned was a professional paper on—what else?—teaching methods. The experts discuss it among themselves to make sure they understand it before undertaking the team task of making sure everyone else understands the concept of the article. It is "pedagogic content knowledge" and the discussion is about how pedagogic content knowledge differs from pedagogic knowledge and content knowledge. The answer: Content knowledge is what the teacher knows, pedagogic knowledge is what the teacher knows about how to teach that knowledge, and pedagogic content knowledge is the way the teacher combines pedagogic knowledge with content knowledge "so as to get ideas across to kids, a way of organizing so they can understand."

I had been visiting schools, departments, and colleges of education for several months at this point, and I had seen a good deal that was less than impressive, but for sheer pretentiousness cloaking the banal, this was quite special. Someone in the class did venture to ask how all this was different from just plain "content" and "method." The professor, an enthusiastic young man in shirtsleeves, moving from table to table checking on the developments in the various groups, was, of course, "glad you asked." It gave him an opportunity to explain: "To avoid eighty years of baggage" attached to those older—and simpler—words.

"Shulman's work is based on Schwab's concept of substantive . . ." leaves most of them glassy-eyed. A couple have contributions to make: "You have to study an entire book, not just a part; all the parts interrelate, you have to connect them . . ." and, "When you study [teach] history you should show how it all fits together . . ." As far as one can tell, these are considered to be appropriate insights on the graduate level in one of the most respected institutions preparing teachers for American schools today.

One of the distinguishing features of cooperative learning seems to be that no one has to learn all about anything. It is, as one member of the class puts it, "good for special ed kids. They come out of their shell better with three than thirty-five." It is also easier for the teacher.

The professor is saying, "Let's get meta here for a minute and analyze what's going on. Did I provide any feedback over here? I hear on-task work at each table. We're doing in-depth learning but not frontal teaching." He is teaching them "how to teach kids to work together in these teams. Assign a role. . . . Here, you be the timer. Give the coach five minutes to make sure the expert clarifies what he means to the group . . ." And he walks around the room watching these grownups acting the child part in this highly structured activity, so many minutes for each "task."

There is, it turns out, something actually interesting in the article they are reading and discussing—a number of case reports of teachers illustrating their "pedagogic content knowledge." They talk about a teacher who is "field-oriented in his background." (One of them calls him "fragmatic." I would like to think this is a clever coinage, but alas . . .) A history teacher whose training was in anthropology, he could only "teach from the text and throw in examples from anthropology." There was "no continuity, no thematic structure, no sense of why are we studying this? He needs to become more flexible, more holistic." Another is praised because "he's done his own thing with books and things like that," not a very sophisticated formulation for a graduate student in education. In this case a high-school history teacher has organized a course around a series of landmark Supreme Court cases. The verdict of the class is that reading the decisions would be "pretty darn difficult for most kids."

Another case report is given of a teacher who organizes an American history course in terms of the American Revolution and "the concept of more people being included in the American democratic process all the time." One of the students objects that this sounds as though Americans were magnanimous, ignores persistent racism, etc., but the professor cuts him off: We're getting away from what matters. The professor isn't concerned with ideas, except for ideas about methods. "This was great," he beams. "No teacher talk." He tells them to think of themselves as "direction givers—monitors, facilitators, not information givers."

With the role-playing part of the class over, the groups disband and members of the class turn their chairs around and replace them in a semblance of rows facing the professor. Freed from the shackles of today's lesson plan, he becomes something of an information giver himself.

Pedagogical content knowledge, he tells them, really comes down to a way of moving from the simple to the more complex. He gives them an example: the distinction between a democracy and a republic is too complex for eighth-graders; the more general idea of popular sovereignty is enough for them at this stage. And he tells them that devising a pedagogical method of their own, having some theory that enables them to organize their subject, a view of its "thematic content," will help them teach better. "Society doesn't give you a lot of pride for being a teacher, so you have to construct your own pride."

The classroom teacher, he reminds them, is relatively unsupervised—a big problem in the public schools. "You can be a in a coma and nobody will notice." One of the students adds, "Especially the kids." He tells them "the research out of Stanford" on the difference between novice teachers and teachers with years of experience does not show a correlation between expertise and years of practice. What it does suggest is that skill is correlated with "a pedagogical model of the content." By which he seems to mean that teachers who have thought about what they do are better than those who haven't.

11

⁓⧉ ——— ⧉⁓

Seattle Pacific University

Private Means and Public Ends

Seattle Pacific University is about fifteen minutes' drive away from the University of Washington but it seems to exist in a different part of the ed school universe. A private Christian establishment, it is one of only three institutions training teachers in the Seattle area. The particular character of its teacher preparation program comes in part from the Methodist church under whose auspices it is run and in part from the marketplace.

The students who come here, whether undergraduates working for a teaching certificate or candidates for a master's degree, are focused on jobs. More than half of the undergraduates are women over twenty-five who already have a college degree. They include a "burnt-out" dentist and a woman who majored in women's studies while raising a family. Among the middle-aged men is a self-styled "house husband" whose career wife worked to provide the major support for the family while he stayed home raising the children and going to college and then law school at night. He says, "We each did what we liked to do best." Many are transfer students from the University of Washington, where they may not have been able to maintain the required grade point average. Others were not accepted there, where enrollment is capped by the limitations of state funding. At this private institution they will have to pay

155

four times the $3,000 yearly tuition charged by the public university. One way students beat the high cost of obtaining teaching credentials here is to attend a community college for two years and transfer for the junior and senior years.

Applicants must pass competency tests in spelling, math, writing, and are observed in introductory course work and as student teachers before being admitted to the second phase of the certification program. This screening theoretically weeds out the least able.

A federally funded continuing education program deals with bilingual staff development. Many of those enrolled are Chinese or Vietnamese who were once teachers but whose documentation was lost and who work in the schools as instructional assistants while studying here toward their certification. The Chinese are the largest non-English-speaking group in the local schools and speak an astounding number of different regional dialects.

One reason for the high cost of tuition in a private institution like this one is that it has to pay for the supervision its students get in their practice teaching internships in private and public schools. They have a more varied experience than their counterparts in the large public institutions, visiting and observing in a wide range of schools, from open-space elementary classes and university experimental special education programs to horizon and other enrichment programs and private Christian as well as public high schools.

It would be hard to say whether the church or the media has the greatest influence on these students. They are reminded of the lessons of "Jesus Christ, master teacher," but equal time is given to such texts as the movie *Stand and Deliver*, and to a *Newsweek* story on the crisis in the schools, a *Wall Street Journal* special supplement on the schools, and a PBS television series on American education, all of which appeared during the week of my visit to SPU.

In a class on Methods of Elementary Math Teaching, prospective teachers manipulate colored wood rods and blocks designed to "conceptualize the foundations of addition and subtraction." There is a pleasure in the rainbow effect of the pieces, but these future teachers are slow to grasp the solutions to the simple problems posed. Understandably, their professor is treating them rather as though they themselves were kindergarteners. They are strikingly different in appearance from their opposite numbers at more prestigious universities. Many of them, for instance, are overweight. They are plain, decent, good-humored, small-town women, to all appearances lacking in the kind of narcissism associated with the urban sophisticates of their generation who have given the word "yuppie" to the language. They are, in short, the teachers of my own middle-western childhood.

Their professor, whom I'll call Dr. Conway, points out to those who are having trouble figuring out how many rods of which size and color are needed to solve the problem he has set—a part of the class that includes both me and Anna, my partner in the group I've been invited to join—that some frustration is necessary for problem-solving habits to be formed. He encourages all of us to try again. "Just because something causes frustration you don't have to purge it from the curriculum," he says. "The aim isn't success but effort."

After class, Professor Conway talks about his students. "They see teaching as a calling, a way to serve. Many of them have already raised a family, and these older women—and a few men—temper the influence of youth. Their seriousness is contagious."

As we talk, the classroom door opens and Anna reappears, out of breath. She has run back up the stairs to tell us she kept thinking about it and has solved the problem we couldn't get. She shows me how. And I think that her perseverance and her pleasure in finally figuring it out are the most important things a child could learn from anyone in the first grade.

Later in the day, I attend a session of what is called "Lab Orientation," the introductory course. It is introductory indeed. At the front of a brand-new handsomely lit auditorium, its rows of comfortable seats holding about 150 students, stands a smiling gray-haired woman with a cheery voice and a gentle, forgiving manner. After a few minutes it becomes clear that judgment is no part of her approach; it might involve disapproval, and the only attitude expressed here is of the Panglossian school. Apologetically, she tells these prospective teachers that she must just point out to them the difference between "student's" and "students'" since many of them have confused the two forms on the papers she is giving back to them. Her eyes remain downcast as she says this, and then she looks up, still smiling, as though she had had to tell them some embarrassing thing it pains her to have to point out, such as the advisability of not belching in public, but now we'll forget about it and go on to other things.

It doesn't get better. They have been asked to set goals for their first week of student teaching. One student says her goal is to learn every child's name by the second day. "Marvelous!" exclaims Professor Pangloss.

Some genuinely interesting things do, however, emerge from this session. For only the second time since beginning my visits to schools of education I hear a reference to the teaching of French. (I realize I had forgotten, in the public school world, about language learning as an aspect of culture and civilization rather than as an ethnic perquisite, a means of enhancing "self-esteem" among non-English speakers.)

All of these students will be visiting inner-city schools in the weeks ahead. Dr. Pangloss tells them it will be "a wonderful multicultural experience," although she feels she must add that they "may be shocked to begin with," until they begin to understand some of the difficulties. "Some of these children have no real homes. They prefer school to home. Their teachers become their parents. They have such an abundance of needs . . . it tears your heart."

She asks them to keep notebooks with pictures, notes, clippings, cartoons, poetry, and prayers. She will check them for organization, grammar, correct spelling. She tells them what size paper to use, to write "in ink on one side of the paper only, with margins." A little laugh punctuates everything she says. She remembers their names and is careful to repeat them each time she responds to a question or comment. "Yes, Bob. Very good, Diane."

During the break, I talk with two of the older students, Doris and Steven. Old friends, they are both products of twelve years of parochial schools as children, have worked at various jobs, earned college degrees, she in women's studies, he in English and history. Both have children. Doris says, "I worked before I got married, raised my kids . . . teaching was what I always wanted to do." She's about to enter what she describes as a tough market for new teachers. She tells me about a substitute teacher she knows "with three M.A.s and five languages—and she can't get a job. Most principals are interested in mediocrity," she says. "I'm going to act real mediocre in my interviews."

After the break the professor talks about the purpose of the notebooks—"to record your reactions to your visitations. How is what you see in private schools different from your public school lab experience? Weigh the advantages and disadvantages of Christian private schools. And you have to think about how you will deal with special children, gifted children." She goes over the sheets she's handed out scheduling the visits to the various schools. Who goes where and when is right there, each group and place clearly designated, but still many of them need to go over it. She has suggested that on their school visits they "think about levels of learning in terms of Bloom's taxonomy." Evidently they have read something besides *Newsweek* then, but the faces around me look blank.

At their last class they had been asked to read selections from the New Testament—the Sermon on the Mount and passages from Matthew and Luke dealing with Christ's teaching—and "to identify the characteristics found in scripture that Jesus Christ demonstrated as a master teacher." As I listen to the comments and to her delighted responses, I begin to understand her approach. It is meant to be religious, and specifically to embody a particular idea of what it is to be Christian. The characteristics the students suggest and which she puts on the board, enlarging a bit on each, are:

- Role model—patient with disciples, nonjudgmental, accepting of all
- Truly understood the level of His learners and went there (task analysis)
- Compassionate attitude to children
- Consistent
- Parables method makes learners think (*"Very* good, Linda!")
- Humble
- Persevering
- Used visual aids (birds, rocks, fields, loaves and fishes)
- Approachable—allowed pupils to touch Him
- Nonviolent
- Respected His followers
- Made all sorts of situations teaching situations ("The motivation was really high")
- Really cared about people
- Commitment to what He was doing
- Confronted a situation and addressed and corrected it but accepted the person ("I like that, Cathy!")
- Anticipatory sets ("Can we have a lesson on the walking on the water part?" one student asks and everyone laughs, including the professor)
- Knew when it was time to retreat and refuel ("I've been waiting for this one! Christ was the perfect model for finding time alone to reflect, to pray. You get very tired after a week in school. . . . I keep my Bible in my car and read for ten or fifteen minutes before school, about how Christ taught. I find it very refreshing, taking time for oneself that way.")

They turn from a consideration of Christ to the teachers they know in this world, listing the characteristics they admire in those who run the classrooms in which they've been visiting. On the board goes another list:

patient
calm
praising
accommodating
sense of humor
trusting
firm but kind
flexible
cares about and loves each kid

"Wonderful!" says our professor. "Good!" "Ah, hah!" Each of the characteristics listed seems to delight her. There is not one mention of knowledge of any kind, or even of any special method of imparting knowledge. She is glad to see them focusing on the positive characteristics of their teachers, she tells them, and she asks them to consider, "What personal characteristics of *yours* are you taking to your labs [classrooms]?"

In the closing minutes of the class, the professor reads Scripture to them. From Matthew (the "wise man, which built his house upon a rock. . . . And it came to pass, when Jesus had ended these sayings, the people were astonished at his doctrine: For he taught them as one having authority . . ."), adding that we should strive to be as Christ would have us, and from Colossians ("Put on therefore, as the elect of God . . . mercies, kindness, humbleness of mind, meekness, long-suffering . . ."), closing with an admonition to them to "remember what Christ taught, to think of yourselves as representatives of the Lord Jesus Christ"—they are snapping notebooks shut, putting papers away in briefcases, struggling into coatsleeves—"as working for the Lord, the Lord Jesus Christ who is going to pay you. He is the one you are really working for." She is still smiling as they troop up the aisles and out the door.

PART SIX

The Southwest

12

❧ —— ❧

The University of Houston

Policies and Prejudices; Learning for Society and Learning for Self

I came to Texas exactly ten years after the publication in *Texas Monthly* magazine, in September 1979, of an article by Gene Lyons called "Why Teachers Can't Teach." A cause célèbre in its time, it called teacher education in Texas—and everywhere else in the country—"a shame, a mammoth and very expensive swindle of the public interest, a hoax, and an intellectual disgrace."

Lyons reported that half of the teacher applicants to the Houston Independent School District scored lower in math and a third of them lower in English than the average high school junior and he blamed the state's sixty-three accredited teacher-training institutions for turning out "teachers who cannot read as well as the average sixteen-year-old, write notes free of barbarisms to parents, or handle arithmetic well enough to keep track of the field-trip money." He accused the teacher colleges of coddling ignorance and, "backed by hometown legislators," of turning out "hordes of certified ignoramuses whose incompetence in turn becomes evidence that the teacher colleges and the educators need yet more money and more power."

He attacked the system that made graduation from an accredited teacher-training program tantamount to certification and heaped scorn on an education bureaucracy, backed by the National Education Association, to whom "to insist upon literacy is considered coercive and potentially harmful" and a proof of "cultural bias." Real knowledge and skills, he maintained, had been replaced by "matters such as sex education, driver training, drug counseling, and the proper attitude toward siblings" by "educationists . . . afflicted with a cultural relativism so profound it has become an intellectual disease.

"Basic, traditional academic disciplines, in which fundamental intellectual skills are supposed to be taught" had, he found, been replaced in teacher education by "a promiscuous choice of courses" that he called "the intellectual equivalent of puffed wheat: one kernel of knowledge inflated by means of hot air, divided into pieces and puffed again." The graduates of the schools of education, "where everyone is transformed into an A student," he charged, "are defrauded into believing they have an education," and he identified the cause of grade inflation and trivial courses (in which "fools dissect, categorize, and elaborate upon the perfectly obvious" and in which it is "virtually impossible to fail") as the system that made the operating budgets of all state colleges dependent on the number of students enrolled.

In programs where "there is no subject matter, only method," Lyons saw enormous amounts of money, energy, and time wasted, and suggested that future teachers could get more useful experience in less time if they were "apprenticed after securing honest college degrees to proven and experienced master teachers in actual classrooms with real kids." When he made the suggestion to a professor of education, the response was, "You're talking about my job."

It was a scathing indictment, and it included the prophecy that fully literate teachers would continue to be the exception and the incompetent the rule as the field moved "toward more specialization and more education courses . . . for an expanded faculty to teach . . . in such growth areas as special education, learning disabilities" and bilingual education, "the going thing these days."

Lyons hoped his article would blow the whistle on the existing system and that "the attack on the Educationists' monopoly over the public schools may have already begun."

And indeed, a series of education battles fought in the Texas legislature in the ensuing years had resulted by 1987 in passage of a bill limiting the number of methods courses for future teachers to eighteen hours, about half the previous requirement, beginning in 1991. Senate Bill 994 also abolished the undergraduate education major. The intention was to have more time for future teachers to acquire a general education in subjects and skills, to become literate and numerate.

The response of the ed school establishment was predictable. The *Journal of Teacher Education*, in its issue of November-December 1988, reported on the new law in an article titled "Assault on Teacher Education in Texas." In addition, the head of the American Association of Colleges for Teacher Education, in an editorial entitled "Outrage in Texas," appearing in the organization's publication *ACCTE Briefs*, reported "hostility," "dismay," and a "numbing effect" among ed school faculty and went on to speak of "a Kafka-like nightmare" in which "shock, anger, and disbelief" were joined with a "feeling of betrayal." To him, any reduction in the time future teachers spend studying pedagogy means that they "will be less prepared to teach," an understandable reaction from those with a vested interest in the teaching of pedagogy.

SB 994 and the reaction to it were very much on my mind when I arrived at the University of Houston to visit its College of Education. With a campus looking as if it could have been ordered by mail, the university is a self-contained entity isolated from urban Houston, primarily a commuter school. Everyone drives here, and the enormous parking areas add to the feeling that one is at a very well-tended mall. The university's enrollment is about 7 percent each black, Hispanic, and foreign, and about 8 percent Asian and Pacific Islander. (Neighboring Texas Southern University, where I would visit next, is a predominantly black institution.)

Here is the dean of the College of Education talking to me at breakfast on my first morning in Houston, in the hotel run by the University's School of Hotel and Restaurant Management: "Our purpose is to develop the skills on which to draw in making decisions. It's competency based. There has to be accountability for delivering certain skills in microteaching. We had become too skills oriented, not reflective, not holistic enough. This has led us to the reflective inquiry approach to teacher education." And so the day begins.

I asked for his thoughts on SB 994. He thought it odd, he said, that the legislature should put a cap on the maximum rather than establishing a minimum for education courses. He described the college's present curriculum; each of its three phases—foundations (sociology, psychology, and philosophy of education), methods, and student teaching—will, under the new law, have to be covered in only six semester hours. The law didn't really affect secondary education majors, who were already required to major in their field, he told me, but it did "cut into the professional education of elementary majors." They have always majored in elementary education. Now they will have to major in interdisciplinary studies—that is, be stronger academically. At the same time, they have to worry about complying with Public Law 94–142, which mandates twenty-three specific requirements regarding the handicapped, and with the demand for a multicultural curriculum.

"This requires familiarity with alternate strategies for teaching concepts, not just telling, but a wider array of courses in how you can teach." I asked for an example. "For instance, the importance of the physical handling of objects related to learning in early childhood." (Why does this require so much time? Why not just illustrate with some examples, then let them practice in the classroom with an experienced teacher to keep an eye on them and give them pointers? It's only such a big deal because those who teach these courses are concerned with protecting their turf.)

I asked him if Ross Perot had been the guiding spirit behind these changes. He said yes, to some extent, but added that the real proximate cause was the negative feelings teachers had expressed about their education—especially methods—courses. They had told the legislature that they found them irrelevant, not helpful. In response to the criticism, the new system provides for the first year of teaching to be an induction year in which new teachers are probationers, working with a mentor teacher. Stirring his coffee, the dean noted that with the cost of the program projected to be 36 million dollars a year, it might well turn out to be a paper tiger, mandated but not funded. Still, he seemed relatively unperturbed by the specter of its implementation. In fact, he thought it might be a good idea— a transition between pre- and in-service. In any case, he expressed none of the "outrage" I had been prepared to hear. His attitude seemed to me to be more one of resignation, born, I ventured to guess, of years of trying to comply with changing and increasingly demanding—if not impossible—aims.

When I come into the room where the Introduction to Early Childhood Education course is already under way they are talking about decision making, problem solving, analytical skills. About "the low-income and culturally varied child" the usual: "holding them back, tracking, stresses them. If you keep them back, you lower their aspirations, you adversely affect their social behavior. You undermine their self-esteem. So don't grade them, don't label them. You have to make them feel good about themselves." Most of this class is conducted in a second language called Euphemism. A child has "auditory process problems" means he doesn't listen. "Think what you are doing to their self-concept." They talk about parents who say, "I want my child to know the alphabet, I want him to know how to read, to add." The parents may think these are good things but early childhood educators say they're pushing. A student refers to "learning-disabled children," stops and says, "That's an offensive label." The professor: "If I was you . . ." A student, confused: "I'm like, what do I do?" With regard to social promotion, another says, "mature-wise, he's slow." This is the language of future teachers of English and literature. A black male teacher says, "You startin' to push 'em on and third-graders can't write their name. We get people walking the streets who can't read and write. Parents know you gotta know how to read, know the math times tables. We live in a competitive society . . ." He's onto the effects of liberal condescension, but he's outnumbered. They go into their routine of "developmentally appropriate . . . learning by doing, by playing, not pushing . . . harmful effects of labeling."

"Okay, here I am labeling," says a young woman, "but my smart kids . . ." and she tells about a test they took, "They didn't score good." She worries about the effects of their frustration. Another, who teaches English as a second language, talks about the importance of gestures and body language, the little helpful things that help you get the idea across. "Rewording something three and four ways, saying, 'We're going to get it.' "

The professor says he's going to hand out copies of an article from *Newsweek* to use as a basis for class discussion. (It's actually *U.S. News and World Report*.) It's an article about a souped-up kindergarten curriculum, with, as the professor puts it, "twice as more emphasis on academics." Of the "classical," traditional low-key kindergarten program, he says, "You can add a flair to a bad curriculum and make it good. That's what we have to do, given all the requirements to teach to the tests."

Someone expresses disapproval of "holiday rituals" in school. They should be replaced with "multicultural content based on their [children's] social experiences." Another suggests that when a parent asks why his child does not do well in academic performance, on reading or math tests, "keep an anecdotal record so you can show the parent how the child led a small group discussion, initiated it and got the other children involved in a discussion of the space shuttle."

You hear the same phrases, the same fads repeated everywhere in the ed school universe. Every place has its icons. At one school they talk about Shulman, in another department it's Madeline Hunter. Here in the course on Generic Teaching Strategies it's Joyce. Not James, of whom few in this room, I was to discover, had ever heard. This Joyce was a local hero, the author of an "instructional system" I would hear more about later in the day.

"In the Houston area," says the professor—call her O'Brien— "we have lots of people for whom English is a second language. We have to watch out for that." She means teaching on their level, not trying to pull them into using more English. She also suggests they look for ideas from other more experienced teachers, such as—her example—"having background music playing in the class-room."

And always, everywhere, the phrase, "The research shows . . ." "The research shows . . ." and on goes the overhead projector. When asked to enumerate the characteristics of a good teacher, these teachers, like almost all the others I have encountered, say, "fair. . .caring. . ." Knowing their subject matter comes last, almost as an afterthought on the list. Professor O'Brien reminds them that some people think the score is authoritarians 10, "warm fuzzies" zero, but they know she's only kidding. They all share "empathy" for the young. The professor says, "We would worry about teenagers who stayed in the library instead of going to McDonald's with their friends."

Between classes, I talked with a young woman on the faculty of UHO who is the coordinator of Phase I, the foundations part of the program. She explained, "The program was designed to move toward social change. Our students ride with the police, interview storekeepers where drug transactions take place, talk to priests, learn about the community's perception of the police, the social stratification of the community and the school. We teach them interviewing techniques, how to ask probing questions, note taking—what you're doing with me right now. . . . Now we are being told what to do by people who are not educators." She saw the new legislation as a result of "anti-intellectual bias in Texas, particularly by business, which wants to take over the business of education." I asked what effect she thought it would have and she replied, "I'm afraid the worst effect will be that we will find ourselves doing things in a way that will make it seem as though what we were doing before wasn't necessary in the first place."

A class on Art in the Elementary School. Many minutes pass in consideration of how to put together a notebook. Then begins a review for an examination to be given the next day. The professor is concerned to "decrease your stress level for the exam." She tells them that if over half the people miss a question, "we'll throw it out." The purpose of art education? Some answers: to develop self-concept, self-esteem, help children learn to express their emotions, use experience rather than abstract thinking. It's "therapeutic." What kind of person does it help to develop. "A self." "Yes, but what kind of a self?" The next student has the right answer: "flexible human beings, open and tolerant of others." I suddenly realize from the singsong intonation—and a quick peek at the notes of the student beside me, in whose notebook appear exactly these words—that these are memorized answers to set questions. The aesthetic aspect? "The aesthetic product is subordinate to the creative process."

"You guys are doing real well," the professor tells them after one of the students has repeated the correct formula. "I'm real pleased. Give him a hand." They go over the kinds of materials an art teacher should have on hand: "stuff to feel, smelly bags . . . It's difficult in our society to have schools provided with everything they should have." The lack of creative expression is a danger to society. Why? It leads to the kind of person who has "poor self-concept, a low achiever," to "stereotyped behaviors," in short—to *conformity.*

They continue to go down the list of questions they will be asked on the exam, rehearsing each answer in the same manner. Why is art vital to the elementary-school child? "Because it is basic to the thinking process. It helps them handle life, become flexible and tolerant. It leads to social and emotional growth. It nurtures creativity through spontaneous self-expression. It moves children from thinking about what is to what might be." The teacher of art is what? "A facilitator, a provider of the appropriate materials and of a place in which to create." It goes on and on. How can the teacher encourage creativity in the classroom? "Not to expect predetermined answers." If any of these men and women around the table see any irony here, they show no sign of it. The aim of art appreciation? "To make the child aware of his environment and that art is all around him. The development of self-awareness."

Mathematics for the Mindless. Well, no. It's actually called Math for Young Children. I've joined a group struggling here to figure out how to make a graph showing in terms of the number of coins they have of various denominations how much money they have in total. An eighth-grader should be able to do this. They keep asking for more direction. The professor says they're doing "task clarification."

They have other things on their minds. What are they going to call their graph? A title has been asked for. The lone white man at the table offers a suggestion. "Why should he name it just because he's a man?" is the response of Letitia, a pretty young Hispanic woman. "We're not going to pay any attention to you, Chuck," she says cheerfully.

The idea here is for these undergraduate elementary-education students to pretend to be children doing the group activity, learning from each other. It is hard to believe that in any other country of the developed world this level—of student and of activity—would be conceivable.

The professor—I'll call him Dr. Grey—plays the game. "Your graph is telling a story. Come to the front of the room, recorders, and tell us the title of your story. And the rest of you, let me see all your eyes up here." And they shuffle up to the front, skinny young women with blank expressions under incredibly elaborate clouds of hair, overweight middle-aged women in shorts and slacks, grinning as they shyly or confidently read out their titles: "How Much Money Do We Have?" "I Wish We Were Richer." "Common Cents." This one delights the professor. "Very good!"

Dr. Grey explains to them the difference between a bar graph and a line graph. They take notes. How do you spell uni-tary, Letitia wants to know. He tells them they are learning "what it is important to know and what it is important to do in order to teach children"— a proposition that seems to be translated by them into the advice that in order to understand children it is best to act like children.

In the class on Social Studies in the Elementary School words and phrases fly around the room: "life-long learners," "higher order concepts," "inquiry process." Nothing wrong with any of those things except that they are inert ideas, in Whitehead's phrase. The same words are heard in every class in every ed school these days. They talk about Bloom's Taxonomy, about open-ended questions and higher-level thinking as opposed to direct questions and knowledge-based systems, but there is little evidence that these words mean anything to them.

Here a professor with a high reputation among his colleagues, several of whom have mentioned him to me, is showing his students how to develop a model of an "instructional unit" of their own for teaching a social studies concept. The concept is that "more primitive peoples satisfy their needs closer to home." They talk about charts, outlines, materials other than textbooks they can assign. They go to the blackboard to show how they would relate people, places, needs, and resources from the local environment and those from far away. The professor feels it necessary to note that "primitive" is becoming "an unpopular word." He apologizes for using it, but he can't think of a substitute.

These student teachers are good-humored, placid, cheerful. Nurturing perhaps. But as one of them says she is "trying to write with this kind of thing," I realize she isn't referring to the use of a pen or other writing implement, she means a generalization.

A course called Effective Use of Time. As I come in, the class is "sharing," at the suggestion of the instructor, some thoughts on cooperative learning. A student, a large black woman I would guess to be in her late thirties, says, "These boys just can't do it. I threw the idea away and took charge." The instructor misses a beat, then comments that it's important to "allow people to feel good about what they say." A student offers an example: a pupil who never made relevant contributions to class discussion. "You'd be talkin' about red grapes and she'd be talkin' about green grass. This time she was almost talkin' about red grapes. Everybody applauded. It helped her self-esteem a lot."

Another example, this time of the importance of understanding the culture from which the pupil comes. About a child who missed school in order to take a trip to Dallas with her family. When the teacher asked whether she'd enjoyed sightseeing, the child explained they'd gone to get her brother out of jail.

We get down to business. We're dealing with "organizing classroom behaviors," with such matters as "how to do an interactive seating chart." The instructor is teaching them SOS, the Stallings Observation System. The system provides them with a new vocabulary, words that lovingly mimic science—variables, coding—to use in "evaluating practice, then analyzing it, then making suggestions for treatment." They will learn how to conduct workshops themselves for other teachers.

An hour is spent in telling them which proportion of class time should be spent on "academic statements" as distinct from "organizing behavior" (telling pupils to get their books out, hand in their papers, etc.) or "social statements" ("making people feel you're glad to have 'em"). How to take snapshots with a polaroid camera at five-minute intervals and then note what everyone was doing at "fmi's" while the teacher was teaching. Record the amount of "involvement in task activities" (translation: paying attention), the percentage of time spent interacting, problem-solving, monitoring, etc. Reduce this, add that.

The overhead transparencies repeat all this, with columns of numbers. The instructor stops herself, asks, "Am I talking to the guys more than the gals?"

At last, a real class. Sitting and listening to this teacher is like coming alive, like black and white film changing to technicolor. You wouldn't have been able to predict this from the course title: Models of Teaching. But that is just what is going on here. A model of teaching.

There are two things involved. The first is the teacher's lively mind and engaging style. Like all good teachers, he is something of an exhibitionist. An enthusiast, he is really interested in his subject and has original and occasionally surprising slants on it. Everyone wakes up in his class. And no amount of methods courses makes a teacher like this. It's his personality together with his knowledge of and passion for his subject that makes him a gifted teacher.

The other thing that makes this class interesting is that it is *about something*. Professor Good is making his points about teaching techniques with actual ideas, and substantial material—the *what* of learning, so seldom present in the ed school classroom. Here he wants to show them ways in which to organize and present a lesson to a high-school history class, and he has handed out a series of short essays, some only a couple of paragraphs long, others consisting of an entire page, on the Pilgrims, the American Revolution, the Articles of Confederation, the Constitution, and the Whiskey Rebellion. It is clear from the class discussion that some of this material is less than familiar to these prospective high school teachers. He is sneaking in some knowledge along with his "models."

In the process of thinking about how to organize and present the material, they have to consider the nature of the ideas shaping the events and the evolving institutions in the early years of this country. He wants them to learn to teach social studies through generalizations, "using the inductive thought process as a way to make sense of the world." Under what circumstances does a challenge to authority lead to rebellion? And he is reminding them of the reading they have done in Hilda Taba, who believes you can teach thinking as logical process, and in Jerome Bruner, who emphasizes teaching concepts. He asks how these ideas fit the Piaget model, in what way Plato is relevant to concept formation.

His own style is markedly to avoid assuming a position of authority himself. He is quick to point out that "I didn't tell you what categories to use" in organizing the data. "Every individual has to decide for himself." In his reluctance to claim any authority for himself, he will say, "May I throw some things out?" and when they try to pin him down on a point, "I didn't say that." He won't judge their answers. He wants to show them the difference between a highly structured authoritarian classroom and one in which "an amorphous group comes up with its own model." It is, however, hard to imagine most of these students being able to make use of this style. They haven't enough knowledge at their command nor do they show any particular evidence of the necessary quickness of mind.

I returned to Professor Good's class the next day. Professor Good is a devotee of Inquiry Training, which he explains to me during the class break as a process of productive questioning in which the teacher gives no answers as correct. The aim is the Platonic one: for the teacher to know how to ask the right questions in order for the pupil to find the answers within his previous knowledge. The trouble is that nobody in this room of about thirty prospective secondary-school social-studies teachers is quite sure just when Prohibition was—before or after World War I. (They will, of course, know less and less as they spend more and more time learning about methods of teaching.) Still, those who, like him, enjoy playing to an audience, and who are interested enough in the world of ideas to go on learning beyond what is required of them for graduation and certification, may be better teachers for the time spent here in this class.

There are many in the education establishment and in academia generally, particularly in the social sciences, who have an investment in schooling as social engineering. They believe that using the schools to teach children to get along with all kinds of people should take precedence over teaching them about the civilization of which they are the inheritors. They are comfortable with using the schools as a means of social leveling through intellectual leveling. If the course is too hard for some, water it down. If some can't pass the test, throw it out.

They have shown a remarkable tendentiousness in the service of ideology, insisting that those who oppose their idea of the purposes of schooling are reactionary bigots; that excellence is a codeword for an exclusivity that is social rather than of mind and spirit; that in fact all ideas, all cultures, all institutions are equally valid, equally important for our children to learn about, equally worthwhile.

The less prestigious the school or college or department of education, the more common sense one hears, the more conservative the attitudes about the relation of school and society, and the less ideology is expressed, ostensibly in terms of method but actually affecting the curriculum as well.

But even in the bastions of correct left–liberal thought on matters pertaining to school and society, where group pressure creates a climate in which it is hard to disagree with one's colleagues, faculty members will tell you in the car on the way to the airport, or in the little off-campus sandwich shop over lunch, that such-and-such policy doesn't really work, that so-and-so's research was carried out in a spirit of "putting numbers to things we've already agreed on." An adjunct professor who had waxed eloquent in class about "less teacher talk" and "functioning as a facilitator" admitted ruefully on a walk across campus that, "Every class I've seen that's worthwhile at this level [undergraduate] was a lecture." He meant only, I think, to criticize the inability of his colleagues to restrain their pedantry. I would agree with his observation, but for a different reason. Few undergraduates, and still fewer students of education, know enough to make a worthwhile contribution to any class discussion.

13

❦ ——— ❦

Texas Southern University

From Segregation to Socialization

Texas Southern University was established in 1947 as a black facility in the racially segregated system then still in place in the South. The current catalogue reads: "Fortunately, constitutional principles have prevailed and historical barriers to admission based upon ethnic identification and color have been dropped. However, programs and expertise developed during those years of enforced segregation now enable us to comfortably address the needs not only of Blacks but also of other ethnic minorities and culturally different students of all races and colors."

The College of Education was established in 1971 and in 1973 TSU was designated a "special purpose institution of higher education for urban programming" by the Texas legislature. The catalogue adds that while the university's social mission is largely associated with regional concerns, "its more global opportunities are reflected by its attraction to students from abroad."

Most of the forty students in the class on Educational Foundations are black, with about half a dozen white students and three or four students from the Middle East and Africa. The first thing that strikes me is that both the professor in his three-piece suit and the students seated around the room are the most conventionally dressed and best-groomed population I'd seen on any of the campuses I'd visited.

175

Their appearance is a statement. "Ladies and gentlemen," the professor I'll call Dr. Rogers begins, and he means it.

Like so many classes in education schools and so many in the public schools themselves, this one begins with a good deal of time spent on what teachers call "housekeeping"—the business of taking attendance and the talk about a coming exam. But the first-name informality I'd seen in most other places gives way here to "Miss Smith" and "Mr. Jones," both in the calling of the roll and in the professor's recognizing students with a comment or a question. The high degree of civility seems oddly matched with the colloquial patterns of speech at first, but soon feels right, reflecting his need to inspire and reassure at the same time. Dr. Rogers tells them the exam will consist of true–false and multiple-choice questions on the first five chapters in their textbooks and that "even if you're late for the exam, we still gonna end on time." He reminds them that there will be no classes on the coming Monday, which is Emancipation Day, known as Juneteenth to black Texans.

The rest of the class time is spent on a review of the last chapter they've read in their textbook, *Introduction to Foundations of American Education.* They go over the text section by section, as if they couldn't be expected to be tested on this material without reading it together.

Discussing the section on school reform, they talk about merit pay. Do you get it, one woman wants to know, for staying after school? "Just stayin' late?" says Dr. Rogers. "No, we're talkin' about above and beyond the teachin' you get paid for according to your contract. You got to participate in activities that enhance teachin' an' learnin'." They talk about going to games after school as a way of participating. "It shows you care about them," says an older teacher. "That you're concerned about the total development of the student. You're interacting with your pupils." Dr. Rogers nods, adds, "You can't *pretend* like you involved."

The students in this black college seem much more practical, more down to earth in their concerns, especially the older, experienced ones. There's less expression of ideological zeal, just as there seems to be more of a middle-class orientation.

"Our students don't have the basic skills," Dr. Rogers tells them. "We got to start doing a better job, ladies and gentlemen. We got to stop passing the buck from the colleges to the elementary school to the high school back to the colleges, which is where the teachers come from. Forget about the blame. We got to take children where we are. We have to be certified and competent. It's obnoxious to have a math teacher and she don't know the concepts. The new standards, they're not all bad. They're good. Putting demands on us." He pauses, then adds, with a wry smile, "This is not a racist statement, but sometimes it does seem like as soon as we come along a ways they put in another exam to put us down again." This is said more in the spirit of those ethnic jokes in which insiders make fun of themselves and comment on their own foibles than with any of the resentment expressed by some of the white left–liberals and young blacks I talked with at large urban universities.

When they come to the section on student rights, Dr. Rogers reminds them that students have responsibilities as well as rights. "You are citizens of America," he says, "and the Constitution protects your rights and you have to know your rights and when you are infringing on others folks' rights. The right to an education—that is a primary right in America, guaranteed to you by the states' constitutions." No talk here about injustice in a racist society.

They go through the text section by section, Dr. Rogers reading the opening line or two and then elaborating. His style is that of a preacher. ("We used to only be able to be teachers or preachers," he says at one point.) One student doesn't understand Dr. Rogers' statement that there are two kinds of students, producers and consumers. He explains, then says, "We will know what you have consumed on Tuesday" (the day of the exam). Another doesn't understand the distinction between the school board and the school district. This is not the first class I've been in where the class goes over a text making sure everyone will be able to repeat what is said on an exam. One difference is in the nature of Dr. Rogers' interpolations. On the due-process right of students not to be suspended without a hearing, he tells them, "Having been a principal, let me share this with you. It's a loophole you won't find in the book." And he tells them they can send home a pupil whose behavior can be considered "detrimental to the health of that individual or any other" in order to "quiet the situation, give the children a chance to calm down. Don't be afraid to call that mother," he tells them. "It's your prerogative." The tips he's giving them will probably be of more use to them in the world of the classrooms they'll be entering than any amount of educational theory.

"Mr. Lewis, Miss Johnson, listen up now, ladies and gentlemen," he quiets them when everyone gets embroiled in an argument over corporal punishment. "When I was a kid, the teacher would tear me up if I did something bad. He'd wear me out. And then when I got home my old man would take up where he left off. I'd say to the teacher, 'Give me two more licks but just don't tell my daddy.'

But times have changed. Today, kids know the law. They can quote it at you—statute, regulation number . . . 'You can't touch me, Mr. Teacher.' "

"Oh, *yes*," adds one of the middle-aged women fervently. "You can't touch 'em. You can't even say, You sit down! You have to say, John, would you *please* sit down. And if he don't, ain't nothin' you can do about it." Another woman tells about a boy sent to the principal, who asked him why he didn't follow the rules, and his response: "Why should I? I don't have to if I don't want to." She adds that when the principal called his parents they said they didn't want to be involved.

The sounds of disapproval and nods of recognition that greet this story tell you it's a familiar one. Dr. Rogers tells them about legislation he says has been in force in Pennsylvania since 1985. "If a kid is late, the *parent* gets a warning. The second time, the parent is fined. The third time, the parent is in court and could do time." (The response is immediate. "Oh, yeah! Good! Yessir!") He goes on, "That says to parents, If you want your child to learn to read, to spell, to count, then send them to us prepared to do so. It puts the onus back on parents for their kids' behavior. *We're* only responsible for their learning." (No self-esteem talk here!) "You have a judge telling parents, Your child is impeding the educational progress of others. You as the parent are responsible."

The discussion moves on to the recent Texas legislation providing that anyone who fails the high school exit exam can't get a driver's license, a law intended to reduce the dropout rate of under-sixteens, the age until which school attendance is mandatory. When a student for whom he clears up a point says, "Thank you, Dr. Rogers," he says, "You welcome, Mr. Foster. Don't forget me in your will, now." The recipe here is a kind of intimate good humor, social liveliness, and decorum. It adds up to civility. One striking note is the juxtaposition of words of wisdom with colloquial grammar: "Kids are more harder on their peers."

(It is instructive to note that the chapter of the textbook entitled "Professional Aspects of Teaching" includes sections on Sex Discrimination, Pregnancy, Child Abuse and Neglect, and AIDS. "Education for Special Populations" deals with blacks and women.)

The concerns here are with practical matters, with how to run a classroom with a minimum of disruption and how to make one's students into good citizens—a phrase I haven't heard in years and am hearing for the first time since I began visiting departments, schools, and colleges of education. These people regard the real enemy as the disappearance of the structured stable family. They disapprove of thirteen-year-old girls who come to school "wearing eye liner and earrings and short tight skirts." They note wearily that it's no use asking to see a student's ID because "the ID's gonna be fake anyway."

A teacher in health education despairs about the teenage pregnancy rate, pleads, "Give 'em advice. They need role models. They're unhappy at home. Their parents are alcoholics and drug addicts." These teachers aren't worried about overriding the rights of students by imposing their values on them. They just wish they could. They share none of the white liberals' illusions about the underclass. They do share with each other common problems, common complaints. They're sharing them so volubly now that Dr. Rogers calls out, "We can all sing together but we can't all talk together." A lady in the front row says, "Ain't that true," and they settle down again. "We movin' right along now," says Dr. Rogers as they move through the chapter.

They talk about not stigmatizing students. Someone suggests not reading the students' records for the first six weeks of the school term in order not to be biased. One of the older teachers says, "Some people will never learn nothin', no matter how much you teach 'em," and one of her neighbors says, "That's right!"

They talk about tenure. Rogers advises them, "Follow the regulations and you won't have to worry about being terminated once you have tenure, but don't lay back and read the papers, don't get lazy. Be more energetic, so you can get a merit pay increase. Be more giving of yourself with those students. Help out with the team, the band, things of that nature." He disapproves of teacher strikes: "Teachers ought to have a code of conduct like doctors and lawyers, take an oath of professionality." About Senate Bill 994, limiting the hours of education methods courses for prospective teachers in Texas, he expresses a wait-and-see attitude. "Time will tell how it will come out."

As he walks them through the chapters of the book, orchestrating the interruptions, questions, personal anecdotes, gripes, one senses the extent to which this class is about community even more than it is about passing Tuesday's exam. One also becomes keenly aware of the distance between the attitudes expressed in this classroom and the belligerence and grievance-collecting of the Ivy League intellectuals and their proteges in social criticism. If things are to go better in the schools, the improvement is more likely to begin with the attitudes about responsibility here than with the attitudes about rights there.

"Close your books," he tells them at the end of the period, "and let me give you your thought for the day." Now he's all preacher, and one senses what has been lost to the black community. "Father's Day is coming up, and our dads are the pillar of strength in our lives. But remember this one thing. A woman was developed from the rib of a man. Not from his foot, to be below him; not from his head, to be above him; but from his rib—to be beside him."

The congregation responds with laughter and with applause from grey-bearded Muhammed and Joseph, a young Nigerian, who have been sharing a book and their evident bewilderment and delight in this foreign culture.

That was Professor Rogers. Now, in a class on elementary school mathematics, I find it has been changed from a class on how to teach arithmetic in the elementary grades to one aimed at improving the teachers' knowledge and understanding of math problems and concepts up through basic algebra. The object: to help prospective teachers pass the exit exam in order to be certified.

The class is being taught by a Ph.D. on loan from NASA, which has its headquarters here in Houston. He is handing back the graded test he gave them in order to appraise their grasp of basic arithmetic. He is trying to be tactful, but it is clear that he is dismayed and unsure of where to begin. I glance at the test paper of the young woman seated next to me. Problem no. 9 reads, "Mr. Diaz bought 10 boxes of alarm clocks for each of his 3 stores. If there are 12 alarm clocks in each box, how many alarm clocks did Mr. Diaz buy?" The possible answers are: "(A) 40, (B) 42, (C) 120, and (D) 360." She has circled (C).

He is illustrating on the board the way an equation can express a ratio, in this case that of the population of Texas to that of the U.S., rounded off. One of the students interrupts. "You mean you'd like us to discuss it?" he asks. "Okay, but there's not a heck of a lot of work here." A few laborious minutes later the student says, Oh, she didn't realize the answer was a ratio. She thought it was a percentage. Everyone seems confused except the instructor. He seems depressed.

And well he might be. At the present time, we are conferring high school diplomas on students who often cannot handle the simplest math operations and who consistently rate at or near the bottom of international comparisons of math performance. In science the story is equally dismal. The National Assessment of Educational Progress found in 1986 that only 41 percent of high school seniors sampled had "some detailed scientific knowledge" or "could evaluate the appropriateness of scientific procedure." And the 1989 International Assessment of Educational Progress report of international comparisons, "A World of Differences," added to the news that American 13-year-olds scored last in math the finding that they tied for last place in science with Ireland and two provinces in Canada.

One might expect that the response of the education establishment would be to demand the higher standards, tougher requirements, insistence on mastery of one level of skills before going on to the next that characterize the systems of the countries whose students so far surpass ours. These students learn what they know they have to—in order to go on in school, in order to graduate, in order to enter college or university.

Instead, the leaders of the world of teaching have decreed that what our students need is *less* drilling and memorization of basic facts and skills, and more "higher order thinking skills," less acquaintance with traditional scientific and mathematical knowledge, and more exposure to concepts. These are the recommendations of the National Council on Science and Technology Education, convened by the American Association for the Advancement of Science and funded by the Carnegie and Mellon foundations, an impressive group if ever there was one. Another prestigious group, the National Research Council, in its report called "Everybody Counts," recommends that, consistent with the educators' goal of reducing "teacher talk," students be encouraged to "work together to find solutions," and that they should make more use of calculators and computers. And the National Council of Teachers of Mathematics recommends retreating even further from practicing sequenced series of calculations, memorization of numerical relationships such as the multiplication tables, repetition, and testing before going on to the next level.

Meanwhile, other voices of the education establishment like that of the Rand Corporation are raised in alarm at the shortages of qualified math and science teachers and blame the situation on low teacher salaries and poor working conditions in the schools. The suggested solution is legislation to provide more tax dollars for scholarships and student loans. What for? To train more teachers in the techniques of socialization, altering the teacher's role from source of knowledge to classroom manager of a learning cooperative designed to provide experiences that will enhance students' self-esteem?

The problem is that our teachers don't know enough math and science to teach it to their pupils. They themselves are products of the system that requires little of its high school graduates and little more of its baccalaureates. Their education courses then train them to be social workers rather than to develop the meager intellectual skills they bring with them to graduate study and beyond, to the classroom.

The trade and technical schools that might exist alongside academic high schools actually high in their scholarly standards and capable of feeding a university system worthy of the name of higher education are of no interest to the architects of egalitarian school policy. And the real losers in this situation are those they most profess to be concerned with helping. In their determination to avoid the charge of "elitism" by providing the same education in the same classroom for everyone, they ignore the needs not only of those youngsters with an academic bent but of those with more practical interests as well. Too often, these students realize they are learning nothing useful to them and leave school, while the very educators who planned their curriculum deplore the soaring dropout rate.

In a class in the Psychology Department dealing with group testing, the professor says, "They will have to come up with a larger pool of words for word association tests used with minority subjects." He is the kind of teacher who talks in an almost uninflected voice without stopping, while students furiously fill their notebooks with as much as they can catch of what he is saying. I think I may have misunderstood him, but no, he tells me after class in a straightforward way that if any test can't be passed by a large group of people, the test has to be changed.

Opening a door to what I thought was a class in progress, I found three students I had seen in the Foundations class that morning looking over their notes together in preparation for the coming exam. They invited me to join them and we talked about what had brought them to TSU, where they were the minority students.

Sandy and Diana were white women in their late thirties or early forties who, having taught ten or a dozen years ago and then stayed home to raise their own children, were back in school acquiring the credits necessary for certification. Jane, also white, was Hispanic in background and presently working as an aide in a bilingual program. She had married right out of high school and now, fifteen years later, was starting her college education.

Sandy, a special education teacher, had been given a scholarship here; Diana was frank about having chosen TSU because of its open enrollment admissions policy. For Jane the choice was both economic and a matter of scheduling; she had to work in both classes and reading between her working day at school and her children's needs. Sandy commented on the level of most of the courses: "Not what you'd expect in college. More like the way it was for my kids in high school. Is your notebook nice—that sort of thing." The black students for the most part "have a different work ethic," she says, "different expectations." Their behavior, Diana comments, "is not always appropriate at the graduate level. In class discussion, they'll go on and on with some personal anecdote that's not really relevant to the issue. They don't generalize."

When I asked why she had chosen to work with the most difficult children, Sandy said, "I *love* special education!" Teaching, she said, and the other two nodded in agreement, was a given calling. Diana said she had a son presently at Harvard ("He could have been a big fish at UT at Austin but he wanted to go East") who planned to teach after graduation. Jane talked about bilingual classes. "They work. They are a bridge to English for these kids from Guatemala, El Salvador, Mexico, who come without a word of English." She thought the problems arose when Spanish was not used as a bridge, when the children were taught all in Spanish or, in presumably "bilingual" classes, by people who didn't really know Spanish.

This led them into the problems of the inner-city schools. "The worst teachers come from other districts to the Houston Independent School District," Diana said. "The ones that can't make it in the other districts. They're glad to have them here." And about ed school, at which this was the second time around for Sandy and Diana. "I ask myself what I ever learned in methods classes to prepare me for teaching," said Sandy. "And the answer is nothing." She says it good-naturedly, like one who has learned to live with the absurdities of life. In the same way that the three of them laugh at the professors of education and administrators they have to deal with. If most of what they do is useless, well, "It's their jobs."

The class in Multicultural Education is a large one. I count around eighty students in the lecture hall. When the professor, a black woman I'll call Professor Carter, asks for help moving the overhead projector, a young man in the front row gets up. "Notice," says Professor Carter, "that no woman moved. We're functioning in a role for which we've been socialized."

The overhead in place and an outline appearing on the screen in front of us, Professor Carter points to the text and says, "We're going to see what happens in a school when teachers ignore the culture from which the children come."

"Teachers who aren't aware of or who ignore cultural differences," she reads from the screen, "create problems in achievement. It's the responsibility of the school to make adjustments. When teachers say we'll carry on business as usual in the cultural orientation we have created, it can lead to transitional trauma." There is no evidence, no discussion, just the "statements of fact" being read from the screen by the professor and assiduously copied into eighty notebooks.

"Let me remind you once again," Professor Carter says, turning back to the class and speaking very slowly, "of the rationale for and goals of multicultural education." She pauses, and then says with emphasis, "The central and overriding one is *to promote equity in student achievement.*"

After a pause during which she looks around to see all hands taking down those words, she resumes her normal tone.

"In 1957 the nation set out to desegregate in order to provide a quality educational experience for all children. We found that desegregating the schools by busing blacks into white schools and tracking them into different programs didn't work, so multicultural education was established. So we're still trying to achieve what we set out to do in 1957." She reads from the screen:

1. Promote academic success for all color, class, and cultural groups.
2. Foster the development of wholesome attitudes about self and others as a basis for building positive interactions with people from all ethnic groups—groups of color and white groups.

At this point a student, a white woman, raises her hand and asks, "But if we're all Americans, all alike in that sense, doesn't stressing the differences promote discrimination?"

"Not if we note and assign *positive* value to the differences," says Professor Carter, and she goes on reading out loud from the screen before us:

3. Create a modified schooling process which manifests the basic principles of democracy.
4. Prepare school learners from every ethnic and income group to function successfully in American society and the broader world community, equipped with the affective and social values, cognitive content and skills required for full participation.
5. Reduce the presence of color, class, and cultural bias in American life. Reduce the pain associated with being the victim of various forms of bias.

6. Raise the level of sensitivity/responsiveness to persons from different cultural and ethnic groups.

The projector is turned off now, and a more informal lecture follows. According to Professor Carter, what she referred to as "the attitudinal pattern" should be part of the curriculum. "The attitude of the Ugly American toward the Third World, the perspective that America is the center of the world, must be changed through the content of social studies in the school curriculum. . . . Research has shown that prejudice lowers self-esteem and that self-esteem is directly related to academic performance. . . . This field of multicultural education began to develop fifteen years ago with the idea of tolerance; now we've gone beyond that to *appreciating* differences. These are the goals in addition to the overriding goal of multicultural education"—and here she pauses and looks at the class. In chorus, they repeat with her—"to provide equity in student achievement."

She goes on, "Lower-income groups have been excluded from student achievement. The research shows that schools create disparity. Class is the determinant of disparity, not ethnicity. Research shows that schools are organized around the values of middle-income groups and their language patterns and cultural experiences. This creates advantages for the middle class. Schools have to make adjustments in their attitudes and values to bring lower-income children up."

Multicultural education, Professor Carter explains, challenges the notion that there is a "model American," the WASP. There is no model group; there are positives associated with each ethnic group and we have to learn to give and take, not all try to become like some model. There are other cultures that don't have some of the problems we have in America, don't, for instance, have "the terrible twos" phase in early childhood, don't have adolescent turmoil. Some African societies socialize their children and teach them skills in ways we could learn from. They don't have the family breakdowns, the incidence of divorce and separation we have. Families are more stable in African and Asian societies, she explains, because the group takes precedence over individuals; a high degree of cooperation helps preserve the group.

"The research also shows," she continues, that "student achievements will conform to teacher expectations. Research has determined this."

She looks over the class. "Any of you?" she asks. "Any of you ever felt this?"

Several hands shoot up. "I used to feel these like negative vibes from this teacher," said one young man. "It really like hurt my self-esteem."

"You felt negative?"

"Yes. I felt negative."

"The hidden curriculum," Professor Carter says, "is what determines who succeeds and who fails. It's a matter of norms, beliefs, and attitudes. The content of the curriculum should relate everything—even math problems—to their life. The pictures in their textbooks should represent their group and not a white middle-class male.

"In addition to the curriculum, the organizational arrangements, the administrative policies, evaluation, assessment, and accountability all need to accommodate to the students.

"The discrepancy between the failure rate of middle-class and lower-class children is caused by a lack of commitment by the schools to the lower-class population of students. You have negative teacher attitudes about kids who can't learn. Why waste time on them? It's not worth it. They can't learn. And there's the way they feel about teen mothers. They blame the parents for not sending us better kids. Well, they're sending us the best kids they have."

I liked the professor's little joke, but I wondered if she really believed it was that simple.

14

The University of Texas at Austin

Tracking, Testing, and Tradition

The University of Texas at Austin is the pride of the nation's third-largest higher-education system, second only to New York and California in the number of colleges and universities in the state. The campus is set within the city and a short walk takes one to the capitol and to streets lined with other buildings of historical and architectural interest. For Texas, this is a city with an impressively visible past. Endowed with equally impressive library and research facilities by oil-rich Texans, the Austin campus has a certain cosmopolitan quality. I wondered, as I made my way to a class on the teaching of reading on my first morning there, if I would find a more enlightened approach to the subject than I had come across up to now.

A visiting lecturer—an experienced first-grade teacher—says apologetically to the students in the class on Reading/Language Arts, "I'm afraid you may find the assignment a bit heavy—too much reading for you to do."

Another visitor, a kindergarten teacher, has come to talk about her system, OLB (for Oral Language Based) Instruction, to this class of undergraduates. She spends a good deal of time playing for them a tape of children's songs, the kind of thing any kid might make up. They set the usual words—this was done in October, so we have bats, witches, goblins—to familiar melodies. She has produced teacher's manuals, games, books dealing with such activities as this one.

This is in fact what good kindergarten teachers have always done. Mine did it half a century ago in the Midwest, my children's were doing these same things a quarter of a century ago in New York's P.S. 40. We read and talked, sang and played in these same ways, but this teacher gives a title to each "activity" and an overall name to the whole and calls it a Program, a System. She talks about Revising, in which children retell a story they've read, adding to it each time they tell it; about Ownership, making a story their own; about Lead-Up Activities to writing their own books. What impresses one is the obviousness of all this.

The new twist, if there is one, is the idea that there is, as she reminds the class, no "wrong." They must beware of comments that might be construed as judgmental. They must beware of observations that might encourage comparisons among the children. They have to show that "everybody is as valuable a member of the group." Once again, they are reminded that they must be sensitive to "dealing with different social and economic groups." There is no discussion of any response to "differences" other than being "sensitive" to them.

A good deal of (expensive) class time is spent watching and listening to video and audio tapes of what they could observe in a supervised classroom as student teachers. The technical paraphernalia seem to serve only to record a lot of superfluous mediocrity and spread it around the ed school world. It's like a mini version of the uses and effects of television in the larger society. Should you really get academic course credit for learning that unused computer paper makes good scrap paper for drawing, or even that "you have to play the political game" in the school to get what you want—free play time, supplies. How is that different from any work situation?

Whether or not it needs to be part of an academic program, some of what she has to tell them is useful. She points out that many children today spend most of their waking day in school; they have breakfast there and stay for the after-school program until picked up by their working parents. "We are a very strong influence on them, and we owe them our best." Discipline, she tells them, will be their biggest problem. She estimates that 25 percent of the children in their classrooms (the greater part of the "special ed" population) will be emotionally disturbed.

Tests, she tells them resignedly, are a fact of life. "They're an objective method politicians can point to, a way of labeling and tracking people." Just that, not a way of appraising what has been learned or how effectively it has been taught. After all, if pupils are not to be judged, why should teachers be?

A number of her pointers are practical, and give these neophytes some idea of what to expect, so that at least they are less likely to go into shock when they leave academia for the world of the inner-city public schools. They will be overwhelmed at first, she tells them, with red tape, and they will have to extend their days in order to talk with parents at 7:30 in the morning or 5:30 in the afternoon. "If they come." Sometimes, she tells them, they will find "that the mother has been killed or the child has moved numerous times or there are different men in the home. With disturbed children, you're going to have problems whatever you do." No one asks how they can be expected to deal with those problems without affecting the rest of the class, impinging on the time and effort necessary to teach them how to read, how to subtract.

Her closing words offer some tips for those about to go out into the education world to seek their fortunes. "Remember, it's more important to make friends with the janitor than the principal. Wait a while before you try to make any changes; change is politically unpopular. Keep your mouth shut and wait for your time. And don't let the bastards get you down."

Later that day I had a talk with the acting dean of the College of Education, who told me, "Our students spend four years getting a B.A. in a subject, then take a fifth year of pedagogy, learning the things teachers need to know about: growth and development, individual differences in attributes and capabilities and how they change, human assessment, cognitive strategies. These things are necessary in any form of social work."

"Then teaching is a form of social work?"

"Oh, yes," she says, and acknowledges, when the question is raised, that the necessity of effecting social change sometimes impedes learning. "But it has to happen then; you can't *not* use the schools as the agencies of social change. It's too convenient."

The problem, she thinks, is the public's evaluation. "You can't ask the schools to do nine different things and then measure only one. We've effected integration. That we have different ethnic groups together in the schools now equals a success." What happens to the life of the mind—to success in terms of academic excellence— is, we seem to agree, another matter.

"Education schools," she says, "have to deal with the problem of beginning teachers—and they are still mostly twenty-one-year-old white girls—who find themselves on their own with the worst classes in the worst schools.

"Ed schools are tightly controlled by regulatory agencies. They have almost no choice in preparatory programs. The word comes down from the legislators to the state board to the local districts. They determine the essential elements of the curriculum and the way education studies must be taught. And beginning teachers will be evaluated testing on teaching behaviors in the classroom.

"To improve learning and teaching, you need better people, and what keeps them out is lack of empowerment. Legislative threats won't do it. Based on what they've seen in their own high school situation, college freshmen don't want to go into teaching. The classroom doesn't inspire bright people to want to teach. They don't see it as a way to use their talents and abilities creatively. They see how teachers are dictated to on what they cover and how they do it. They see that the principal talks to them like children.

"If you measure the dropout rate you'll probably find that it was close to 90 percent in 1910, and it's 33 percent now. The question is, what do the dropouts do? We are in the midst of a social upheaval that's part of the transformation to the information age. We're experiencing an unprecedented rate of change."

She sees a ray of hope in the developing educational technology. Used to teach what? I ask. She talks enthusiastically about interactive computer programs, videodiscs that will teach "social skills, decision making about drugs and alcohol, put the student in the midst of a situation like a party, where he has to decide whether to take drugs, whether to drink, confront him with the consequences of his behavior, show him the reasons for ways of avoiding them. It can even," she says, seeming awed by the possibility, "insert the student's face in the picture as the actor!"

Next, the dean addresses herself to the issue of how ed schools could be made better. It's a circular problem, she says, "a catch 22." The faculties of schools of education, she maintains, are more "mixed," more uneven than those of other colleges and department. "There are a lot of weak academicians, good old boys, and there are too many schools. Sixty-seven institutions in Texas are involved in the preparation of teachers in one program area or another."

Her suggestion is to reallocate resources by selecting certain institutions to continue and reapportioning the available resources among them. "The problem is that every legislator wants to have a teacher-training institution in his district so everyone can go to one in his hometown. As things are now, you have a school somewhere with two programs and 2,000 people, and here at the University of Texas you have twenty-seven programs with 51,000 students and fifty-one faculty members. The standards are set so the bottom person in the state can pass. Quality is pushed down to the level of the least efficient component.

"The answer is to select a set of education schools in the way we have medical schools, of which there are six in the state, to set the standards for admission and for graduation high, and to support and fund them adequately. At present, ed school has the poorest funding and resources of all—lower than business, lower than engineering. The answer is to stop pouring money into poor programs with poor faculty."

For all her thoughtfulness about the issues facing educators and how they might best be addressed, and even though she has been functioning very effectively as acting dean, I am told that she is unlikely to be given the permanent appointment. The reason is that she is "not minority."

While I was on campus the school paper, *The Daily Texan,* suggested that in order not to "scare away" minority students, the university had best concern itself with dispelling its reputation as a "white" school (no concern expressed about whether it is a *good* school or not). The article implied, with the aid of graphs showing the comparatively low percentage of minority populations enrolled on this campus, that the percentage in itself demonstrated that the school was "racist." Detailing a panoply of intensive recruiting programs designed to encourage and give aid to minority students, the article suggested that these programs have not succeeded in attracting larger numbers of minority students even when they are accepted, because they are "afraid that they can't look to graduate."

The Social Studies professor seems quick-minded, with a sense of humor. Her students, on the other hand, are almost all young women—there are few men, very few Hispanics, no blacks—who would not, to put it charitably, qualify as intellectuals. In fact, "air heads" is the expression that comes to mind watching them chew gum, comb their hair, look off into space. And listening to them ask the kinds of questions that they should themselves be answering for young children.

Once again, we are preparing for a test. The professor proposes to the class to "walk you through" the distinctions they have been learning between generalizations, concepts, facts, and skills. Someone wants to know how this is different from Madeline Hunter's system. Her other professors use the Madeline Hunter format. She seems concerned that she might have to learn another whole "system."

Professor Boyd, as I'll call her, reassures her. It is all consistent, a matter of grasping the logic of teaching, seeing what needs to be taught first, what next. Several questions make it clear that some of the students don't grasp the difference between a generalization and related concepts. One wants to know where they are supposed to "get our facts from." The professor says they can get their facts from a movie, a song, a reference book, or a textbook. Their fact lesson will provide clear directions for their students in the form of handouts. And she now hands out to them such a sheet of instructions, at the same time projecting it on the overhead screen and reading to them what it says there.

These girls are nervous, querulous, defensive. Examination anxiety? She reassures them. They all understand about demonstration, guided practice, then independent practice, don't they? Glum looks. Don't they? Well, then, she will show them all this is no different from Madeline Hunter.

She shows them how what she is saying corresponds to a Madeline Hunter lesson. The professor's concern at this moment is to relieve the students' anxiety about having to learn something new. They have trouble with the simplest directions. Patiently, she goes through the description of a sample lesson they might present: showing a film on the life of Stephen F. Austin; telling their pupils what they're looking for—what facts are to be considered relevant, such as dates, the identities of individuals, their significant contributions; distributing handouts; possibly arranging for a guest speaker on the topic. She explains how to make use of the overhead projector, how to have pupils copy from it. She provides them with a sample of how to head their papers.

Nevertheless, Robin cannot quite get the series of steps involved in telling her anticipated pupils what to do. She's having trouble distinguishing the facts from the skills lessons. Patiently, the professor explains again the distinction between stating what they're studying and describing how to present it, how to fill out the cards she's asked for so she can review their grasp of lesson planning. Robin looks blank.

A student asks for an example of a "knowledge question." The answer is, "Well, an example might be how a particular teaching program—say, Widening Horizons—works."

Professor Boyd summarizes. The logical sequence of learning as developed by Bruner, by Taba. They have read about these systematizers in a textbook. Why? Why should they even know these names since they don't read the works themselves? What relation does it have to their teaching for them to know the names and the formulas and slogans? It's just something to test them on, one suspects. And in the end they may know the difference between a generalization and a concept but not the causes of the War of 1812 or the way commerce and transportation interacted in opening up the West. They haven't read either of Lincoln's inaugural speeches. They don't know how many years separated the two world wars. They don't know when the peak years of immigration occurred, or what brought the newcomers here from so many other parts of the world. Those are not things they are taught or tested on or, if they were, they have already been forgotten. Some time in the recent but already misty past, the social scientists and the educational psychologists captured the teacher-preparation field.

After class I talked with Professor Boyd, a woman with a quarter-century of experience in the school of education. She has seen fads come and go. She explains that the Madeline Hunter system has been accepted and adapted by the Texas schools—where it is called "the lesson cycle"—"because it gives them a commonly accepted set of skills that can be appraised" for purposes of the state's requirement for teacher evaluation.

I asked about the students. How have they changed over the years? She tells me about one who came to her office recently to complain about having been given a *B* for the course. Professor Boyd had felt she was stretching it at that. The young woman's writing had been no more than acceptable, her classroom contributions barely adequate. When she pointed this out to the student, her reply was, "You didn't give me a model." When Professor Boyd showed her an examination question left blank, the young woman said indignantly, "You didn't tell us that."

Boyd thinks the trouble began with the social promotion policies in the early 1960s. "It came along with busing. You couldn't fail anybody because it might warp their personalities. Now the pupil says, 'Why should I work? I'll pass anyway.' There's no challenge in the public elementary schools." She tells about a friend who teaches in a Dallas school where over half the pupils were honors graduates. "Everyone has to be perfect. We don't allow anyone the opportunity to fail. But how," she asks, "can you appreciate your successes without the possibility of failure?"

It is the learning theorists who have captured the high ground in ed schools, claiming for themselves the status of true academics, as the researchers. The "ed psych" people, as they are known to their colleagues who transmit their findings to the prospective classroom teachers, are as far from substantive knowledge (what is known, as distinct from how one gets to know things) about anything except their own field, as it is possible to be. This makes for a rather solipsistic discipline, in which specialists have more and more to say about less and less.

Impressive phrases abound in the office where I sit talking with a young professor I'll call Dr. Hayes. I am here because in the dean's letter confirming the arrangements for my visit to the school she said, "Dr. Jane Hayes has just returned from what she described as the most important and exciting conference on teacher education that she has ever attended. At the conference were the national leaders in the teacher education [sic], and Dr. Hayes said that they made some important observations and recommendations regarding the integration of what is known about learning and teaching into what is known about teacher education and schooling. I thought you might find a conversation with Dr. Hayes quite useful to you."

I did, in fact, though not in the way she meant. What I heard was a description of a presentation by education professor Lee Shulman, the gist of which, as reported by Dr. Hayes, was that "to understand teaching you have to appreciate the complex variables . . . foundation studies are like the basement the rest is built on . . . you begin with the case study presentation . . . analyze student and teacher interaction on video . . . ask what is the stance of the learner . . . what could the teacher do in this situation . . . reflect on the variables . . ."

A concrete example of a practical use here: "Analyzing the philosophy behind the policy statements of lawmakers. Does the curriculum fit the policy? How can it be interpreted at different levels? Rather than reading what Plato did, this kind of activity is useful in decision making. It reflects reality just now. That's the way philosophy of education courses should be taught."

And now we not only have the philosophy of history, literature, or science displaced by the philosophy of education, but the philosophy of education itself is to drop historical reference for "reality just now." How will it be understood? In what perspective? That's not a hard question to answer: in the light of agreed-on political goals. Lacking any tradition, with no sustaining belief in the value of a liberal education, the "ed psych" learning theorists have no authority to appeal to except "research," most of which is trivial when it isn't obvious, and much of which is in the service of political aims rather than objective knowledge.

PART SEVEN

Back East

15

❧ ——— ❧

New Jersey's Alternative

The Way Out?

New Jersey's Provisional Teacher Program was in its fifth year when I saw it in operation in the summer of 1989. A pioneer on the alternate certification route, the program takes eligible college graduates who want to teach and immediately puts them into a classroom, where they have full-time one-on-one supervision by an experienced mentor teacher for a month, and less intense but close supervision by a support team for a full school year. During that time, they also take 200 hours of instruction on evenings and weekends in teaching methods and techniques and related matters. They learn about classroom management, lesson planning, discipline, use of the prescribed curriculum, and how to find and use other kinds of resources. At the end of a year of full-time teaching, if they have passed the National Teacher Examination at the required state level and satisfactorily completed the 200 hours of course work, they are eligible for regular certification in the subject that was their college major if they plan to teach in high school, or in generic teaching if they'll be teaching elementary grades. The point is that they have to have majored in some subject area, not in education.

The purpose of the program is to get people into the classroom who might not think the investment of time and money required by traditional graduate education programs worth their while. The real question is whether such alternatives attract not only more but better teachers.

The group I sat in with were intelligent, highly motivated, and high-spirited. It was now the end of the school year, and they were sharing anecdotes—horror stories about children, parents, and principals as well as moments of triumph—and making plans for an end-of-year celebration complete with T-shirts that would read "NJ Provisional Teacher Program—The Road Less Taken." They seemed to have acquired a grasp of how to juggle the many responsibilities of a classroom teacher and to be facing what lay ahead for them with enthusiasm. The only trouble with them was that they didn't seem to know very much more than the graduate ed students I'd seen and talked with.

A young man whose bookish demeanor and interest in teaching English in high school seemed at first glance to be impressive said about the difficulty of teaching both writing skills and grammar: "It's hard, hard to . . . like, disseminate?—is that the word I want, disseminate?—mix together . . ." He pauses, evidently at a loss, and the lecturer offers, "Integrate?" Relieved, he says, "Yes, integrate."

Other locutions from a single evening's output: "One of the kids are in the hallway . . . If you aks other teachers . . . Her father was like puttin' her down . . . I be doing the planning . . . I'm not going to argue with no parent." These are the words of men and women, white and black, all of them college graduates who are going to be teachers. When I expressed mild surprise at what I'd heard here to one of the administrators of the program, she replied somewhat wryly, "Colloquial English is the thing now," adding, "the grammar you and I learned isn't taught anymore." She also told me that some of these provisional teachers, and this surprised me, "were superstars of their graduating classes from good colleges, including some Ivy League schools."

During a typical school year in the Provisional Teacher Program, one evening was devoted to testing and measurement instruments. Copies of various kinds of tests were distributed and discussed with the provisional teachers. Afterward, they practiced discussing test results in a parent–teacher conference. They took turns being the teacher with the lecturer of the evening, an education faculty member at one of the state colleges with years of high-school teaching experience, playing the role of the parent. In another class, they were asked to formulate their educational philosophy, then to compare it with that of their school district. In another, they acquainted themselves with the various audiovisual aids that might be available in their school and how each of them might be used. Still another class dealt with how different learning theories might be applied to distinctive classroom situations. All of these hours were devoted to something of immediate practical use to the classroom teacher.

On one summer evening I sat in with a group that met in a stifling classroom in the high school of a small New Jersey town. They had come from cities and suburbs where they were teaching elementary and high school classes. There were more women than men, and more whites than blacks, but more men and more blacks than in most education classes I'd been in. I had been told that one of the effects of this program had been to attract increasing numbers of minority students—22 percent, as compared with 10 percent of the state and 5 percent of the national enrollment in teacher training. "They may not think of teaching while they're in school," one of the program administrators said of the black and Hispanic students, "and then they graduate into the real world and decide they'd like to teach."

The crash course that would enable them to do so with a minimum of delay and expense was led on this evening by a lecturer from a state college with many years of high-school teaching experience behind him. He spent the first hour and a half on the topic of planning, talking about the different ways in which a high school teacher concerned with graduation requirements in his subject and an elementary teacher concerned with an entire spectrum of subjects both had to plan their objectives in content and skills for September to June, then for each marking period, finally for every single day, and how their goals and expectations should be set, evaluated, and revised when necessary. "You can't just have an idea of what you're going to cover over the year and then wing it day by day, figuring you'll get there somehow. If you do that you're neglecting your professional responsibilities. And when you bring the day's lesson to closure," he reminds them, "you have to have a way of evaluating what they've understood."

As the evening progressed, judging by the response of the class, they were learning a good deal that would really be useful in teaching. The comments of both lecturer and class actually reflected the realities of the world of the schoolroom.

"Judy, as a fourth-grade teacher you have to cover the whole nine yards of subjects: English—well, they call that language arts now—spelling, writing, vocabulary—they don't learn to diagram sentences anymore, do they, it's a shame—reading, math, science, social studies . . .

"I remember when we were first married my wife taught sixth grade, and she'd start planning and reading and grading on Sunday when we got home from church and it would take up every moment from the time she got home from school until late every night up till Friday, when she'd crash."

Martha, who's black and teaching in an inner-city elementary school, complains about textbooks: "I wish they'd get a *writer* to write them. The way they're written, they make the history so *boring*."

The lecturer agrees. "It's not just the style, there are no *ideas* in them. They should talk about things like the effect of the frontier on the American spirit. Kids can deal with that."

Linda says, "You start at the beginning of September with ten kids and you end up with forty. You better not write the names in ink in your grade book, they come and go so fast."

The lecturer nods. "And you've got paperwork up the kazoo. You have to fill out a form for everything. And meetings. The beginning-of-the-year 'Let's Get 'Em' meeting. The Association meeting. The district meeting on drugs and alcohol that's required by law now . . ."

"What's the first thing you want to try to achieve in September?" he asks them. Laura answers immediately: "Order." Mona says, "Getting to know them, who they are."

Meanwhile, Carol, who teaches physical education, wants to share with the rest of us her goal for the new school year, which is to think of "less competitive games. Show you can have fun without having winners and losers."

After the break the subject was discipline. What to do about chronically tardy kids? "Write the parents a note and tell them the latest educational research shows kids who come to school on time do 95 percent better . . ." After the laughter, Diane persists. What about giving out on-time stamps? No good. It makes the children who don't get them feel bad about themselves. Maybe the kid has a parent who can't get out of bed in the morning. It's not the kid's fault. Avoid confrontations. If a kid habitually comes to school unprepared? If he doesn't bring a pencil, lend him one. Or rent him one. Maybe have him leave a shoe in place of the pencil, get it back when he returns the pencil. Avoid confrontation. Maybe he'll remember next time. It's hard to get them to pay attention. How do you get them to focus so you can teach? Send troublemakers to the assistant principal? No good. He may not back you up, and then where are you? After-school detention? "That's not always a punishment. For some of these kids, nobody's home. Being with you is wonderful." Make them work during detention? Make them sit still and do nothing?

The talk turns to violence and the movement for conflict resolution in urban schools. Instead of the principal or vice principal imposing discipline (it can get confrontational), "a student team might adjudicate fights."

Nina tells about a fight that broke out between two girls in the junior high school where she is teaching. "One of them was banging the other's head on the floor and she could have cracked it wide open. Not one adult made a move. Not one. The assistant principal was right there, too. I got in between them and stopped it and took the one of them down to the AP's office. And he's like, oh, you're brave!"

Donna speaks up. "I don't know what to do. I have kids in my class who can't speak, can't move. I have others who can read and do multiplication. In the same group." At this, Elena turns to her and says, "I have a blind, deaf child. I don't know what to do with him. I just go over and touch him every once in a while." For a minute, nobody says anything. Then the lecturer breaks the silence. "None of us can imagine," he says quietly, "at least I can't imagine—what it must be like not to be able to see, to hear . . ." All of us must be wondering the same things. What it's like for the teacher, for Elena. What can she do for this child? How much of her energy, the resources needed to teach the children able to learn from her, is spent. Is it worthwhile, or a waste?

After the class, I went up to the lecturer. I wanted to tell him how much I had enjoyed the class. He was apologetic; he wanted me to know he'd read Goodlad. "Too much teacher talk," he said ruefully. "I did too much of the talking today. Why should they listen to *me* all the time?" He thought, he said, that cooperative learning was a good idea. An idea whose time had come—surely I could never disagree with that.

Some time after I'd visited the alternative program in New Jersey, I attended a national conference on alternative teacher certification convened in Washington, D.C., by the Department of Education's Office of Educational Research and Improvement of Practice.

The New Jersey people put their case first and the early sessions were characterized by their almost evangelical enthusiasm. They had found a way to improve the quality of people going into teaching, and they were here to spread the word among other education professionals. They must have known they would face a hostile phalanx of entrenched ed school aparatchiks, to whose power and prestige they constituted a threat, but I was unprepared for the resistance that would be put up later in the day to their approach to the question of what a beginning teacher should be expected to know.

The New Jerseyans' answer, of course, was that if you knew your subject, you could learn the pedagogy while you were on the job—that ideally the learning and the doing should take place together. They told how, when they first announced the plan to recruit teachers from among those just out of college and from the business community, providing mentors to coach them in the classroom, local newspapers predicted dire results. One indignant editorial writer said they would wind up with "dogs, drunks, or derelicts." Others warned of "pointy-headed intellectuals" who would be insensitive, uncaring.

New Jersey's Commissioner of Education was able to report that most critics were won over in the first six months of the program. "We brought in top-flight faculty. Board [of Education] members and legislators could see it was a grass-roots experiment that worked." In the four years since the program had been under way, he pointed out, it had not been necessary for the state to issue one single emergency certificate. All of the teachers in the alternate-route program were now from among those scoring in the top fourth of the National Teacher Examination, and their scores in English, social studies, math, and science were higher than those of the traditional-route teachers, those with degrees in education. But those had moved up too, presumably because of the competition. It was that competition which could break the monopoly of the mediocre put in place by the education school establishment.

The competition consisted of members of Phi Beta Kappa and Magna Cum Laude graduates of Ivy League colleges, of an editor with years of publishing experience, an art curator from Yale, a religion major from Dartmouth, recent graduates of Williams, Stanford, Northwestern, Brown, and other schools as far away as London, of a lawyer, a playwright, a critic, someone who had experience in educational television, another in government, another in engineering. Technological expertise, community activities, and public service were represented by such people as an honors graduate of Harvard and a former teacher of history and mathematics, another of naval science and several of various languages. It was, the Commissioner announced with justifiable pride, "a gold mine of talent."

Questions were raised by members of the audience. What was the percentage of minorities among the recruits? Twenty-one percent, most of them recruited in colleges. How many dropped out after the first year? Four percent (in contrast to 18 percent of "regular" first-year teachers). The low dropout rate was attributed to the high degree of collegial support provided by the mentoring system. The principal and three teachers in the school provide a "support team" to counsel the new teacher and offset the feeling so many novice teachers complain of—being "lonely in the classroom."

Someone referred to the recruits as "unqualified." That was the big question. What makes a teacher qualified, or as members of this audience liked to put it, a "professional." Having been licensed automatically as a graduate of an accredited school of education? Having paid one's dues by going through the bureaucratic maze of red tape? Belonging to a union?

Recruits to the program must have college degrees with an academic major, pass a written test, and then receive eighty hours of intensive instruction before taking on a classroom. "It works," is the simple summing-up of New Jersey's top education official.

By the end of 1989, twenty-two other states had established some kind of alternate route to teaching credentials. Panelists from some of them talked about their experiments with alternative certification. Classes in a highly effective special school for gifted students in Louisiana are taught by a former attorney, an engineer, a pharmacist, an artist, a writer. None has had any education courses.

That, precisely, remains a sticking point. Questioners ask in baleful tones about the number of "minorities" among the recruits, and about what proportion of them go into inner-city schools. (Everything in the educationist mentality today is oriented to inner-city schools and their problematic students. There is an unquestioned assumption that it is the obligation of every teacher to take on those problems, to be first and foremost a social worker coping with the urban underclass. The meanest tones are used to speak of teachers who "desert" in order to teach in suburban schools. Nobody dares to ask why they should not, why it is unacceptable to want to teach motivated students, to provide the stimulation out of which comes the stretching of minds, the intellectual creativity necessary if a culture is to produce anything in the way of novelty, invention, leadership. To ask such questions is to be branded insensitive at best, racist at worst.)

Delegates from other states are heard from. In Texas there are so many applicants—from fifty in the first year the program was announced to over five thousand in the next—they are able to take only "the cream of the crop." We hear about computer programmers, Broadway dancers, medical doctors, who are "more mature, more motivated," who make a conscious commitment in changing professions. Dallas and Houston's Independent School District are taking advantage of the fifty-year-old educated adult with life experience and of the edge his twenty years with IBM has given him over the graduate with four years of college who often goes into teaching by default.

In the next breath—taking the requisite loyalty oath—the Texas delegates hasten to assure everyone that these stalwarts are without exception "committed to the urban inner-city experience," to special education, to bilingual education. We hear about the NASA computer programmer who wanted "to work with people, not machines" in the schools of Pennsylvania, which has had alternative certification since 1969 and actually has a surplus of science and math teachers. Someone from Texas suggests sending a few there, where they have a shortage of science and math teachers. And once again we hear about the "critical shortage of minority science and math teachers" all over the country. "Intellectual achievement and life experience are all very well"—the inevitable question from the floor—"but what about loving and caring?"

At least it's almost time for lunch.

The president-elect of the American Association of Colleges for Teacher Education asks for "quality control," suggesting that alternative programs should be monitored by others than those who run then, i.e., by their arch rivals, the schools of education. Someone points out (a fact that has indeed gone unremarked by me) that a bachelor's degree is not necessarily a bachelor of arts degree—it can be a professional degree, for instance in engineering, and is therefore no guarantee of a background in liberal arts or of any particular distribution of credits such as would insure even a minimum acquaintance with history, literature, languages.

Finally someone asks about the children. How are they performing? The question refers to pupils in Houston's inner-city schools. Have they been helped or hurt? The answer is inconclusive ("no significant differences in student achievement"). Everyone is free to go off to lunch with the opinions with which he came.

In the afternoon the crème de la crème of the ed school establishment took over. First to speak was a young woman whose voice and bearing exuded such confidence in her own charm and in the rightness of her position that she need hardly have told us that she was "a charismatic teacher." And went on to show us. An assistant professor at the prestigious midwestern university whose college of education has become synonymous with the movement to "professionalize" teaching, she directs student teachers and is herself an elementary classroom teacher. In her third-grade classroom, she proudly told us, she waited for the children to get the idea themselves that a piece of graph paper corresponding to the square-patterned floor of the classroom could be used to make a diagram of the room. "It took them three days to figure it out." She showed no hesitation at all in telling us that she had flunked the student teacher (she recounted with relish the number of degrees he held and where they were from) who taught in a traditional way, not "my way." He didn't seem to get the idea that the children should "organize the concepts" themselves, which would lead to "deeper understanding," and he had failed to see that "we are dealing with a new kind of population that can't learn in the old status-quo ways." The audience still reeling from this bit of wisdom, she went on to say that "a good teacher has to be a scholar of teaching, not a scholar of history" [or English, or science] "in order to teach my way." Anyone who thought she deserved some kind of prize for arrogance hadn't reckoned on the speaker who followed her.

Like Professor Charisma, he was a member of the establishment in good standing, an official of a large and wealthy foundation that has funded and directed much of the research and reporting on schools and teachers since the 1960s. He said he was going to read us some rules of good teaching. A good teacher, he read out in a deadpan voice, corrects mistakes right away; groups children in small homogenous groups; defines, explains, and gives examples; uses drills and practice; requires students to raise their hands before answering; praises students who do well. . . . "Teaching this way," he announced clearly and with emphasis, "is *unethical* and *immoral*." Why? "Because we may be teaching disproportionately those who need most to know what we have to teach." And "teaching rests on a foundation of development and psychology of learning."

Dr. Foundation next declared, "I think about poor and disadvantaged children. Society has an obligation to them." From his tone it was clear that he had not even considered the possibility that others who think about them might have different ideas about how best to serve them.

"Teachers," he declaimed, "need to know *how* to teach, not something to teach." To which Professor Charisma added, "What I know has nothing to do with whether I'm a good teacher."

Among comments from the floor were those made by Dean Hawley of Peabody College, arguably the nation's premier undergraduate school of education. What he had to say was, "You can't improve teaching just by improving teacher education. There are too many other things going on [in the society and in the schools]." Teaching, he asserted, is not "a learned field" like law or medicine [to be mastered by study]. "You become a good teacher practicing teaching in the classroom."

These rather mild and not unreasonable statements of opinion differing from theirs so enraged Professor Charisma and Dr. Foundation that they moved from the arena of civil discourse to ad hominem attack. Dr. F. called the somewhat surprised-looking dean "anti-intellectual" and lectured him in a reproachful tone to the effect that "we owe more to poor youngsters . . . the ones most likely to get bad teachers." Professor C. put her oar in with, "People learn in different ways. We have to prepare teachers to deal with different cognitive styles. . . . Paper and pencil tests are useless for the kinds of understanding required of a teacher. . . . A teacher should always be thinking about teaching." Always? Never even a little about the subject being taught? No, it's only "commitment and care" for children that count.

"My graduate students," Professor Charisma confides, "think a teacher is supposed to be the person with the answer. They come to me with the attitude that says, If I don't know, I'll go off and get the answer." Her tone makes it clear that she quickly disabuses them. Dr. Foundation asserts that "alternative certification is a quick-fix solution. It will just paper over the problems. We have to attract older people, but we should make them go the same route. We seem to be saying," he sums up with a smirk, "that smart people don't go into teacher education, dumb ones do, and the problem is to get the smart ones into teaching." He gets a laugh at this from his audience, but the laughter is more conspiratorial than cheerful—and may haunt us all for a long time to come.

In Conclusion

Teaching, Knowledge, and the Public Good

Wherever I went in my year of crisscrossing the country from one college or university to another, whether in public institutions or on private campuses, in urban centers or rural areas, I found a striking degree of conformity about what is considered to be the business of schools and the job of teachers. Everywhere I visited, in new concrete structures and old stone halls of ivy, among undergraduates or older students, I heard the same things over and over again. And failed to hear others.

Everywhere, I found idealistic people eager to do good. And everywhere, I found them being told that the way to do good was to prepare themselves to cure a sick society. To become therapists, as it were, specializing in the pathology of education. Almost nowhere did I find teachers of teachers whose emphasis was on the measurable learning of real knowledge.

Hardly anywhere did I find a sense that any kind of knowledge is valuable in itself or more valuable than any other, a fact which ceased to surprise me once it became clear that among teacher-educators today, the goal of schooling is not considered to be instructional, let alone intellectual, but political. The aim is not to produce individuals capable of effort and mastery, but to make sure everyone gets a passing grade. The school is to be remade into a republic of feelings—as distinct from a republic of learning—where everyone can feel he deserves an *A*.

In order to create a more just society, future teachers are being told, they must focus on the handicapped of all kinds—those who have the greatest difficulties in learning, whether because of physical problems or emotional ones, congenital conditions or those caused by lack of stimulation in the family or lack of structure in the home— in order to have everyone come out equal in the end. What matters is not to teach any particular subject or skill, not to preserve past accomplishments or stimulate future achievements, but to give to all that stamp of approval that will make them "feel good about themselves." Self-esteem has replaced understanding as the goal of education.

Thus the education of teachers has not only been politicized; it has been reoriented toward what is euphemistically called "special education." The ed school culture today is dominated by the diagnosis of learning pathologies and the development of learning therapies— methods for dealing with, if not actually teaching anything to, the various kinds of children with learning difficulties. It is no longer acceptable to think in terms of different systems for different kinds of students of differing degrees of ability and motivation, since it is no longer learning that is at the center of the educational enterprise but, increasingly, the promotion of "equity."

Where the goal of the teacher is to promote self-esteem in everyone in equal measure, performance will no longer count for much. Nor will it seem to matter much what is taught. What is coming increasingly to fill the time and occupy the attention of those being trained to teach are those "instructional strategies" that will enable them to cope with the various kinds of handicapped students they must be prepared to pass along through the same system, without suggesting that they may not be performing at the same level as the more able students. What happens to those more capable or motivated students is hardly anyone's concern.

Where the purpose of the educational system is to promote "self-esteem" regardless of actual accomplishment, substitutes for accomplishment must be found. In the current political climate the chief substitute for measurable individual achievement has become emphasis on the (superior) characteristics of the racial or ethnic subgroup to which one belongs. As a result, the emphasis is shifted from the common values of the larger society to identification with the special interests—and perceived grievances—of this or that racial

or ethnic groups. And membership in a particular group becomes a more important qualification for teaching than expertise or experience. Thus the ubiquitous concern in teacher education for more "minority teachers" rather than for more good teachers of science, math, history, or literature, no matter who they are or where they come from.

As separatism is emphasized and content trivialized, accountability is ignored. Testing, in the ed school world, is almost as bad as "tracking." No one wants to know the actual results of these policies—whether they really help poor students, how they affect the bright and the gifted. The ed school establishment is more concerned with politics—both academic and ideological—than with learning.

Since what matters is not whether or not anyone has learned anything, but that no one fail to pass, the threshold is lowered as required for almost anyone to get by—in the schooling of teachers as well as in the schools in which they will teach. After all, special methods, not specific subject matter, is what they will be expected to demonstrate.

Meanwhile, any criticism of this state of affairs is met with the charge of elitism or, worse still, racism. No one in the ed school universe dares publicly to advocate a curriculum that resists the "cooperative learning," the "multicultural" and "global" approach that is often a thinly disguised rejection of individualistic democratic values and institutions and of the very idea that underneath all our variety of backgrounds we Americans have been and should continue to become one nation, one culture. That aim and, in fact, any knowledge or appreciation of that common culture and the institutions from which it derives, I found to be conspicuously absent in the places that prepare men and women to teach in our country's public schools today.

The only way to have better schools is to get better teachers. We will never improve schooling, no matter how many reports by commissions, panels, and committees prescribe whatever changes in how the schools are structured or how reading or math is taught, until we improve teacher education. What we have today are teacher-producing factories that process material from the bottom of the heap and turn out models that perform, but not well enough. What we need is to sacrifice quantity for quality, both in the institutions that educate teachers and their graduates. The institutions should be essentially academic, and their graduates should be judged by how much they know, not just how much they care.

If we expect to attract better applicants, they will have to be able to look forward to being paid well; to being given a measure of independence from administrators, politicians, and special-interest groups; and to being able to advance in their profession according to their achievement in a more narrowly defined job. That means as teachers of reading and writing skills, of history, science, math, literature—not as social workers, baby-sitters, policemen, diagnosticians, drug counselors, psychotherapists. They will have to be able to anticipate the challenge presented by gifted students, and not be expected to devote most of their attention and efforts to remediation for the slow, the weak, the apathetic, the hostile. That does *not* mean we give up trying to educate those pupils, it only means we stop trying to do so at the expense of those who can and want to learn and give teachers the opportunity of helping them do it.

But we will never have better teachers until the quality of education at our colleges and universities improves, providing better educated candidates for teaching as for all else. More exacting college and university entrance requirements would necessitate higher standards for high schools in order to meet them, and eventually for elementary schools, which would have to provide literacy and numeracy, in order to prepare for high school. Better schools and better teachers are inextricable. As long as colleges accept high school graduates only 30 percent of whom have had four years of English and three years each of math, science, and social studies, their degrees will mean little. A more exacting core curriculum in our high schools is indispensable for the preparation of those who would be teachers. That means no longer automatically passing students from one elementary grade to the next regardless of performance in order to bolster their self-esteem. It means our college and university students would no longer be learning things they should have learned in high school—and sometimes even before that.

At present, our teacher-training institutions, the schools, colleges, and departments of education on campuses across the country, are producing for the classrooms of America experts in methods of teaching with nothing to apply those methods to. Their technique is abundant, their knowledge practically nonexistent. A mastery of instructional strategies, an emphasis on educational psychology, a familiarity with pedagogical philosophies have gradually taken the place of a knowledge of history, literature, science, and mathematics. Little wonder then that in so many of our high schools those subjects have given way to courses in filmmaking, driver education, and marriage and family living. Neither possessing nor respecting knowledge themselves, how can teachers imbue their students with any enthusiasm for it? Nowhere in America today is intellectual life deader than in our schools—unless it is in our schools of education.

Next to the media in general and television in particular, our schools of education are the greatest contributor to the "dumbing down" of America. They have been transformed into agencies for social change, mandated to achieve equality at all costs, an equality not of opportunity but of outcome. No one can be tested because no one must fail.

At the same time they denigrate the history of the institutions that made us the nation that we are, a nation that they must surely notice people want to come to from all over the world and that few leave voluntarily for other parts. While faced with educating the waves of immigrants who persist in wanting to come and live here, they misprize the Western civilization that defined our political institutions and the cultural ideas and artifacts it gave rise to. They have moved from the ideal of integration back to separatism. They have replaced a civic ethos with an emphasis on one's special racial, ethnic, or linguistic group or on one's self, on "multicultural" and bilingual education and "self-esteem." They demean the immigrant and the poor by saying they can't become part of what has gone before and enriched others, can't appreciate the accummulated wisdom of the past, that we have to ask less of them, bend the rules for them, if they are to enter the mainstream. They are too impatient or have too little confidence in them to encourage the underachieving to work to better their situations while educating the next generation for further success. And ultimately they leave them hopeless in the face of the disappearance of the family structure that nourished such patterns in previous generations.

We have set aside equality of opportunity—the idea of opening doors to anyone—and replaced it with equality of results. Everyone has to pass, to be promoted, to enter college, to get a degree. And so a degree has come to mean little more than that one is alive and has applied for one.

That is why alternative certification programs are no panacea for the ills that affect our schools. The good news about these programs is that they provide a way to circumvent the unnecessary baggage imposed by the ed school curriculum, leaving room for substantive learning instead. The bad news is that the people coming out of these programs are only as good as the education they themselves have had—which brings us back full circle to the cumulative inadequacies of an educational system whose erosion of standards has left the average college degree meaning very little and the average college graduate not particularly rich in substantive learning.

Another solution that has been proposed for the problem of quality control of teachers is a national proficiency examination designed to function like the national board exams in medicine and the bar exams in law, a somewhat questionable analogy, since teaching is not a profession with its own specific body of knowledge. The idea is to establish uniform criteria for selection, training, and placing of qualified teachers by means of standard assessment measures for entrance, during, and at the end of their academic and "clinical" preparation. This, it is said, would make teaching a more selective occupation and provide a rationale for higher salaries and career advancement based on proven ability rather than automatic seniority.

Is the attempt to "professionalize" the already overbureaucratized and unionized teaching occupation a good idea? If we have learned anything from the social history of this country in the last half-century, it is that policies and programs often have unforeseen and unintended results. It is possible that legislating standards for teachers will attract some who are better qualified; at the same time it might discourage those maverick adults from outside the system who would like to teach and would be good at it but are unwilling to go through the process of meeting arcane and time-consuming certification requirements. Why make it harder for talented and knowledgeable individuals to be absorbed into the system by extending those requirements on a national basis? Why not let local school districts respond to their needs as they arise? This could be done using their own selection criteria and procedures for on-the-job appraisals.

Everything they need to know about how to teach could be learned by intelligent people in a single summer of well-planned instruction. As it now stands, only individuals with three years of teaching experience are eligible to take the tests for board certification, which virtually closes the door to those outside the existing ed school–state certification route. What is needed is a truly independent board, independent both of the educational bureaucrats and the government. Its members ought to be liberal educators, not union officials, and its money ought to come from the private sphere rather than legislatively dictated federal funds.

We have impoverished ourselves as a nation by failing to nurture a liberally well-educated citizenry that includes a scientifically and technologically literate labor force. To do so we would have to put in place a curriculum that begins in the earliest grades to teach children history and literature, mathematics and science, music and foreign languages. And to do that we would need to see to it that all teachers have a solid liberal education that includes all of the above.

The graduates of those institutions which educate teachers are a long way from fitting that description today.

In a work such as this, one ought to be expected to follow criticism with constructive suggestions, not just to say how bad things are but how they might be made better. My tour of the ed school world left me depressed about our country's future, but not entirely demoralized. The nature of the problem, once defined, suggested its own solution. It is a very tall order, and my optimism is not exactly boundless where it comes to the question of whether there is a national will—even a national interest—sufficient to turn things around. But there is a way to do it.

It is a matter—and nothing less will do it—of raising standards all along the spectrum of schooling from first grade to graduate study. It means redefining the purpose of schooling again, from primarily agencies of political change and social work to primarily transmitters of the culture and of the kinds of knowledge and skills required to extend it. Only in that way can we break into the cycle of pupil-to-teacher-to-pupil in order to increase learning in America and have a more informed and more productive citizenry, men and women who possess and value knowledge and use it to lead richer lives and enrich the future through study and invention, exploration and interpretation.

We need to upgrade standards throughout the educational system, from elementary school and secondary school all the way up through college and university. Education and public policy expert Chester E. Finn of Vanderbilt University has suggested a national common curriculum—a core of learning including reading and writing ability, competency in math and understanding of science, knowledge of history and literature, that every student should be required to demonstrate in order to be admitted to college. The specifies of the curriculum and supplementary subjects would remain a matter for individual schools and communities to decide on. But there should be clear and testable norms. No child should be passed from one grade to another without demonstrating by means of a dependable system of testing that he or she knows what is supposed to be learned in that grade. There is nothing wrong with "teaching to the test" if the test is a good one, if it tests what matters, and if teachers have flexibility in preparing for it—in how they teach students to write a clear paragraph, relate events in history, or solve an equation.

As in other industrialized countries, students should have to take meaningful courses and make good grades in them in order to pass and go on to higher education and desirable jobs. Certainly it would provide us with better teachers, because it would raise the level of the pool of applicants. And as in those other countries so far ahead of us today in what their students learn and what their citizens can produce, there would have to be different channels of schooling for different students with different interests and abilities, each of them open to everyone, but none of them "dumbed down" so as to fit everyone. And every individual would be assured of an education that neither pushes some out because it is designed for a level of performance they cannot meet or holds some back because it has been designed with the least able in mind, the inevitable consequence of insisting on artificially equalized achievement rather than equality of opportunity.

weak curriculum

In 1989 the National Endowment for the Humanities reported that it is possible to graduate from 77 percent of the nation's colleges without ever studying a foreign language, from 45 percent without ever taking a course in American or English literature, from 41 percent without studying mathematics and from 38 percent without ever having taken a history course.

Not everyone wants or needs to study chemistry or classics beyond a certain point. We need to make sure that everyone with an interest and the potential ability has the opportunity, but there is a limit to how much we can equalize the life circumstances of every individual and we cannot pretend that there is not wide variation in individual endowment, in inclination and ability—even within families, let alone larger groups. We can, in line with legislation now pending in Congress, establish teaching scholarships and fund a teacher corps to encourage people to work with the least advantaged students so as to help those who want help, but we must stop corrupting the entire educational system by lowering standards so that the least able and the least motivated can be said to "pass."

If teachers themselves have had to work hard at learning to get where they are, there is more chance children will begin to learn early in life that success is related to effort, something the pupils of other countries who so consistently outperform American students know well. They are expected to do well, and by and large they do. Their teachers do not encourage them to think of themselves as victims nor do they worry overmuch about their self-esteem. They worry instead about understanding and remembering. Some of them manage to understand and remember enough to deal with sophisticated mathematical and scientific material at an age when too many American students are dropping algebra in favor of driver education. The outcome has much to do with character, something that it used to be considered part of a teacher's qualifications to possess and to demonstrate.

In addition to upgrading the entire system by raising standards both for entry and exit, we should separate the training of teachers of the very young, where nurturing capacity is appropriate, from that of older students, where subject mastery counts most. Primary teachers may be caregivers, but while these categories need not necessary be mutually exclusive, teachers of older students should be intellectually able. In a world in which there is a lot to learn, they must know something well and be able to teach it effectively.

The essential thing is to engage the child in the learning process, and the best hope for doing that is the teacher who has something to teach and can convey, inspire, and motivate the child to learn it—in the earliest years by playing both on children's desire to please her and their satisfaction in their own mastery, their sense of accomplishment, and in the later years by engaging older children in ways that make ideas intrinsically interesting to them.

There is room for an upgraded undergraduate education major for teachers of primary/elementary grades only. However, a meaningful liberal arts degree in an academic subject followed by a period of supervised practice teaching ought to be the requirement for high school teachers.

While there is a measure of altruism involved in choosing to teach the young, and a degree of gratification to be gotten from it, teachers have to be able to expect, like anyone else, to be compensated in money and prestige and decision-making power for doing their job well. Career ladders, mentor teacher positions, and merit pay are means to this end. If we want to attract better people, and keep them from deserting the classroom for the administrative office, we have to offer them better prospects both in terms of salary and satisfaction.

The greatest complaint teachers have isn't low pay but the humiliations to which they are subject by a large, inflexible bureaucracy which stifles their initiative—the very thing we want to encourage in the service of the curriculum. Ideally, there would be a core curriculum from the earliest grades on, with decisions about how best to implement it made at the classroom level by individual teachers. As long as there is accountability in the form of an examination system—one leaning heavily on written expression and not just on objective tests—for appraising outcome in student achievement, teachers need to be able to make use of their own discretion. A good part of the fun of teaching—what makes it a pleasure and not a chore—lies in the ability to exercise that discretion. A student teacher in a Detroit inner-city school, full of imaginative ideas about how to reach her pupils but forced to follow someone else's lesson plan using a prescribed textbook and worksheets, said to me, "I might as well be on the assembly line." She and others like her will either move to a school in another district or leave the field.

And last but hardly least is the need to remove from the job some of its nonteaching aspects and make it a more possible profession. The kind of people we ought to be attracting are interested primarily in imparting knowledge and incidentally in contributing to young people's character through their example. Those who want to be social workers, policemen, physical or psychological therapists, or child-care workers should enter those fields, which should be separated from that of teaching. At the very least, a teacher should be able to count on the fact that her pupils are amenable to learning what she has to teach.

A measure of dignity for the classroom teacher could be ensured by such things as smaller classes in the early grades, teams of teachers trading insights and help with problems, mentor teachers to guide novices, and paraprofessionals or teaching interns to help with all the housekeeping chores that secretaries or aides can do just as well.

No amount of restructuring or empowerment, no amount of money spent on salaries or programs, will make much difference until we place knowledge itself at the center of the educational enterprise. At the present time, knowledge—real knowledge in the form of facts, not "thinking skills" or feelings of self-worth—is about the least concern of the professional education industry. It despises "mere facts," chronology, traditions, rules, memorization, practice—all of which are dirty words in education today. It prizes "cognitive skills," self-determination, creative thinking. As though anything really creative could go on in an empty head. But what choice is there when teachers themselves don't know beans about anything? The only possible fallback position is the progressive emphasis on being a "facilitator" of "cognitive strategies" for problem solving. This trend, fashionable in schools, colleges, and departments of education all over the country, along with the preference for self-expression over self-control, is a particularly cruel disservice to the many disadvantaged youngsters who are being deprived of the very habits and background knowledge that could enable them to make it in the modern world. For all our children, it is a catastrophe.

How to teach English literature should be the concern of professors of English, not experts in curriculum and instruction. The methodology can best be integrated with the subject itself, with the subject as the main focus, not the methodology. Everything you need to know about how to teach English—that can be taught didactically—can be learned within the framework of an undergraduate English major. What can't be learned that way is most of what counts, and it is learned in context, on the job, by trial and error with an experienced teacher looking over one's shoulder and offering pointers. A professor of English can suggest ways of making Chaucer come alive for tenth-graders. A mentor teacher can show how it's done. The new teacher can try things out. These are all useful. What is not useful is a course in theory divorced from the daily practice. How you teach *Moby Dick* or binomial theory requires some art, some individual style and judgment in the interaction between a teacher and a specific set of individual pupils. It requires being at home enough with the subject matter and alert enough to the responses of the students to have considerable latitude in how one teaches each lesson each day.

Those who call for higher standards are accused of being discriminatory—elitist, if not racist. Of course, standards imply having to meet them, and some will do so while others will not. As long as success or failure depends on effort and achievement and no one is excluded from the chance to make that effort and achieve the best results of which he is capable, the criticisms are misleading. The real racists are those who assume members of minority groups are not capable of the same effort and achievement as anyone else, that they need different rules. So convinced are they that members of minority groups will fail that they are prepared to change the rules for everyone to ensure the same outcome for everyone. It is a low outcome, and it demeans the minorities, the rest of the society, and the very idea of education, which if it means anything means possessing knowledge.

That is what schools are for, because that is what schools can do. They can transmit knowledge—of how to read and compute, of what the sciences tell us about the nature of the world and what the philosophers and poets tell us about the nature of men and women, of what countries have in common and how they differ, what a string quartet, a cathedral, a fresco are made of. What they can't do—or can't do well—is what families, psychotherapists, ministers, social workers, and police are trained to do. What the politicization of the schools has led to is the usurpation of the teacher's role by that of the so-called helping professions.

We must finally recognize that we may not be able to educate everyone in the same way. Individuals differ widely in many ways. To suit their education to their interests and capacities is not to assign any of them to the ash heap. On the contrary, it will make their schooling more useful in terms of their lives after school and make it possible to educate those who are capable of more and whose talents and energies are too often wasted in the present craze for an equity that pretends there are no meaningful differences in how much children can learn.

To say that every child or young man or woman has the same capacity and the same motivation for learning, and that it is the fault of schools and teachers that so many do not, is to be blind to the realities of human life as it is being lived all around us in America today. And this applies as much to the suburban as the inner-city cultures, to the wasting effects of television abuse as much as the wasting effects of drug abuse. Teachers complain that affluent parents who are too busy with their careers or too tired at the end of the day to show up for open-school night, PTA meetings, or a teacher conference are as common these days as poor and uneducated parents whose indifference to their children's education keeps them away.

If our children's schools are not meeting our expectations, let alone our hopes for them, much of the reason lies with the institutions that prepare men and women to teach in them. The most prestigious of them are largely concerned with academic reputation within the university setting, competing for funds with the professional schools of law and medicine, and cranking out enormous amounts of research, much of it trivial, with much faculty time and energy going into writing grant proposals and designing model projects. Little of this helps the classroom teacher.

The worst of the ed schools are certification mills where the minimally qualified instruct the barely literate in a parody of learning. Prospective teachers leave no more prepared to impart knowledge or inspire learning than when they entered.

In between these extremes there stretches a wide range of programs, most of which have in common a set of required courses on methods of teaching and theories of learning that are deadly dull. There is almost universal agreement among teachers, who say they are too much, too soon. What teachers find useful in their preparatory training is practice teaching and advice from experienced teachers. What they get in the methods courses means little to them until they get into the classroom. And even then what they find useful that can be learned from lectures, readings, and classroom discussion could probably be taught in one intensive summer or a single year of evening classes. Anyone who couldn't learn it in one full-time year shouldn't be thinking of becoming a teacher.

Why then the years of pedagogical training, which produce people who have a lot of information about how to teach but have little or nothing to teach? The answer lies in the vested interests of the accredited schools, colleges, and departments of education, graduation from which is tantamount to certification in most states. It lies in the tendency of legislative bodies, unions, state, district, and local school boards to prefer the status quo. It lies in the inertia which tends to perpetuate all established institutions once they have taken hold. The status quo is a system that does *not* produce the teachers we need, the best teachers our children could have.

The public school, once charged with the task of transmitting the common culture and imparting the skills required to understand it, participate in it, and extend it, has come to be seen instead by those who prepare men and women to teach in it as an agency of social change. No longer is there said to be a common culture, but a multiplicity of cultures, each of equal value and significance. The function of the schools is to achieve educational equity as a means to social and economic equity. Not equality of opportunity but equal grading is the accepted goal, and objective standards are agreed to be an obstruction to that goal since not everyone does equally well by them.

The accepted means to the end of everyone doing well is the encouragement of self-esteem, which is achieved through being taught about oneself and about one's own community by people as much as possible like oneself and of the same community. The sense of "otherness" is to be banished, since in this scheme any distinction, any differentiation, is looked upon as invidious, if not odious.

The idea of a common culture stretching from the ancients to our own times, bequeathing a literature, a history, a body of knowledge, and a set of traditions that define our political institutions and are of unique value is said to be a myth kept in place by the powers that be in the service of domination, of keeping the lower classes in their place and of exploiting them. Hardly anywhere, among those who shape the aims of our public schools today, does one hear a word about love of classical learning, music, drama.

The people who become "educators" and who run our school systems usually have degrees in education, psychology, social sciences, public administration; they are not people who have studied, know, and love literature, history, science, or philosophy. Our "educators" are not educated. They do not love learning. Naturally enough, they think of the past as dead because it has never been alive to them. And they will not bring it to life for their pupils.

The single most important factor in an individual's education is his teachers. All of us remember particular individuals who influenced and inspired us and gave direction to our lives. Not buildings, programs, curricula, philosophies of education, but men and women who by virtue of their personalities and their love of some discipline, some book, some kind of learning, opened the world to us, and showed us things we had not seen before, gave life a meaning it had not had before. What we need if we are to touch the minds of children, rescue the public school system and the democracy it should nourish, are inspiring teachers. They are precisely what the present system militates against. Although they exist here and there, they do what they do in spite of the present system of preparation and in spite of all the odds against them which that system presents.

Isn't it time we changed it?

Index